The Chief AI Officer's Handbook

Master AI leadership with strategies to innovate, overcome challenges, and drive business growth

Jarrod Anderson

The Chief AI Officer's Handbook

Copyright © 2025 Packt Publishing

All rights reserved. No part of this book may be reproduced, stored in a retrieval system, or transmitted in any form or by any means, without the prior written permission of the publisher, except in the case of brief quotations embedded in critical articles or reviews.

The author acknowledges the use of cutting-edge AI, such as ChatGPT, with the sole aim of enhancing the language and clarity within the book, thereby ensuring a smooth reading experience for readers. It's important to note that the content itself has been crafted by the author and edited by a professional publishing team.

Every effort has been made in the preparation of this book to ensure the accuracy of the information presented. However, the information contained in this book is sold without warranty, either express or implied. Neither the author, nor Packt Publishing or its dealers and distributors, will be held liable for any damages caused or alleged to have been caused directly or indirectly by this book.

Packt Publishing has endeavored to provide trademark information about all of the companies and products mentioned in this book by the appropriate use of capitals. However, Packt Publishing cannot guarantee the accuracy of this information.

Group Product Manager: Niranjan Naikwadi
Publishing Product Manager: Nitin Nainani
Book Project Manager: Aparna Nair
Senior Editor: Rohit Singh
Technical Editor: Rahul Limbachiya
Copy Editor: Safis Editing
Proofreader: Rohit Singh
Indexer: Rekha Nair
Production Designer: Jyoti Kadam
DevRel Marketing Executive: Vinishka Kalra

First published: January 2025

Production reference: 1271224

Published by Packt Publishing Ltd.
Grosvenor House
11 St Paul's Square
Birmingham
B3 1RB, UK.

ISBN 978-1-83620-085-7

www.packtpub.com

To Paula,

Your unwavering love, patience, and belief in me have been the cornerstone of my journey. Thank you for standing by my side through every challenge and triumph, for grounding me when I needed it most, and for inspiring me with your own strength and grace. This book is as much yours as it is mine—dedicated to the woman who makes every achievement meaningful.

With all my love,

Jarrod

Foreword

When Jarrod Anderson and I first crossed paths at Microsoft, it was clear that we shared more than a passing interest in technology—we were kindred spirits, driven by a mutual fascination with AI's transformative potential. Our conversations often veered into the big questions: How can AI reshape industries, empower individuals, and solve problems that seem insurmountable? Yet, while we both delighted in these philosophical musings, we never lost sight of the practical implications—the tangible ways AI could drive meaningful change, not just for our companies but for the broader industry.

Jarrod is a visionary. He has a remarkable ability to see the forest and the trees simultaneously, balancing high-level strategy with extraordinary attention to detail. Whether it was debating how to integrate AI seamlessly into business workflows or brainstorming ideas to push the limits of what's possible, Jarrod's enthusiasm and depth of knowledge always stood out. His expertise is matched only by his commitment to empowering others, making him the perfect guide for anyone embarking on the journey of AI leadership.

The Chief AI Officer's Handbook is not just a manual; it's a manifesto for forward-thinking organizations that understand the urgency of harnessing AI's power. Consider this: economic projections suggest AI could inject $2.6 to $4.4 trillion annually into the global economy, as reported by McKinsey & Company. Moreover, the automation of half of all work could arrive a decade earlier than previously expected. The message is clear: AI is not an optional upgrade; it's a fundamental shift that will define the future of business.

But there's more to AI adoption than technology. A Gartner poll from June 2024 revealed that while 55% of organizations have an AI board and 54% have a designated AI leader, only a small fraction of those leaders hold the title of Chief AI Officer. This statistic underlines a critical gap in leadership—a gap this handbook is designed to fill. It's a call to action for organizations to invest in dedicated, strategic AI leadership capable of navigating the complexities of this new era.

Jarrod doesn't just talk about AI—he lives it. His career has been a testament to the idea that AI is as much about culture and strategy as it is about algorithms and data. He has an innate ability to demystify complex concepts, turning them into actionable insights that drive results. This book is a reflection of his approach: practical, insightful, and deeply attuned to the challenges and opportunities facing today's organizations.

What sets Jarrod apart is his focus on people. In a world increasingly captivated by the capabilities of machines, Jarrod reminds us that technology should serve human needs, not the other way around. His book goes beyond the technical aspects of AI to address the cultural, ethical, and strategic dimensions that are often overlooked. It's a roadmap for leaders who want to create not just smarter organizations but also more resilient, adaptive, and human-centered ones.

As you turn the pages of this handbook, you'll discover not just a guide to implementing AI but also a blueprint for transformative leadership. You'll learn how to craft an AI vision, align it with business goals, and foster a culture of innovation and ethical accountability. More importantly, you'll gain the tools to turn abstract possibilities into concrete outcomes.

Whether you're a seasoned executive or an emerging leader, this book will challenge you to think differently about AI—not as a tool to be deployed but as a strategic force that can redefine the very fabric of your organization. Jarrod has written a book for the dreamers and the doers, for those ready to lead the way into an AI-powered future.

It's time to embrace the possibilities. The future isn't waiting, and neither should you.

Jeff Winter

VP of Business Strategy, Critical Manufacturing

Contributors

About the author

Jarrod Anderson is the Chief Artificial Intelligence Officer at SYRV.AI. He is a visionary and transformative leader in AI. With over three decades of experience, he has led AI teams at multiple Fortune 50 companies. Now dedicated to cutting-edge AI agents and agentic systems, he pushes AI's boundaries to drive innovation, efficiency, and growth. At SYRV.AI, he leads his team to achieve groundbreaking advancements across industries, envisioning a future where AI is integral to business strategy and operational excellence. His expertise spans agriculture, finance, energy, and manufacturing, where he has integrated AI solutions to solve complex challenges and create new opportunities, delivering exceptional value to clients and partners worldwide.

About the reviewers

Rahul Zende, a principal data scientist, specializes in applied AI and **machine learning** (**ML**). He works for a leading US financial institution, studied at the UW in Seattle, and has worked across diverse sectors including banking and finance, research, and technology. Rahul's career showcases multiple awards and recognitions and contributions to multiple prestigious research outcomes, and he often judges, speaks, or reviews at top events, publications, and competitions. Optimistic for the future of AI and ML, Rahul is a prolific influencer in this space through his work in large-scale enterprise initiatives, commitment to mentoring budding professionals, and sharing insights as a respected voice at national and international events, and publications.

Sri Bhargav Krishna Adusumilli is a visionary technologist, celebrated for redefining the boundaries of AI, blockchain, and IoT innovation. As the co-founder of Mindquest Technology Solutions LLC and an award-winning enterprise architect, he merges technical brilliance with entrepreneurial spirit. A prolific author and inventor, Sri Bhargav's work includes patents, industry-defining books, and thought leadership recognized by global platforms such as Forbes and IEEE. Known for mentoring future innovators and spearheading transformative projects at top organizations, he is a beacon of inspiration, driven by a mission to harness technology for societal impact and progress.

Soumo Chakraborty is a principal architect for AI Client Services at Fractal. He has 18 years of experience in leading transformation projects such as platform and data migration, AIOps, and MLOps, and is now leading the GenAI and LLMOps area. His technical breadth has evolved from the days of on-premises IT infrastructure to cutting-edge technologies using AI and ML, which makes him a trusted client partner. He leads the solutioning for complex data and MLOps deals, provides consultation to "first of a kind" GenAI proposals, and delivers innovation to clients. He advocates ethical AI practices and applies them to business use cases. Soumo holds one patent in ML.

This effort is dedicated to my family who motivates me to rise, and to all my well-wishers.

Table of Contents

Preface   xix

Part 1: The Role and Responsibilities of the Chief AI Officer

1

Why Every Company Needs a Chief AI Officer   3

The strategic necessity for a CAIO	4
Bridging the gap – from vision to execution	4
Driving innovation	4
Cohesive and impactful AI efforts	5
Ensuring compliance and ethical AI use	5
The changing landscape of data and AI	6
The competitive advantage	6
Building a data-driven culture	6
Navigating the AI ecosystem	7
The evolving role of the CAIO	7
Embracing the CAIO era	8
The strategic importance of AI leadership	**8**
Integrating AI into business strategy	8
Navigating AI implementation challenges	9
Driving cross-functional collaboration	9
Ensuring continuous improvement and adaptability	9
Enhancing decision-making with AI	10
The transformative power of AI leadership	10
AI leadership and the future of business	11
Alignment of AI initiatives with business goals	**11**
Strategic vision and AI integration	11
Establishing clear objectives and metrics	12
Cross-functional collaboration and alignment	12
Continuous evaluation and adjustment	12
Leveraging data and insights	12
Building a culture of alignment	13
The role of leadership in alignment	13
The strategic impact of alignment	13
Reflection and practical next steps	**14**
Key questions for reflection	14
Practical next steps	15
Summary	**16**
Questions	**17**
References	**17**

2

Key Responsibilities of a Chief AI Officer — 19

The problem – pain points and challenges — 20
The complexity of AI technologies — 20
Rapid technological advancements — 21
Ethical and regulatory concerns — 21
Cultural and organizational resistance — 22
Resource allocation and skill gaps — 22
The need for a clear AI vision — 23

The solution – step-by-step implementation — 23
Step 1 – Developing a clear AI vision and strategy — 23
Step 2 – Navigating technological complexity — 24
Step 3 – Addressing ethical and regulatory challenges — 24
Step 4 – Cultivating a culture of AI adoption — 25
Step 5 – Strategic resource allocation and skill development — 25
Step 6 – Establishing robust infrastructure and processes — 26

Case study – transforming operations at APEX Manufacturing and Distribution — 26
Initial situation — 26
Steps taken — 27
Results achieved — 30

Reflection and practical next steps — 30
Reflecting on core insights — 31
Critical assessment — 31
Practical next steps — 31
Moving forward — 32

Summary — 33
Questions — 33
References — 33

3

Crafting a Winning AI Strategy — 35

The problem – pain points and challenges — 36
Misaligned objectives — 36
Lack of clear KPIs — 36
Measuring ROI — 37
Integration with existing processes — 37
Talent gap — 37
Data quality and governance — 37
The significance of the problem — 37

The solution – a step-by-step implementation — 38
Step 1 – developing a clear AI vision and strategy — 38
Step 2 – creating a detailed roadmap — 38
Step 3 – identifying KPIs — 39
Step 4 – measuring ROI — 39
Step 5 – ensuring seamless integration — 40
Step 6 – building and sustaining AI talent — 40

Hypothetical case study – transforming operations at APEX Manufacturing and Distribution — 41
Initial situation — 41
Steps taken — 41

Results achieved	44	Moving forward	46
Reflection and practical next steps	**45**	**Summary**	**47**
Reflect on core insights	45	**Questions**	**47**
Critical assessment	45	**References**	**48**
Practical next steps	45		

4

Building High-Performing AI Teams — 49

The problem – pain points and challenges	**50**	Step 1 – recruiting top AI talent	55
		Step 2 – structuring your AI team for success	55
Talent scarcity	50	Step 3 – fostering a culture of innovation and collaboration	56
Structuring the AI team	51		
Fostering a culture of innovation	51	Step 4 – integrating AI initiatives with business processes	56
Integration with existing business processes	52		
Measuring success	52	Step 5 – measuring success and iterating	57
The significance of the problem	53	**Hypothetical case study – transforming APEX's manufacturing and distribution with AI**	**58**
Solution and process for building exceptional AI teams	**53**		
Identifying the right talent – curiosity, creativity, and imagination	53	Steps taken	58
		Results achieved	60
Providing the right environment – impact and control	54	**Reflection and practical next steps**	**61**
		Summary	**62**
Step-by-step implementation for building a high-performing AI team	**54**	**Questions**	**63**
		References	**63**

Part 2: Building and Implementing AI Systems

5

Data – the Lifeblood of AI — 67

The problem – pain points and challenges	**68**	Ensuring data quality – the devil is in the details	70
Data collection – the first hurdle	69	Maintaining data integrity – the trust factor	70
Data management – an ongoing battle	69	Leveraging big data – turning volume into value	71

Table of Contents

The solution and process – implementation	**71**
Data collection and management	72
Ensuring data quality	74
Maintaining data integrity	75
Leveraging big data and data analytics	76
Case study – APEX Manufacturing and Distribution	**77**
Data collection and management	78
Ensuring data quality and integrity	79
Leveraging big data and advanced analytics	80
Results achieved	81
Memorable insights	81
Reflection and practical next steps	**81**
Reflecting on core insights	82
Critical assessment questions	82
Actionable next steps	82
Summary	**83**
Questions	**84**
References	**84**

6

AI Project Management   87

The problem – pain points and challenges	**88**
Scope creep – the silent project killer	88
Resource allocation – balancing expertise and time	89
Technology integration – the jigsaw puzzle of systems	89
Data quality and availability – the fuel for AI	90
Change management – navigating organizational resistance	90
Analytical insight with a relatable touch	91
The solution and its implementation	**91**
Managing AI projects from concept to deployment	91
Agile methodologies for AI	93
Overcoming common AI project challenges	94
A checklist for identifying and mitigating challenges	96
Hypothetical case study – APEX Manufacturing and Distribution	**97**
Initial situation	97
Step-by-step implementation	97
Results achieved	99
Relatable anecdotes and motivational insights	99
Reflection and practical next steps	**100**
Summary	**101**
Questions	**102**
References	**102**

7

Understanding Deterministic, Probabilistic, and Generative AI   103

The problem – pain points and challenges	**105**
Navigating the deterministic AI landscape	105
The complexity of probabilistic AI	105
Unleashing the potential of generative AI	106
Integrating AI into existing business processes	107

Personal anecdote – the AI learning curve	107	Step 3 – implementing probabilistic AI for inventory management	114
Overcoming challenges	107	Step 4 – implementing probabilistic AI for predictive maintenance	115
The solution and implementation	**108**	Step 5 – implementing generative AI for design innovation	115
Deterministic AI	108	The transformative results at APEX Manufacturing and Distribution	116
Probabilistic AI	109		
Generative AI	111		
Hypothetical case study – APEX Manufacturing and Distribution	**112**	**Reflection and practical next steps**	**117**
Step 1 – identifying pain points and setting objectives	113	**Summary**	**119**
		Questions	**119**
Step 2 – implementing deterministic AI for quality control	113	**References**	**119**

8

AI Agents and Agentic Systems 121

What are AI agents?	**122**	Step 2 – choosing the right architecture	131
Understanding agentic systems	123	Step 3 – developing perception and action mechanisms	131
Evolution of AI agents	123		
The role of machine learning	124	Step 4 – implementing decision-making algorithms	132
Integration with IoT	124		
Potential applications	124	Step 5 – testing and validating	132
Real-world applications of AI agents	124	Step 6 – deploying and monitoring	132
		Step 7 – continuous improvement	133
The problem – pain points and challenges	**126**	**Hypothetical case study – APEX Manufacturing and Distribution**	**134**
Complexity and integration	126	Initial situation	134
Data privacy and security	127	Steps taken	134
Ethical considerations and bias	127	Results achieved	135
Resistance to change	128	Relatable anecdotes and insights	136
High costs and ROI uncertainty	128		
Lack of expertise	128	**Reflection and practical next steps**	**136**
Insights on agentic systems	129	Reflective questions	136
Early development – experimentation, learning, and adoption	129	Critical assessment	137
		Practical next steps	137
Personal anecdote – navigating the AI terrain	130	**Summary**	**138**
The solution and implementation	**130**	**Questions**	**139**
Step 1 – defining objectives and goals	130	**References**	**139**

9

Designing AI Systems — 141

The problem – pain points and challenges — 143
- Data quality and bias — 143
- Complexity and integration — 143
- Ethical and legal concerns — 144
- Scalability and maintenance — 144
- Human-AI collaboration — 144
- Security risks — 144
- Personal anecdote – learning the hard way — 144
- The stakes are high — 145

The solution – step-by-step implementation — 145
- Step 1 – defining clear objectives — 145
- Step 2 – gathering and preparing quality data — 146
- Step 3 – selecting the right algorithms and tools — 146
- Step 4 – developing and training your model — 146
- Step 5 – ensuring ethical and fair AI — 147
- Step 6 – integrating and deploying your AI system — 147
- Step 7 – monitoring and maintaining your AI system — 148
- Best practices for AI system design — 148
- Human-centered AI design — 148

Hypothetical case study – APEX Manufacturing and Distribution — 149
- Initial situation — 149
- Step-by-step implementation — 149
- Results achieved — 152

Reflection and practical next steps — 153
Summary — 154
Questions — 155
References — 155

10

Training AI Models — 157

AI model training – from data to insights — 158
- The importance of data selection — 158
- The art of feature engineering — 158
- The training process — 159
- Model evaluation — 159
- Continuous learning and improvement — 159
- Unexpected insights — 159

The problem – pain points and challenges — 160
- Data quality and availability — 160
- Feature engineering complexity — 160
- Model selection and tuning — 160
- Computational resources — 161
- Interpretability and trust — 161
- Ethical and legal considerations — 162
- Continuous learning and maintenance — 162
- Integration with business processes — 162
- Scaling AI solutions — 163
- User adoption and feedback — 163

The solution and process – step-by-step implementation — 163
- Step 1 – selecting the right algorithms — 163
- Step 2 – model training and optimization — 165
- Step 3 – handling bias and fairness in AI — 167

Hypothetical case study – APEX Manufacturing and Distribution	169
Initial situation	169
Step-by-step implementation	169
Results achieved	172

Reflection and practical next steps	172
Summary	173
Questions	174
References	174

11

Deploying AI Solutions 175

The problem – pain points and challenges	176
Scaling from prototype to production	176
Managing CI/CD for AI	177
Ongoing monitoring and maintenance	177
Integrating AI with business processes	178
Addressing ethical and compliance issues	178

The solution and implementation process	178
From prototype to production	178
CI/CD for AI	179
Monitoring and maintaining AI systems	180
Aligning AI with business processes	181

Navigating ethical and compliance issues	181

Hypothetical case study – APEX Manufacturing and Distribution	182
Step 1 – assessment and prototype development	182
Step 2 – scaling from prototype to production	183
Step 3 – implementing CI/CD for AI	183
Step 4 – monitoring and maintenance	184
Results achieved	184
Relatable anecdote – the turning point	184

Reflection and practical next steps	185
Summary	188
Questions	188
References	189

Part 3: Governance, Ethics, Security, and Compliance

12

AI Governance and Ethics 193

The problem – pain points and challenges	194
Bias and fairness	194
Lack of transparency	194
Accountability	194

Data privacy and security	195
Ethical decision-making	195
Regulatory compliance	195
Compelling examples	195
Personal anecdotes	196

The solution and process – implementation	**196**	Client's initial situation	199
		Steps taken	200
Understanding AI ethics	196	Results achieved	202
Building ethical AI frameworks	197	**Reflection and practical next steps**	**203**
Governance of AI solutions and capabilities	198	**Summary**	**205**
Hypothetical case study – APEX Manufacturing and Distribution	**199**	**Questions**	**205**
		References	**206**

13

Security in AI Systems — 207

The problem – pain points and challenges	**208**	AI in cybersecurity	212
		Addressing AI vulnerabilities	212
Data breaches and privacy concerns	208	**Hypothetical case study – APEX Manufacturing and Distribution**	**214**
Model vulnerabilities and adversarial attacks	209		
Data poisoning and integrity	209	Client's initial situation	214
Model inversion and privacy risks	209	Steps taken	214
Lack of explainability and transparency	210	Results achieved	216
The rapid evolution of threats	210	Anecdote	217
Personal anecdotes	210	**Reflection and practical next steps**	**217**
The solution and process – implementation	**211**	**Summary**	**218**
		Questions	**219**
Securing AI models and data	211	**References**	**219**

14

Privacy in the Age of AI — 221

he problem – pain points and challenges	**222**	**The solution and process – implementation**	**225**
Data collection and consent	222	Understanding AI and data privacy	225
Data security and breaches	223	Implementing privacy-preserving AI	226
Compliance with regulations	223	Regulations and best practices	227
Data minimization and retention	223	**Hypothetical case study – APEX Manufacturing and Distribution**	**228**
Anonymization and de-identification	224		
Ethical use of AI and data	224	Client's initial situation	228

Steps taken	229	Reflection and practical next steps	234
Results achieved	232	Summary	235
Detailed implementation and continued success	233	Questions	236
		References	236
Long-term impact	234		

15

AI Compliance 237

The problem – pain points and challenges	238	Navigating legal and regulatory requirements	242
Complex and evolving regulations	238	Building a culture of compliance and accountability	243
Data privacy and security	239		
Transparency and explainability	239	**Hypothetical case study – APEX Manufacturing and Distribution**	**244**
Bias and fairness	240	Client's initial situation	245
Accountability and governance	240	Steps taken	245
Integration with existing systems and processes	240	Results achieved	249
Resource constraints	241	Reflection and practical next steps	249
The solution and process – implementation	241	Summary	250
		Questions	251
Ensuring AI compliance with industry standards	241	References	251

Part 4: Empowering AI Leadership with Practical Tools and Insights

16

Conclusion 255

The transformative power of AI	256	The road ahead for Chief AI Officers	258
Key themes and insights	257	Visionary leadership	258
The profound impact on business strategies	257	Ethical stewardship	258
		Strategic innovation	259
Improving customer experiences	257	Summary	259
Enhancing operational efficiency	257	References	260
A clear vision of AI's potential	258		

17

Appendix 261

Glossary of AI terms 261
Recommended readings and resources 266

Books 266
Academic papers and articles 267
Online courses and tutorials 267
Websites and blogs 267
Professional organizations and communities 268
Conferences and events 268
Podcasts and videos 268
Government and regulatory resources 268
Research institutions 269
Tools and platforms 269
Additional resources 269
Educational platforms 270
Community forums 270
Ethics and policy resources 270
Industry reports 270
Key journals and publications 270

Templates and frameworks 271

NIST AI Risk Management Framework (AI RMF) 271
AI strategy development template 272
AI Project Management Framework 273
Ethical AI Implementation Framework 274
Data Governance Framework 275
AI Capability Maturity Model 276
AI Vendor Selection Framework 277
AI Ethics and Compliance Checklist 278
AI Skills and Competency Framework 279
AI Investment Evaluation Template 280

Assessments 283

Chapter 1 – Why Every Company Needs a Chief AI Officer 283
Chapter 2 – Key Responsibilities of a Chief AI Officer 284
Chapter 3 – Crafting a Winning AI Strategy 285
Chapter 4 – Building High-Performing AI Teams 286
Chapter 5 – Data – the Lifeblood of AI 287
Chapter 6 – AI Project Management 288
Chapter 7 – Understanding Deterministic, Probabilistic, and Generative AI 289
Chapter 8 – AI Agents and Agentic Systems 289
Chapter 9 – Designing AI Systems 291
Chapter 10 – Training AI Models 292
Chapter 11 – Deploying AI Solutions 292
Chapter 12 – AI Governance and Ethics 293
Chapter 13 – Security in AI Systems 294
Chapter 14 – Privacy in the Age of AI 294
Chapter 15 – AI Compliance 295

Index 297

Other Books You May Enjoy 308

Preface

In an era of rapid technological evolution, **artificial intelligence** (**AI**) has emerged as a transformative force, reshaping industries and redefining possibilities. Yet, harnessing AI's potential is no simple task—it demands a unique blend of strategic vision, technical understanding, and ethical stewardship. *The Chief AI Officer's Handbook* is designed to guide leaders through this complex terrain, providing the tools and insights needed to thrive in a world increasingly driven by AI.

The Chief AI Officer's Handbook offers a comprehensive approach, combining strategic insights, technical knowledge, and ethical considerations. Unlike other AI books that focus solely on the technical or abstract, this handbook bridges the gap, providing practical frameworks, case studies, and actionable advice to empower leaders. It guides you through the evolving role and responsibilities of a **Chief AI Officer** (**CAIO**)—from crafting AI strategies and building high-performing teams to implementing AI systems and ensuring governance and compliance.

Before exploring this book, a foundational understanding of AI and its basic concepts, such as machine learning and data analytics, is beneficial. Familiarity with business strategy and leadership principles will also enhance your ability to apply the teachings effectively. This knowledge is optional but will enable you to appreciate the strategic insights and practical guidance provided fully.

By the end of this journey, you will possess a deep understanding of the strategic, technical, and ethical dimensions of AI leadership. You will be equipped to develop and execute effective AI strategies, build and manage high-performing AI teams, implement advanced AI systems, and ensure ethical and compliant AI practices within your organization. Ultimately, this book will empower you to leverage the transformative power of AI to drive innovation, solve complex business challenges, and achieve sustainable growth.

Welcome to the future of leadership. Welcome to the role of the CAIO.

Who this book is for

The Chief AI Officer's Handbook is tailored for CAIOs, business leaders, AI and data science professionals, IT managers, entrepreneurs, consultants, academic leaders, policymakers, and general business professionals. This diverse audience seeks to understand not only the technical intricacies of AI but also how to leverage AI to solve real-world business problems, drive innovation, and achieve strategic goals. This book provides comprehensive insights into AI strategy, team building, project management, ethical considerations, and practical implementation, making it an invaluable resource for harnessing AI's transformative power.

What this book covers

Chapter 1, Why Every Company Needs a Chief AI Officer, is where you will discover why AI leadership is critical for businesses to remain competitive in a rapidly evolving landscape. This chapter examines the pivotal role of a CAIO in aligning AI initiatives with organizational objectives to drive innovation and deliver measurable impact.

Chapter 2, Key Responsibilities of a Chief AI Officer, is where you will gain a clear understanding of the multifaceted responsibilities that define the CAIO role. From crafting an AI vision to ensuring ethical practices and advocating for AI adoption, this chapter delves into the essential duties that enable a CAIO to lead transformative change within an organization.

Chapter 3, Crafting a Winning AI Strategy, explores the key elements of a successful AI strategy and provides practical steps for defining AI goals, integrating them into business processes, and demonstrating return on investment. You will learn how to align AI initiatives with overarching business strategies for sustained success.

Chapter 4, Building High-Performing AI Teams, uncovers the secrets to assembling and leading a dynamic AI team. This chapter offers insights into attracting top talent, structuring teams for maximum impact, and cultivating a culture of innovation and collaboration to ensure long-term organizational success.

Chapter 5, Data – the Lifeblood of AI, helps you to understand the foundational role of data in AI systems. This chapter explores data collection and management methods, ensuring data quality and integrity, and leveraging big data and analytics to drive AI success.

Chapter 6, AI Project Management, is where you will navigate the complexities of managing AI projects from concept to deployment. This chapter provides practical advice on using agile methodologies, addressing common challenges, and ensuring the smooth execution of AI initiatives.

Chapter 7, Understanding Deterministic, Probabilistic, and Generative AI, unpacks the key concepts and techniques behind deterministic, probabilistic, and generative AI. This chapter provides clarity on these approaches and their practical applications in various industries.

Chapter 8, AI Agents and Agentic Systems, explores the transformative potential of AI agents and agentic systems in automating and enhancing decision-making. This chapter introduces their core principles, offers guidance on implementation, and addresses the challenges and opportunities they present.

Chapter 9, Designing AI Systems, provides insights into best practices for designing AI systems that balance technical excellence with human-centric considerations. This chapter emphasizes creating solutions that are functional, ethical, and user-friendly.

Chapter 10, Training AI Models, is where you will learn the essential steps to train effective AI models, from selecting the right algorithms to optimizing performance and addressing bias. This chapter ensures your AI systems are both efficient and fair.

Chapter 11, *Deploying AI Solutions*, helps you move from prototypes to production with confidence. This chapter covers strategies for deploying AI systems, integrating continuous deployment practices, and maintaining performance and reliability over time.

Chapter 12, *AI Governance and Ethics*, examines the critical role of ethics in AI development and deployment. This chapter explores how to build ethical AI frameworks, ensure responsible governance, and align AI capabilities with organizational and societal values.

Chapter 13, *Security in AI Systems*, addresses the unique security challenges of AI systems. This chapter covers securing AI models and data, leveraging AI in cybersecurity, and mitigating vulnerabilities to protect both systems and users.

Chapter 14, *Privacy in the Age of AI*, helps you understand the interplay between AI and data privacy in today's world. This chapter provides insights into implementing privacy-preserving AI, navigating regulatory landscapes, and adhering to best practices for safeguarding sensitive information.

Chapter 15, *AI Compliance*, teaches you how to ensure compliance with industry standards and legal requirements. This chapter emphasizes building a culture of accountability, navigating regulatory complexities, and integrating compliance into AI initiatives seamlessly.

Chapter 16, *Conclusion*, reflects on AI's transformative potential and profound impact on businesses and society. This chapter highlights the journey ahead for CAIOs, emphasizing their role in shaping the future through innovation, ethical leadership, and strategic foresight.

Chapter 17, *Appendix*, points you to where you can find additional resources, tools, and references to support your journey as a CAIO. This chapter includes supplementary materials to deepen your understanding and provide practical guidance for applying the concepts explored throughout the book.

To get the most out of this book

Before diving into *The Chief AI Officer's Handbook*, you should have a foundational understanding of AI and its basic concepts, including machine learning, data analytics, and the general landscape of AI technologies. Familiarity with business strategy and leadership principles is also beneficial, as the book integrates these with AI applications. While technical proficiency is not a prerequisite, having a basic grasp of how AI systems function and their potential impact on business operations will enable you to fully appreciate the strategic insights and practical guidance provided. This foundational knowledge ensures that you can effectively apply the book's teachings to drive innovation and solve complex problems within your organization.

Conventions used

There are a number of text conventions used throughout this book.

`Code in text`: Indicates code words in text, database table names, folder names, filenames, file extensions, pathnames, dummy URLs, user input, and Twitter handles. Here is an example: "Leverage libraries such as `scikit-learn`, `TensorFlow`, and `PyTorch` to implement and experiment with various algorithms."

Bold: Indicates a new term, an important word, or words that you see onscreen. For instance, words in menus or dialog boxes appear in **bold**. Here is an example: "They must balance the excitement of new AI possibilities with practical considerations of feasibility and **return on investment** (**ROI**)."

> **Tips or important notes**
> Appear like this.

Get in touch

Feedback from our readers is always welcome.

General feedback: If you have questions about any aspect of this book, email us at `customercare@packtpub.com` and mention the book title in the subject of your message.

Errata: Although we have taken every care to ensure the accuracy of our content, mistakes do happen. If you have found a mistake in this book, we would be grateful if you would report this to us. Please visit `www.packtpub.com/support/errata` and fill in the form.

Piracy: If you come across any illegal copies of our works in any form on the internet, we would be grateful if you would provide us with the location address or website name. Please contact us at `copyright@packt.com` with a link to the material.

If you are interested in becoming an author: If there is a topic that you have expertise in and you are interested in either writing or contributing to a book, please visit `authors.packtpub.com`.

Share Your Thoughts

Once you've read *The Chief AI Officer's Handbook*, we'd love to hear your thoughts! Scan the QR code below to go straight to the Amazon review page for this book and share your feedback.

https://packt.link/r/1-836-20085-4

Your review is important to us and the tech community and will help us make sure we're delivering excellent quality content.

Download a free PDF copy of this book

Thanks for purchasing this book!

Do you like to read on the go but are unable to carry your print books everywhere?

Is your eBook purchase not compatible with the device of your choice?

Don't worry, now with every Packt book you get a DRM-free PDF version of that book at no cost.

Read anywhere, any place, on any device. Search, copy, and paste code from your favorite technical books directly into your application.

The perks don't stop there, you can get exclusive access to discounts, newsletters, and great free content in your inbox daily

Follow these simple steps to get the benefits:

1. Scan the QR code or visit the link below

https://packt.link/free-ebook/9781836200857

2. Submit your proof of purchase
3. That's it! We'll send your free PDF and other benefits to your email directly

Part 1: The Role and Responsibilities of the Chief AI Officer

In an era where AI is reshaping industries, the **Chief AI Officer** (**CAIO**) has become essential for driving innovation, aligning AI initiatives with business goals, and ensuring ethical and effective implementation. This part explores why every organization needs a CAIO, the key responsibilities of this transformative role, and the foundational steps to crafting a winning AI strategy and building high-performing AI teams. It sets the stage for understanding how the CAIO can unlock AI's full potential to create lasting value.

This part has the following chapters:

- *Chapter 1, Why Every Company Needs a Chief AI Officer*
- *Chapter 2, Key Responsibilities of a Chief AI Officer*
- *Chapter 3, Crafting a Winning AI Strategy*
- *Chapter 4, Building High-Performing AI Teams*

1
Why Every Company Needs a Chief AI Officer

There are only two types of companies in this world, those who are great at AI and everybody else. If you don't know AI, you are going to fail, period, end of story. You have to understand it, because it will have significant impact on every single thing that you do. There's no avoiding it

– Mark Cuban

Imagine this: a leading company experiences a significant setback when its new **artificial intelligence** (**AI**)-powered customer service system crashes during the busiest sales season. What was once seen as a model of efficiency is now overwhelmed, leaving thousands of customers frustrated and generating a flood of negative reviews. The company lost millions in revenue, all because its AI system wasn't prepared to handle the surge in demand or adapt to changing customer behaviors. The root cause? A lack of strategic oversight and foresight in AI management.

Imagine if a **Chief AI Officer** (**CAIO**) had been in place—someone focused on anticipating challenges, optimizing AI strategies, and ensuring the technology evolves alongside the business. With a CAIO at the helm, this crisis could have been averted, turning a potential failure into a seamless success. This situation underscores the critical need for a CAIO, highlighting their role in driving innovation, maintaining operational resilience, and securing a competitive edge in today's fast-paced market. The presence of a CAIO can make the difference between catastrophic failure and extraordinary success.

In this chapter, we will cover the following topics:

- The strategic necessity for a CAIO
- The strategic importance of AI leadership
- Alignment of AI initiatives with business goals

By the end of this chapter, you will gain a clear understanding of how a CAIO can drive innovation across the organization, ensure AI initiatives are strategically aligned and cohesive, and foster sustainable, long-term business success.

The strategic necessity for a CAIO

In today's fast-paced, technology-driven world, the need for a dedicated CAIO is more pressing than ever. Companies are increasingly realizing that AI is not just a tool but a transformative force that can redefine business models, enhance customer experiences, and drive operational efficiency [1]. However, harnessing AI's full potential requires strategic oversight and integration into the business's core operations, a task ideally suited for a CAIO.

A CAIO ensures that AI initiatives align with the overarching business objectives. This alignment is crucial because AI projects can become disjointed and fail to deliver expected value without it. The CAIO also ensures that AI efforts are innovative and impactful, driving tangible business results.

Bridging the gap – from vision to execution

One of the most critical roles of a CAIO is to bridge the gap between technical teams and executive leadership. This unique position requires deep technical knowledge and strategic business acumen. The CAIO ensures that AI strategies are not just visionary but also executable. They translate complex AI concepts into actionable business plans that resonate with C-suite executives, ensuring that AI initiatives receive the necessary support and resources.

With a CAIO, companies can easily align their AI ambitions and their business goals. Technical teams might focus on the latest advancements without considering how these innovations fit into the larger strategic picture. Conversely, executives may need to understand technical complexities to set ambitious AI goals fully. A CAIO is a crucial intermediary, ensuring that both sides are aligned and working toward the same objectives.

The role of a CAIO involves more than just translating technical jargon into business language. It requires an in-depth understanding of the company's vision and an ability to foresee how AI can drive this vision forward. The CAIO must constantly evaluate the potential of emerging AI technologies and assess their fit within the company's strategic framework. Doing so ensures that AI initiatives are ambitious, achievable, and aligned with the company's long-term goals.

Driving innovation

Innovation is the lifeblood of any competitive enterprise, and a CAIO is at the forefront of driving this innovation through AI. They foster a culture of experimentation and learning, encouraging teams to explore new AI applications and solutions. By staying abreast of the latest advancements in AI technology and methodologies, the CAIO ensures that the company remains ahead of the curve.

The CAIO's role in driving innovation also extends to identifying and nurturing AI talent within the organization. They create continuous learning and development pathways, ensuring the company's AI capabilities constantly evolve. This focus on talent development is critical in maintaining a competitive edge in the rapidly changing AI landscape.

A CAIO must also cultivate an environment where creative thinking is encouraged and risk-taking is seen as an essential component of innovation. They must balance the excitement of new AI possibilities with practical considerations of feasibility and **return on investment (ROI)**. This balance is crucial in fostering sustainable innovation that drives long-term business success.

Cohesive and impactful AI efforts

A CAIO ensures that AI initiatives are not isolated experiments but part of a cohesive, strategic plan. They oversee the integration of AI across various functions, ensuring that each project contributes to the company's long-term goals. This holistic approach maximizes the impact of AI investments, turning isolated successes into company-wide transformation.

Without a cohesive strategy, AI projects can become siloed, leading to fragmented efforts that fail to realize their full potential. A CAIO coordinates these efforts, ensuring that AI initiatives are aligned with the company's strategic vision and that resources are allocated efficiently. This coordinated approach enhances the overall impact of AI on the business.

A CAIO's strategic oversight involves setting clear priorities for AI initiatives, establishing governance frameworks, and implementing robust project management practices. By doing so, they ensure that AI projects are executed efficiently and deliver measurable business value. This approach transforms AI from a series of experimental ventures into a core component of the company's strategic agenda.

Ensuring compliance and ethical AI use

In an era of increasing regulatory scrutiny and ethical concerns, a CAIO ensures that AI is used responsibly and compliantly. They stay ahead of regulatory changes, ensuring AI systems adhere to the latest standards and guidelines. This proactive approach prevents compliance crises that can devastate businesses.

The CAIO's responsibility extends beyond compliance to ethical considerations. They ensure that AI systems are designed and implemented fairly, transparently, and without bias. This involves setting up ethical guidelines, conducting regular audits, and fostering a culture of ethical AI use within the organization. Ensuring ethical AI practices builds trust with customers and stakeholders and mitigates risks associated with biased or unfair AI outcomes.

The CAIO must also navigate the complex landscape of global data privacy laws and regulations. They must ensure that the company's AI systems comply with these regulations while delivering business value. This involves implementing robust data governance frameworks and ensuring that data is collected, stored, and used in ways that protect individual privacy and uphold ethical standards.

The changing landscape of data and AI

The landscape and use of data are rapidly evolving, with AI playing an increasingly active role in data management, analysis, and utilization. Data has become the backbone of modern enterprises, driving decisions, strategies, and innovations. However, the data's sheer volume and complexity require advanced AI capabilities to extract meaningful insights and drive actionable outcomes.

A CAIO is pivotal in navigating this data-rich environment. They ensure that AI technologies are leveraged to manage and analyze data effectively, transforming raw information into strategic assets. This involves implementing AI-driven data analytics, predictive modeling, and **machine learning (ML)** algorithms that enhance decision-making and operational efficiency.

Furthermore, the CAIO oversees the integration of AI with data governance frameworks, ensuring that data is used responsibly and compliantly. This integration is crucial as data privacy and security concerns become more pronounced. The CAIO ensures that AI systems adhere to data protection regulations and ethical standards, safeguarding the organization and its stakeholders [2].

As AI becomes more embedded in data processes, the CAIO's role expands to ensure data integrity and quality. They must implement systems that validate and clean data, ensuring that AI models are built on reliable and accurate information. This focus on data quality is essential for maximizing the effectiveness of AI applications and driving insightful business decisions.

The competitive advantage

Having a CAIO provides a significant competitive advantage. Companies with a CAIO are better positioned to leverage AI for strategic growth, operational efficiency, and customer satisfaction. They are more agile in responding to market changes and regulatory requirements and can better manage risks associated with AI deployment.

A CAIO ensures that AI initiatives are implemented, scalable, and sustainable. They monitor the performance of AI systems, making necessary adjustments to optimize outcomes and ensure long-term success. This ongoing oversight is crucial in maintaining a competitive edge in an AI-driven market.

A CAIO's strategic vision helps the company identify new market opportunities and stay ahead of competitors. The company can differentiate itself in a crowded marketplace by leveraging AI to enhance product offerings, improve customer experiences, and optimize operations. The CAIO's ability to anticipate and respond to emerging trends and challenges in the AI landscape further reinforces this competitive edge.

Building a data-driven culture

A CAIO is instrumental in building a data-driven culture within the organization. They promote the use of data and AI across all levels of the business, ensuring that accurate and relevant insights inform decision-making. This cultural shift is critical for maximizing the value of AI investments.

Creating a data-driven culture involves more than just implementing AI technologies; it requires a fundamental change in how the organization operates [3]. The CAIO champions this transformation, encouraging employees to embrace data and AI in their daily workflows and decision-making processes. This cultural shift enhances the organization's ability to leverage AI for strategic advantage.

The CAIO fosters this culture by promoting data literacy and ensuring employees at all levels have the skills and knowledge to work effectively with data and AI. This involves providing training and resources, creating opportunities for collaboration, and establishing clear guidelines for data use. By building a data-driven culture, the CAIO helps the organization unlock the full potential of its data assets.

Navigating the AI ecosystem

The AI ecosystem is complex and constantly evolving. A CAIO navigates this ecosystem, identifying opportunities for partnerships, collaborations, and investments. They stay abreast of emerging technologies and trends, ensuring the company remains at the forefront of AI innovation.

Navigating the AI ecosystem involves understanding the broader landscape of AI research, development, and application. The CAIO actively engages with academic institutions, research organizations, and industry consortia to stay informed about the latest advancements and best practices. This engagement ensures the company is well positioned to adopt and leverage cutting-edge AI technologies.

The CAIO is also crucial in identifying and nurturing strategic partnerships with AI vendors and technology providers. These partnerships can provide access to new AI tools, platforms, and expertise, enhancing the company's capabilities and accelerating its AI initiatives. By building a solid network within the AI ecosystem, the CAIO ensures that the company remains at the forefront of AI innovation.

The evolving role of the CAIO

As AI continues to evolve and reshape industries, the role of the CAIO will become even more critical. The CAIO will lead AI initiatives and drive the organization's overall digital transformation. They will play a key role in shaping the company's strategic direction, ensuring that AI is seamlessly integrated into every aspect of the business.

In the future, we expect the CAIO's role to expand further, encompassing responsibilities such as managing AI ethics, driving AI literacy across the organization, and fostering a culture of continuous innovation. The CAIO will be a crucial driver of business growth, ensuring that the company remains competitive in an AI-driven world.

The CAIO will also need to address new challenges and opportunities arising from the convergence of AI with other emerging technologies, such as quantum computing, blockchain, and the **internet of things (IoT)** [4]. By staying at the cutting edge of these technological advancements, the CAIO can help the company leverage new possibilities and maintain its competitive edge.

Embracing the CAIO era

As we move deeper into the AI era, the importance of having a CAIO cannot be overstated. The CAIO is the linchpin that connects AI initiatives with strategic business goals, ensuring that AI is not just a technological tool but a driving force for transformation and growth. By investing in a CAIO, companies are not just future-proofing their operations but also positioning themselves to thrive in an AI-driven world.

The era of the CAIO is here, and those who embrace it will lead the way in innovation, efficiency, and strategic growth. The transformative power of AI, guided by the expertise and vision of a CAIO, will shape the future of business and society, creating new opportunities and solving complex challenges in ways we have yet to imagine. The CAIO's role is essential in navigating the complexities of AI, ensuring that businesses harness their full potential responsibly and effectively. Embracing the CAIO era means committing to a future where AI drives continuous improvement, innovation, and success.

The strategic importance of AI leadership

In an era where technological advancements occur at an unprecedented pace, the strategic importance of AI leadership cannot be overstated. As enterprises strive to harness the transformative power of AI, the role of CAIO emerges as a cornerstone for driving AI initiatives that are seamlessly aligned with business objectives. The CAIO is not merely a technical expert but a strategic leader who understands the intricacies of AI and its potential to revolutionize business operations and strategy.

Integrating AI into business strategy

AI leadership begins with integrating AI into the broader business strategy. This integration is not a one-off task but an ongoing process that requires a deep understanding of the business landscape and AI technologies' capabilities. A CAIO brings this dual expertise, ensuring that AI initiatives are technologically sound and strategically relevant.

The CAIO's strategic vision allows them to identify areas where AI can create the most value, whether enhancing customer experience, optimizing operations, or driving innovation. By aligning AI initiatives with business goals, the CAIO ensures that AI becomes an integral part of the company's strategic plan rather than a series of isolated projects.

For example, in a retail business, AI can analyze customer data to identify purchasing trends and personalize marketing efforts [5]. In manufacturing, AI-driven predictive maintenance can minimize downtime and improve efficiency. The CAIO identifies these opportunities and ensures that AI initiatives are directed toward achieving these high-impact outcomes.

Navigating AI implementation challenges

Implementing AI within an organization is fraught with challenges, from technical hurdles to resistance to change. Effective AI leadership is crucial in navigating these challenges and ensuring the successful deployment of AI solutions. The CAIO plays a vital role in overcoming these obstacles by fostering a culture that embraces AI and providing necessary resources and support to AI projects.

One of the primary challenges in AI implementation is integrating new AI systems with existing technologies and workflows. The CAIO must ensure that AI solutions are compatible with the company's current infrastructure and that they enhance rather than disrupt existing operations. This requires careful planning, robust testing, and ongoing monitoring.

Resistance to change is another significant barrier to AI implementation. Employees may be wary of AI technologies, fearing job displacement or increased workloads. The CAIO addresses these concerns by clearly communicating the benefits of AI, providing training and support, and involving employees in the AI journey. By fostering a culture of collaboration and continuous learning, the CAIO ensures that AI initiatives are embraced across the organization.

Driving cross-functional collaboration

AI initiatives often span multiple departments and require cross-functional collaboration. The CAIO is instrumental in breaking down silos and fostering a collaborative environment where different teams can work together toward common AI goals. This collaborative approach enhances the effectiveness of AI initiatives and ensures that AI solutions are tailored to each department's specific needs and objectives.

The CAIO facilitates cross-functional collaboration by establishing clear communication channels, setting shared goals, and promoting a culture of teamwork. Regular meetings, workshops, and collaborative platforms help ensure that all stakeholders are aligned and engaged in the AI journey. By bringing diverse perspectives and expertise together, the CAIO ensures that AI initiatives are comprehensive, innovative, and effective.

For instance, AI-driven data analytics can improve patient outcomes in a healthcare organization by providing doctors with real-time insights. However, collaboration between IT, data science, and clinical teams is essential for this to be effective. The CAIO ensures these teams work together seamlessly, leveraging their expertise to develop and implement AI solutions that deliver tangible benefits.

Ensuring continuous improvement and adaptability

In the rapidly evolving field of AI, continuous improvement and adaptability are vital for maintaining a competitive edge. The CAIO is responsible for fostering a constant learning and innovation culture, ensuring that the organization remains agile and responsive to new developments in AI technology.

This involves keeping abreast of the latest advancements in AI and regularly evaluating and refining AI strategies and initiatives. The CAIO ensures that the organization consistently leverages the most effective and efficient AI solutions and that AI strategies align continuously with the changing business landscape.

Continuous improvement requires a commitment to ongoing education and development. The CAIO promotes training programs, workshops, and partnerships with academic institutions to ensure the organization's AI capabilities constantly evolve. By fostering a culture of continuous learning, the CAIO ensures that the organization remains at the forefront of AI innovation [6].

Adaptability is equally vital in the dynamic field of AI. The CAIO must be prepared to pivot strategies and initiatives in response to new developments, challenges, and opportunities. This requires a flexible approach to AI leadership and a willingness to experiment, take calculated risks, and learn from failures. By embracing adaptability, the CAIO ensures that the organization can navigate the complexities of the AI landscape and seize new opportunities as they arise.

Enhancing decision-making with AI

AI leadership's most significant contribution is enhancing the organization's decision-making processes. The CAIO leverages AI to provide actionable insights and predictive analytics that inform strategic decisions. This data-driven approach ensures that business decisions are based on accurate and up-to-date information, reducing uncertainty and enhancing strategic outcomes.

By integrating AI into decision-making processes, the CAIO helps the organization react to current challenges and anticipate future opportunities and threats. This proactive approach is essential for maintaining a competitive advantage in today's fast-paced business environment.

AI-driven decision-making involves using advanced analytics, ML algorithms, and predictive modeling to analyze vast amounts of data and generate insights. These insights can inform various strategic decisions, from market expansion and product development to resource allocation and risk management. The CAIO ensures that these AI capabilities are leveraged effectively, providing the organization with a powerful tool for strategic planning and execution.

The transformative power of AI leadership

The transformative power of AI leadership lies in its ability to drive strategic alignment, foster innovation, and enhance operational efficiency. The CAIO, as the embodiment of AI leadership, plays a critical role in guiding the organization through the complexities of AI implementation and ensuring that AI initiatives deliver tangible business value.

AI leadership is not just about managing AI projects; it's about embedding AI into the very fabric of the organization's strategic vision and operational processes. The CAIO's strategic oversight ensures that AI is leveraged to its fullest potential, driving continuous improvement and positioning the organization for long-term success.

The CAIO's influence extends beyond the technical aspects of AI. They are pivotal in shaping the organization's culture, values, and vision. By championing AI and fostering a culture of innovation and collaboration, the CAIO ensures that AI initiatives are technologically advanced and aligned with the organization's core principles and objectives.

AI leadership and the future of business

As AI continues to evolve and reshape industries, the strategic importance of AI leadership will only grow. The CAIO will be crucial in guiding organizations through the complexities of AI adoption, ensuring that AI initiatives are aligned with business objectives, and driving continuous improvement and innovation [7].

The future of business will be defined by those who can effectively harness the power of AI. The CAIO, as the strategic leader of AI initiatives, will be at the forefront of this transformation, ensuring that organizations are well equipped to navigate the challenges and opportunities of the AI era.

In conclusion, the strategic importance of AI leadership is evident in its ability to integrate AI with business strategy, navigate implementation challenges, drive cross-functional collaboration, ensure continuous improvement, and enhance decision-making. As the strategic leader of AI initiatives, the CAIO is indispensable in modern enterprises, guiding them through the complexities of the AI landscape and ensuring that they harness the full potential of AI to drive innovation, efficiency, and growth. The CAIO's role is essential in navigating the complexities of AI, ensuring that businesses harness their full potential responsibly and effectively. Embracing the CAIO era means committing to a future where AI drives continuous improvement, innovation, and success.

Alignment of AI initiatives with business goals

In the realm of modern enterprise, the alignment of AI initiatives with overarching business goals is a critical determinant of success. Ensuring that AI efforts are cohesive, impactful, and strategically integrated with business objectives is essential for driving innovation, enhancing operational efficiency, and achieving organizational goals. This alignment is not merely a technical endeavor but a strategic necessity that requires thoughtful planning, robust frameworks, and continuous evaluation.

Strategic vision and AI integration

A clear and comprehensive strategic vision is the starting point for aligning AI initiatives with business goals. This vision must articulate how AI will support and enhance the company's mission, objectives, and long-term goals. The CAIO plays a pivotal role in shaping this vision, ensuring that AI initiatives are not pursued in isolation but integrated into the broader strategic framework of the organization.

A well-defined strategic vision is a roadmap for AI initiatives, guiding their development and implementation. It ensures that AI efforts are focused on areas that will deliver the most significant business value, whether by enhancing customer experiences, optimizing supply chains, or driving product innovation. By embedding AI into the strategic vision, the CAIO ensures that AI initiatives are aligned with the company's priorities and objectives.

Establishing clear objectives and metrics

Establishing clear objectives and metrics for success ensures that AI initiatives align with business goals. These objectives should be **specific**, **measurable**, **achievable**, **relevant**, and **time-bound** (**SMART**). They should align with the company's strategic priorities and provide a clear framework for evaluating the success of AI initiatives.

The CAIO defines these objectives and ensures they are communicated across the organization. This involves setting performance indicators, benchmarks, and milestones that align with business goals and provide a clear path for measuring progress and success. By establishing clear objectives and metrics, the CAIO ensures that AI initiatives are focused, accountable, and aligned with the overall business strategy.

Cross-functional collaboration and alignment

AI initiatives often require collaboration across multiple departments and functions. Ensuring these initiatives are aligned with business goals requires effective cross-functional collaboration and alignment. The CAIO plays a crucial role in fostering this collaboration, breaking down silos, and ensuring that all stakeholders are aligned and engaged in the AI journey.

Effective collaboration involves regular communication, shared goals, and joint planning. The CAIO must establish clear communication channels and create opportunities for cross-functional teams to collaborate on AI initiatives. This collaborative approach ensures that AI efforts are aligned with the needs and objectives of different departments, enhancing their overall impact and effectiveness.

Continuous evaluation and adjustment

The dynamic nature of AI and business environments requires continuous evaluation and adjustment of AI initiatives. Ensuring AI efforts align with business goals necessitates ongoing monitoring, evaluation, and refinement. The CAIO is responsible for establishing robust evaluation frameworks and processes that enable continuous assessment and improvement of AI initiatives.

Continuous evaluation involves tracking progress against defined objectives and metrics, identifying areas for improvement, and making necessary adjustments to keep AI initiatives on track. This iterative approach ensures that AI efforts remain relevant, effective, and aligned with the evolving business landscape. By fostering a culture of continuous improvement, the CAIO ensures that AI initiatives are agile and responsive to changing business needs and opportunities.

Leveraging data and insights

The alignment of AI initiatives with business goals is deeply rooted in leveraging data and insights. Data-driven decision-making is at the heart of successful AI implementation. The CAIO ensures that AI initiatives are informed by accurate, timely, and relevant data, providing the insights needed to drive strategic decisions and achieve business objectives.

This involves establishing robust data governance frameworks, ensuring data quality, and leveraging advanced analytics to extract actionable insights. The CAIO must ensure that data is integrated across the organization and accessible to all relevant stakeholders. By harnessing the power of data, the CAIO ensures that AI initiatives are based on solid foundations and aligned with business goals.

Building a culture of alignment

Achieving alignment between AI initiatives and business goals requires a cultural shift within the organization. The CAIO plays a crucial role in building a culture of alignment, where AI is seen as a strategic enabler rather than a standalone technology. This involves promoting a shared understanding of AI's strategic value, fostering collaboration, and encouraging a holistic approach to AI implementation.

Building a culture of alignment involves engaging employees at all levels, providing training and resources, and creating opportunities for collaboration and innovation. The CAIO must lead by example, demonstrating the strategic importance of AI and its role in achieving business goals. By fostering a culture of alignment, the CAIO ensures that AI initiatives are embraced and supported across the organization.

The role of leadership in alignment

Leadership is crucial in ensuring that AI initiatives align with business goals. The CAIO and other senior leaders must provide strong leadership and direction, setting the tone for AI adoption and integration. This involves articulating a clear vision, establishing strategic priorities, and ensuring that AI initiatives have available resources and support.

Effective leadership involves strategic planning and active engagement with AI initiatives. Senior leaders must champion AI efforts, communicate their strategic importance, and ensure they are integrated into the business strategy. By providing strong leadership, the CAIO ensures that AI initiatives are aligned with business goals and positioned for success.

The strategic impact of alignment

Aligning AI initiatives with business goals has a profound strategic impact. When AI efforts are cohesive, impactful, and aligned with business strategies, they drive significant value and competitive advantage. This alignment ensures that AI initiatives are technologically advanced and strategically relevant, delivering tangible benefits and supporting the organization's mission and objectives.

Organizations can harness AI's full potential to drive innovation, enhance efficiency, and achieve strategic objectives by ensuring that AI initiatives are aligned with business goals. The CAIO plays a crucial role in this alignment, guiding AI efforts, fostering collaboration, and providing continuous improvement. Through strategic alignment, the CAIO ensures that AI initiatives are both successful and transformative, positioning the organization for long-term success in an AI-driven world.

Reflection and practical next steps

Before we conclude this chapter, let's take a moment to reflect on the key insights presented about the vital role of a CAIO and the strategic importance of AI leadership in today's business landscape. The central message is clear: AI is not just a technological trend; it is a transformative force that, when aligned with business objectives, can drive innovation, enhance operational efficiency, and provide a competitive edge. Now, it's time to think about how you can translate these ideas into action, whether you are leading an organization, managing a department, or working on a personal project.

Start by asking yourself: How well are AI strategies integrated into your organization or workflow? Do you see AI as a critical driver of business growth, or is it still treated as an isolated initiative? The CAIO's role is to ensure that AI is not just another tool but an integral part of your company's vision and strategy. Reflect on how your organization approaches AI leadership and whether the same level of strategic oversight is being applied. Is there someone focused on aligning AI initiatives with business goals, or could this be a gap in your current setup?

Key questions for reflection

Reflect on these key questions to assess your AI maturity, strategic alignment, leadership, compliance, and culture of innovation:

- **What is your organization's current AI maturity level?** Consider how embedded AI is within your core operations. Is it being used effectively to support strategic goals, or is there untapped potential that could be explored further?

- **How is AI leadership structured in your company?** Is there a clear figure, such as a CAIO or similar role, responsible for overseeing AI projects, ensuring alignment with business objectives, and driving innovation? Or do these responsibilities fall between various teams without cohesive direction?

- **How aligned are your AI initiatives with your business strategy?** Are AI projects contributing directly to key objectives such as revenue growth, customer satisfaction, or operational efficiency, or are they disconnected from your broader goals?

- **What steps are being taken to ensure compliance and ethical AI use?** Do you have frameworks to ensure your AI systems are transparent, fair, and aligned with regulatory requirements? If not, how can this be improved to avoid potential risks in the future?

- **Are you fostering a culture of innovation through AI?** Is your team encouraged to explore new AI technologies and approaches, or are they operating within traditional, risk-averse boundaries? How can you inspire a more experimental mindset that leverages AI to solve complex problems creatively?

With these questions in mind, let's turn to practical next steps to help you move from reflection to action.

Practical next steps *Great Idea*

Align your organization's AI efforts with these key steps to strengthen leadership, drive innovation, and ensure ethical, strategic impact:

1. **Conduct a comprehensive AI audit:** Start by assessing your organization's current state of AI. This audit should examine how AI is used across different departments and functions, identifying strengths and gaps. Are AI projects siloed or part of a cohesive, organization-wide strategy? By taking stock of your AI initiatives, you'll be better positioned to identify areas for improvement or expansion. This can also reveal opportunities where a dedicated CAIO could add significant value by ensuring alignment between AI initiatives and business goals.

2. **Establish AI leadership or strengthen existing leadership**: If your organization does not have a CAIO or a similar leadership role focused on AI, consider the benefits of establishing one. As we've seen, a CAIO bridges the gap between technical teams and executive leadership, ensuring that AI projects are strategically aligned and operationally feasible. Even if a full-time CAIO is not an option, assigning a senior leader with clear AI oversight responsibilities can improve strategic alignment and execution. This leader would ensure that AI initiatives consistently deliver measurable value and fully integrate into the company's broader objectives.

3. **Foster a culture of continuous AI innovation**: AI-driven innovation requires a forward-thinking culture that embraces experimentation and learning. Encourage your teams to explore new AI applications and methodologies by creating an environment where taking calculated risks is accepted and encouraged. One way to achieve this is by establishing "innovation labs" or dedicating resources to small pilot AI projects that can test new ideas without the pressure of immediate success. The goal here is to create a sandbox where experimentation leads to breakthrough innovations that could have a significant impact on your business.

4. **Align AI initiatives with strategic business goals**: To ensure that AI initiatives contribute meaningfully to business outcomes, establish clear objectives for each project that are directly tied to organizational goals. This requires defining **key performance indicators** (**KPIs**) and success metrics for each AI initiative. The CAIO, or a similar AI leader, should regularly review these metrics to ensure projects are on track and delivering value. For example, if a project aims to improve customer service response times through AI-driven automation, track metrics such as customer satisfaction scores, response times, and cost savings. Continuous alignment and course correction will ensure AI remains a strategic enabler rather than an isolated effort.

5. **Enhance cross-functional collaboration**: AI initiatives often span multiple departments, requiring close collaboration between technical teams, business leaders, and operational staff. Ensure that AI projects are not confined to specific departments but are collaborative efforts that draw on the expertise of different areas within the organization. Establish regular cross-functional meetings or task forces to ensure that AI projects are aligned with the needs and priorities of all stakeholders. For example, a successful AI-driven sales optimization project might involve input from marketing, IT, and sales teams to ensure that all relevant perspectives are incorporated into the solution.

6. **Ensure compliance and ethical AI use**: In an age of increasing scrutiny over data privacy and ethical AI usage, it's critical to build frameworks that ensure your AI systems comply with regulatory standards and operate ethically. Designate a team or individual responsible for staying up to date on emerging regulations and ethical considerations in AI. This can include regular audits of your AI models to check for bias, transparency, and fairness. By proactively addressing these issues, you can avoid reputational and financial risks that come with non-compliance or unethical AI practices.

7. **Leverage data to drive AI-enhanced decision-making**: The CAIO should ensure that AI is integrated into decision-making processes by leveraging data-driven insights. AI can provide predictive analytics and real-time data that improve the quality and speed of business decisions. This requires setting up systems where AI-generated insights are made accessible to decision-makers at all levels of the organization. For instance, predictive maintenance in manufacturing can drastically reduce downtime by providing data-driven insights into equipment performance. Encouraging data literacy and providing training will help employees make the most of these insights, improving overall business outcomes.

8. **Cultivate a data-driven and AI-enabled culture**: AI leadership isn't just about the technology; it's about fostering a cultural shift within the organization toward embracing AI and data at all levels. A CAIO can lead this cultural transformation by promoting data literacy, encouraging data-driven decision-making, and ensuring that employees across all functions understand how AI can benefit their daily operations. Consider implementing training programs, workshops, or certification opportunities to build data skills across your organization. As more employees become comfortable working with AI, you'll find that innovative ideas and improvements emerge from all levels of the business.

9. **Implement continuous improvement processes**: AI technologies and methodologies evolve rapidly, and your AI strategy must evolve with them. Establish a framework for continuous evaluation of your AI systems to ensure they remain effective and aligned with your business objectives. This might include regular performance reviews, gathering feedback from end users, and benchmarking AI systems against industry standards. By maintaining a flexible, adaptable approach to AI leadership, you'll ensure your organization can pivot as new technologies or challenges arise, keeping your AI initiatives relevant and impactful.

Summary

In this chapter, we explored the growing importance of having a dedicated CAIO in organizations navigating the complexities of today's AI-driven landscape. You saw how a CAIO plays a pivotal role in aligning AI initiatives with overarching business goals, ensuring that these efforts not only deliver technical excellence but also drive strategic outcomes such as innovation, operational efficiency, and competitive advantage. We discussed how the CAIO serves as a vital bridge between technical teams and executive leadership, ensuring that AI projects are cohesive, impactful, and sustainable. This role also involves fostering a culture of innovation, managing compliance and ethical concerns, and promoting a data-driven decision-making process. As you reflect on these key takeaways, consider how focused AI leadership could enhance your organization's ability to leverage AI more effectively.

Looking ahead, the next chapter will provide a detailed exploration of the **key responsibilities of a CAIO**. We'll break down the essential duties of a CAIO, from setting AI strategy to managing teams, and discuss how this role ensures the successful implementation of AI initiatives across all levels of the business. It's time to dive into the day-to-day responsibilities that make this leadership position indispensable in the modern enterprise.

Questions

1. What is the primary role of a CAIO within an organization, and why is it considered essential in today's business environment?
2. How does a CAIO help bridge the gap between technical teams and executive leadership?
3. What are some key ways a CAIO can drive innovation through AI initiatives?
4. Why is aligning AI initiatives with overall business goals important, and what risks arise if this alignment is lacking?
5. In what ways does a CAIO ensure compliance with regulatory standards and promote ethical AI use?
6. How does a CAIO contribute to building a data-driven culture within an organization, and why is this critical for long-term success?
7. What challenges might a CAIO face when implementing AI initiatives, and how can they overcome these challenges?
8. Why is continuous improvement important in AI leadership, and how does a CAIO foster this within their organization?
9. What are some examples of how AI can enhance decision-making processes, and what role does the CAIO play in this enhancement?
10. How can a CAIO ensure cross-functional collaboration when implementing AI initiatives across different departments?

References

1. *Crucial Steps for Organizations to Prepare for the AI Revolution*. leadersdialog.com. `https://leadersdialog.com/?session=tba-15`.
2. Adelakun, B. O., Majekodunmi, T. G., & Akintoye, O. S. (2024). *AI and ethical accounting: Navigating challenges and opportunities. International Journal of Advanced Economics*. doi.org. `https://doi.org/10.51594/ijae.v6i6.1230`.
3. *Why A Data-Driven Culture Is Critical To Your Business*. elnion.com. `https://elnion.com/2023/05/24/why-a-data-driven-culture-is-critical-to-your-business/`.

4. Kejriwal, M. (2022). *What Is on the Horizon? Future of Business and Finance.* doi.org. `https://doi.org/10.1007/978-3-031-19039-1_6`.

5. *Revolutionizing Business: The Impact Of Artificial Intelligence For Enterprises.* como-evitar.net. `https://como-evitar.net/revolutionizing-business-the-impact-of-artificial-intelligence-for-enterprises/`.

6. *Wanted: Chief AI Officer. Hungry Workhorse.* hungryworkhorse.com. `https://hungryworkhorse.com/business-management/wanted-chief-ai-officer/`.

7. *Unlocking the Power of AI: Transforming Business Processes with Automation.* isidroavila.com. `https://isidroavila.com/index.php/2023/07/17/unlocking-the-power-of-ai-transforming-business-processes-with-automation/`.

2

Key Responsibilities of a Chief AI Officer

It's going to be interesting to see how society deals with artificial intelligence, but it will definitely be cool

– Colin Angle

Imagine this: in 2023, a leading financial institution implemented an AI-powered fraud detection system, reducing fraudulent transactions by 70% within the first 6 months. Behind this success was a **Chief AI Officer** (**CAIO**) orchestrating the integration of advanced algorithms with the company's operations, ensuring that the technology not only worked but delivered real value. This is just one example of how pivotal the CAIO's role can be.

In another scenario, consider a global retail giant that leveraged AI to personalize customer experiences, resulting in a 25% increase in sales. The CAIO played a crucial role in aligning AI initiatives with business goals, ensuring seamless implementation and continuous improvement. These are not isolated cases; they represent the CAIO's growing influence and critical importance in modern businesses.

In an era where AI is transforming industries from healthcare to finance, the responsibilities of a CAIO are both vast and vital. They are the visionaries crafting a comprehensive AI strategy, the guardians ensuring ethical compliance, and the champions driving AI adoption across the organization. But how does one navigate these multifaceted responsibilities? How do you balance strategic oversight with the hands-on involvement needed to execute complex AI projects?

Consider the complexities a CAIO faces daily: integrating AI into existing business models, staying ahead of technological advancements, and managing the ethical implications of AI decisions. They are responsible for ensuring that AI systems are not only effective but also fair, transparent, and aligned with the company's values and legal requirements.

Moreover, the CAIO must foster a culture of AI adoption within the organization. This involves not only advocating for AI's potential but also addressing employees' fears and misconceptions. While many executives recognize AI's transformative potential, few employees feel prepared for this shift. Bridging this gap is a key responsibility of the CAIO, requiring strong leadership and communication skills.

This chapter delves into the core responsibilities of a CAIO, providing a clear framework for understanding and excelling in this role. Whether stepping into the position for the first time or looking to refine your approach, this guide offers practical advice on balancing the big picture with the details, ensuring your AI initiatives are innovative, ethical, and impactful.

We will explore how to develop a robust AI vision that aligns with your organization's goals, manage the execution of AI projects, and navigate the ethical and regulatory landscapes. Additionally, we'll provide insights into fostering an AI-friendly culture and ensuring your team is on board with the AI-driven changes.

In this chapter, we will cover the following topics:

- Strategic AI vision and implementation
- Navigating technological and ethical challenges
- Fostering AI adoption and organizational transformation
- Case study – AI transformation in manufacturing

By the end of this chapter, you will gain a comprehensive understanding of the key responsibilities of a CAIO, the common challenges in implementing AI strategies, and how to develop a structured approach to AI implementation. You will also learn to recognize the impact of AI on organizational efficiency and performance and apply insights from a real-world case study to your initiatives. Together, we will explore what it truly means to be a CAIO and how to harness the transformative power of AI, equipping you with the tools and strategies to lead your organization confidently into an AI-powered future.

The problem – pain points and challenges

In today's hyper-competitive business environment, integrating AI is no longer a luxury – it's a necessity. However, the journey to effectively harness AI is fraught with challenges, and the CAIO stands at the epicenter of these complexities. Businesses face significant hurdles in understanding, implementing, and maximizing the potential of AI, making the CAIO's role both critical and challenging.

The complexity of AI technologies

Understanding these challenges is the first step toward overcoming them. By addressing these pain points head-on, CAIOs can lead their organizations toward a future where AI is not just a tool but a cornerstone of strategic growth and innovation. The significance of these challenges cannot be overstated; they represent the critical obstacles that must be navigated to unlock AI's full potential. As we explore each of these areas in depth, CAIOs will be better equipped to transform their organizations and achieve sustainable competitive advantage through AI.

One of the primary challenges businesses encounter is the sheer complexity of AI technologies. AI encompasses a broad spectrum of tools and techniques, from machine learning algorithms predicting customer behavior to natural language processing systems interacting with users in human-like ways. For instance, a global study by McKinsey found that only 20% of companies have adopted AI at scale, largely due to difficulties in understanding and integrating these technologies into existing workflows [1].

The CAIO must navigate this complexity, ensuring the right technologies are chosen and effectively implemented to drive business value.

Moreover, the diversity of AI applications means that CAIOs must be well-versed in various AI methodologies and how they can be applied across different business functions. For example, predictive analytics can transform marketing strategies, while computer vision can revolutionize quality control in manufacturing. Each application requires a deep understanding of the technology and the specific business context. The CAIO must bridge these gaps, translating complex technical concepts into actionable business strategies.

Rapid technological advancements

The rapid pace of AI development presents another significant challenge. What is cutting-edge today might be outdated tomorrow. This creates a continuous learning curve for CAIOs, who must stay abreast of the latest advancements while anticipating future trends. According to Gartner, by 2025, GenAI will be a workforce partner for 90% of companies worldwide [2]. CAIOs must be strategic thinkers and agile leaders, capable of pivoting quickly as new opportunities and challenges arise. For example, a company that fails to adopt the latest AI-driven customer service technologies may quickly fall behind competitors that provide more personalized and efficient customer interactions.

The speed of AI advancements also means CAIOs must cultivate a culture of continuous learning within their organizations. This involves staying updated with the latest research and development and fostering an environment where employees are encouraged to upskill and embrace new technologies. Failure to do so can result in a skills gap, where the organization cannot fully leverage AI's potential, thereby missing out on competitive advantages.

Ethical and regulatory concerns

Ethical and regulatory considerations add another layer of complexity to the CAIO's responsibilities. Using AI in business decisions can lead to unintended consequences, such as biased algorithms reinforcing existing inequalities. A notable case involved a major tech company whose AI recruiting tool was found to discriminate against female candidates, leading to widespread criticism and the eventual abandonment of the tool [3]. Ensuring that AI systems are fair, transparent, and compliant with regulations is daunting, but it is essential for maintaining trust and credibility. The CAIO must establish robust governance frameworks to monitor and address these ethical challenges.

Moreover, the regulatory landscape for AI is continuously evolving. Governments worldwide are increasingly scrutinizing AI applications to ensure they do not harm consumers or exacerbate social inequalities. For example, the European Union's **General Data Protection Regulation (GDPR)** has significant implications for how companies handle data used in AI systems. The CAIO must ensure that the organization's AI initiatives comply with these regulations, often requiring working closely with legal and compliance teams to navigate the complex legal terrain.

Cultural and organizational resistance

Fostering a culture of AI adoption within an organization can be challenging. Employees may resist AI initiatives due to fear of job displacement or skepticism about the technology's benefits. A survey by PwC revealed that 68% of executives believe AI will drive significant changes in the workforce, but only 31% of employees feel AI will increase their productivity [4]. This disconnect underscores the importance of effective change management and communication in promoting AI adoption. The CAIO must advocate for AI's potential and address these fears and misconceptions, ensuring that the entire organization is aligned with and supportive of AI-driven initiatives.

Creating an AI-friendly culture requires clear communication about AI's benefits and how it can enhance rather than replace human capabilities. For instance, AI can automate routine tasks, allowing employees to focus on more strategic and creative aspects of their jobs. The CAIO must spearhead these communication efforts, highlighting success stories and demonstrating tangible benefits to foster a positive attitude toward AI.

Resource allocation and skill gaps

Another significant challenge is the allocation of resources and addressing skill gaps. Developing and implementing AI solutions requires substantial technology, talent, and investment in training. Many organizations struggle to find skilled AI professionals, and the cost of building an in-house AI team can be prohibitive. According to a report by Deloitte, 68% of surveyed executives cited talent shortages as a significant barrier to AI adoption [5]. The CAIO must strategically allocate resources, identify areas where AI can deliver the most value, and invest in developing in-house capabilities or seeking external partnerships.

The CAIO must also prioritize which AI projects to undertake based on potential ROI and alignment with business goals. This involves making tough decisions about resource allocation, especially in organizations with limited budgets. The CAIO must balance immediate needs with long-term strategic goals, ensuring that AI investments drive sustainable growth.

The need for a clear AI vision

Finally, a clear AI vision and strategy can hinder AI adoption. Many organizations embark on AI projects without a comprehensive plan, leading to fragmented efforts and suboptimal outcomes. The CAIO must develop a clear AI vision that aligns with the organization's overall business strategy, setting measurable goals and defining a roadmap for achieving them. This involves identifying high-impact AI use cases and ensuring that the necessary infrastructure and processes are in place to support AI initiatives.

A well-defined AI strategy acts as a north star, guiding the organization's efforts and ensuring all AI initiatives are cohesive and aligned with broader business objectives. The CAIO must articulate this vision clearly to all stakeholders, from the boardroom to the front lines, to ensure everyone understands the strategic importance of AI and their role in its implementation.

The role of the CAIO is pivotal in addressing these challenges. By developing a clear AI vision and strategy, ensuring ethical compliance, fostering a culture of innovation, and effectively managing resources, CAIOs can guide their organizations through the complexities of AI implementation. In the following sections, we will delve deeper into these responsibilities, providing practical advice and insights to help CAIOs navigate the multifaceted landscape of AI leadership.

The solution – step-by-step implementation

Implementing an effective AI strategy requires a meticulous, step-by-step approach. Here's a comprehensive guide to address the key challenges and drive successful AI integration in your organization.

Step 1 – Developing a clear AI vision and strategy

This step includes the following aspects:

- **Strategic alignment**: Collaborate with executive leadership to align AI with the organization's long-term goals. This involves engaging in strategic discussions to understand business priorities and identify how AI can support these objectives. For instance, if the goal is to enhance customer experience, AI strategies might focus on personalized interactions and predictive analytics to anticipate customer needs.
- **Roadmap development**: Create a detailed roadmap outlining specific AI projects, timelines, and milestones. Start with pilot projects to demonstrate quick wins and build confidence. The roadmap should include short-term, medium-term, and long-term goals, providing a clear path forward. For example, a roadmap might start with implementing AI-driven chatbots and gradually expand to more complex AI applications such as predictive maintenance.
- **Measurable outcomes**: Establish clear metrics to measure the success of AI initiatives, such as performance improvements, cost savings, or revenue growth. Regular reviews and adjustments based on these metrics help keep AI initiatives on track. This structured approach ensures that all AI efforts are cohesive and aligned with business objectives, reducing the risk of fragmented or misaligned projects.

Step 2 – Navigating technological complexity

Let's go through what this step includes:

- **Technology assessment**: Conduct a thorough evaluation of existing technologies to identify gaps and opportunities. This involves evaluating the current technology stack, understanding the data landscape, and identifying areas where AI can add value. For example, a retailer might need advanced recommendation systems to improve product suggestions, while a manufacturer might benefit from predictive maintenance tools to reduce downtime.

- **Solution design**: Design AI solutions tailored to business needs, selecting suitable algorithms, tools, and platforms. Detailed feasibility studies and pilot projects help refine these designs before full-scale implementation. For instance, AI algorithms for customer segmentation can be tested on a smaller scale before being applied across the entire customer base.

- **Implementation support**: Provide hands-on support during implementation to ensure seamless integration with existing systems. This includes working closely with IT teams, providing training and support, and troubleshooting issues during deployment. Regular check-ins and iterative development cycles ensure challenges are quickly addressed, minimizing disruption.

Step 3 – Addressing ethical and regulatory challenges

This step requires addressing the following:

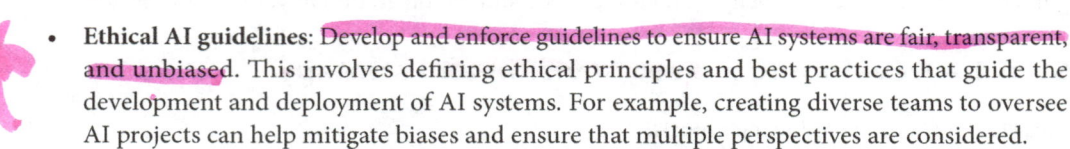

- **Ethical AI guidelines**: Develop and enforce guidelines to ensure AI systems are fair, transparent, and unbiased. This involves defining ethical principles and best practices that guide the development and deployment of AI systems. For example, creating diverse teams to oversee AI projects can help mitigate biases and ensure that multiple perspectives are considered.

- **Compliance monitoring**: Continuously monitor AI systems to ensure compliance with evolving regulations, such as GDPR. This includes regular audits, risk assessments, and implementing controls to ensure AI systems comply with legal and regulatory requirements. Proactive engagement with regulatory bodies and staying updated on new legislation helps maintain compliance.

- **Stakeholder engagement**: Engage with diverse stakeholders to understand and address ethical concerns, fostering a culture of accountability and trust. This involves involving a wide range of perspectives in the AI development process, including those of employees, customers, and external experts. Transparency initiatives, such as public reports and open dialogues, can further build trust and demonstrate a commitment to ethical practices.

Step 4 – Cultivating a culture of AI adoption

For this step, you need to take care of the following:

- **Communication plans**: Develop clear communication plans to articulate the benefits of AI and address employee concerns. This involves regular updates, town hall meetings, and Q&A sessions to keep employees informed and engaged. Transparent communication helps demystify AI and dispel myths, making the technology more approachable.
- **Training programs**: Implement comprehensive training programs to upskill employees and foster a culture of continuous learning. These programs cover technical skills, such as data science and machine learning, and soft skills, such as change management and ethical considerations. Interactive workshops, online courses, and hands-on projects help reinforce learning.
- **Success stories**: Highlight early wins and success stories to build momentum and support for AI initiatives. Showcasing tangible benefits and positive outcomes can build trust and enthusiasm for AI across the organization. Regularly celebrating these successes and recognizing contributors helps sustain motivation and engagement.

Step 5 – Strategic resource allocation and skill development

Here are the activities involved:

- **Resource planning**: Identify high-impact AI projects and strategically allocate resources to maximize ROI. This includes evaluating the potential return on investment for different AI initiatives and prioritizing those that offer the greatest value. Detailed cost-benefit analyses and scenario planning help ensure optimal resource allocation.
- **Talent acquisition**: Help recruit and train AI talent, either by building in-house capabilities or through strategic partnerships. This involves identifying skill gaps, recruiting top talent, and providing ongoing training and development opportunities. Partnering with educational institutions and industry bodies can help source and nurture emerging talent.
- **Continuous learning**: Promote a constant learning and development culture to keep pace with AI advancements. This includes providing access to online courses, workshops, conferences, and other learning opportunities to ensure that employees stay up to date with the latest developments in AI. Encouraging participation in AI communities and networks can also enhance knowledge sharing and innovation.

Step 6 – Establishing robust infrastructure and processes

The final step involves the following:

- **Infrastructure investment**: Invest in scalable IT infrastructure and robust data management practices to support AI initiatives. This includes cloud platforms, data storage solutions, and data processing capabilities. For instance, using cloud platforms such as AWS, Google Cloud, or Azure can provide the flexibility and scalability needed for AI initiatives.

- **Process optimization**: Optimize workflows for efficiency and implement processes for continuous improvement. This includes streamlining workflows to integrate AI solutions effectively and implementing continuous improvement and iteration processes. Regularly reviewing and refining these processes ensures that AI initiatives remain efficient and effective.

- **Security and data privacy**: Prioritize security and data privacy to protect the organization's foundation. Implement robust security measures and data governance frameworks to safeguard sensitive information and ensure compliance with data protection regulations. This is crucial for maintaining trust and integrity in AI systems.

By following these step-by-step guidelines, organizations can effectively develop a clear AI vision, navigate technological complexities, address ethical and regulatory challenges, cultivate a culture of AI adoption, strategically manage resources, and establish robust infrastructure and processes. This comprehensive approach empowers CAIOs to lead their organizations through the complexities of AI integration, ensuring that AI becomes a cornerstone of strategic growth and innovation.

Case study – transforming operations at APEX Manufacturing and Distribution

Throughout this book, we will use the hypothetical company APEX Manufacturing and Distribution as a recurring example to illustrate the concepts and strategies discussed. By following APEX's journey, we aim to provide detailed, professional insights into the practical application of AI within a business setting. This approach allows us to present actionable strategies and real-world scenarios, making complex AI concepts more relatable and easily understood.

Initial situation

In early 2023, APEX Manufacturing and Distribution – a prominent player in the industrial sector – faced significant challenges in its operational efficiency. APEX served a diverse client base across multiple regions as a company specializing in producing and distributing high-quality industrial machinery. However, the company struggled with numerous inefficiencies in its production and distribution processes, leading to delays, increased costs, and customer dissatisfaction.

The high demand for their products led to bottlenecks in the production line, frequent equipment failures, and a lack of real-time visibility into operations. These issues affected the company's profitability and eroded its competitive edge. The leadership at APEX recognized that a fundamental transformation was essential to maintaining their market position and improving operational efficiency. They sought an innovative solution to streamline processes, enhance productivity, and reduce operational costs.

Steps taken

The transformation journey began with a comprehensive assessment of the current operational landscape. This phase was crucial to understanding the depth of the issues and identifying specific areas where AI could make the most significant improvements.

The key findings during this assessment included the following:

- **Production delays**: There were frequent delays in the production line due to equipment failures and inefficient scheduling. These delays caused significant backlogs and affected delivery timelines.
- **High maintenance costs**: Significant costs incurred due to unplanned maintenance and equipment downtime. Maintenance teams were often reactive rather than proactive, leading to costly repairs and replacements.
- **Lack of real-time data**: Inadequate real-time visibility into production processes, leading to suboptimal decision-making. Managers lacked the necessary data to make informed decisions quickly.
- **Customer dissatisfaction**: Delays and inefficiencies lead to lower customer satisfaction and potential loss of business. Customer complaints increased, and satisfaction scores were consistently below expectations.

Building on these findings, the following actions were implemented to address the issues identified and drive improvement.

Developing a clear AI vision

With these insights, in collaboration with the CAIO, APEX's leadership developed a clear and ambitious vision for integrating AI into their manufacturing and distribution operations. The objective was to deploy AI-driven solutions that streamline production processes, enhance equipment maintenance, and provide real-time operational insights.

The strategic goals included the following:

- **Predictive maintenance**: Implement AI-driven predictive maintenance to anticipate equipment failures and reduce downtime. This would shift the maintenance approach from reactive to proactive.
- **AI-enhanced scheduling**: Use AI to optimize production scheduling and improve efficiency. This included creating dynamic schedules that could adapt to real-time changes in production conditions.

- **Real-time monitoring**: Deploy AI-powered real-time monitoring systems to provide visibility into production processes. This would allow managers to make data-driven decisions on the fly.
- **Staff training**: Equip staff with the skills needed to work alongside AI tools, ensuring a smooth transition and effective use of new technologies. Training programs were designed to foster a culture of innovation and continuous improvement.

Creating a detailed roadmap

To turn this vision into reality, a detailed roadmap was crafted. This roadmap delineated the path forward, highlighting short-term, medium-term, and long-term goals with specific milestones and deliverables for each phase.

The roadmap highlights are as follows:

- **Phase 1 (0–3 months)**: Deploy AI-driven predictive maintenance systems to address the most critical equipment issues. Focus on quick wins to demonstrate the benefits of AI. This phase also included initial staff training to ensure readiness for AI integration.
- **Phase 2 (3–6 months)**: Integrate AI-enhanced scheduling tools to optimize production processes and reduce delays. Roll out comprehensive training programs for staff to ensure they can use the new tools effectively.
- **Phase 3 (6–12 months)**: Implement AI-powered real-time monitoring systems to provide complete visibility into production operations, further enhancing efficiency and decision-making. This phase would also involve refining and scaling the initial implementations based on feedback and performance data.

Implementing the solution

We can divide the implementation process into multiple phases, as discussed next.

Phase 1 – Deploying predictive maintenance systems

The journey began with developing and deploying AI-driven predictive maintenance systems designed to monitor equipment health, anticipate potential failures, and proactively schedule maintenance:

- **Developing predictive models**: Detailed models were created to analyze equipment data and forecast potential failures. These models were based on historical maintenance records and real-time sensor data. Advanced machine learning algorithms were employed to increase the accuracy of predictions.
- **Testing and iteration**: The predictive maintenance system underwent rigorous testing to ensure accuracy and reliability. This testing phase involved real-world scenarios to validate the system's performance. Feedback from maintenance teams was incorporated to refine the system.

- **Full deployment**: After successful testing, the predictive maintenance system was rolled out across all production facilities, significantly reducing unplanned downtime and maintenance costs. The deployment was accompanied by detailed documentation and training sessions for maintenance staff.

Phase 2 – Integration and training

Following the successful deployment of the predictive maintenance systems, the next step was integrating AI-enhanced scheduling tools and training the staff. This included the following:

- **AI-enhanced scheduling**: AI algorithms were developed to optimize production schedules, considering various factors such as order priority, machine availability, and maintenance schedules. These algorithms helped reduce production delays and improve overall efficiency. The scheduling system was designed to be dynamic, adjusting in real time to changes in production conditions.
- **Comprehensive training programs**: Training programs were designed and implemented to help staff understand and effectively use the new AI tools. These programs included the following:
  - **Hands-on workshops**: Interactive workshops provided practical experience with the AI tools, allowing staff to familiarize themselves with the new systems. These workshops included real-world scenarios and problem-solving exercises.
  - **Online training modules**: Self-paced online modules offered detailed insights into the functionality and benefits of AI in manufacturing operations. These modules were available on-demand, allowing staff to learn independently.
  - **Ongoing support**: A support hotline and regular Q&A sessions were established to address any issues or concerns during the transition period. Continuous feedback loops ensured that training materials were updated and relevant.

Phase 3 – Real-time monitoring

The final phase focused on implementing AI-powered real-time monitoring systems to provide complete visibility into production processes and enhance decision-making. This was achieved with the following:

- **Data collection and integration**: Data from various sources, including sensors and production logs, was aggregated to build a comprehensive dataset for analysis. This data was crucial for developing accurate monitoring systems and predictive models.
- **Development of monitoring systems**: AI-driven monitoring systems were developed to analyze real-time data and provide actionable insights into production processes. These systems helped identify bottlenecks and optimize operations. Advanced visualization tools were used to present data in an easily understandable format.

- **Implementation and feedback**: The monitoring systems were implemented across all facilities, and feedback was collected to refine and improve the system further. Continuous improvement cycles ensured that the system evolved to meet the needs of the production teams.

Results achieved

The implementation of AI-driven solutions led to significant hypothetical improvements in APEX Manufacturing and Distribution's operations, reflecting the real-world results that can be achieved with such technologies:

- **Reduced downtime and maintenance costs**: The predictive maintenance system reduced equipment downtime by 40%, leading to substantial cost savings. The ability to proactively anticipate and address equipment issues minimized unplanned maintenance and improved overall production efficiency. This shift from reactive to proactive maintenance also extended the lifespan of critical machinery.
- **Improved production efficiency**: The AI-enhanced scheduling tools optimized production schedules, reducing delays and increasing throughput. This led to a 25% improvement in production efficiency, allowing APEX to meet customer demands more effectively. The dynamic scheduling system ensured production lines operated smoothly despite unexpected issues.
- **Enhanced real-time visibility**: The monitoring systems provided complete visibility into production processes, enabling better decision-making and operational control. This improved transparency led to more efficient operations and quicker identification and resolution of bottlenecks. Managers could now make data-driven decisions that optimized production flow and resource allocation.
- **Increased customer satisfaction**: With reduced delays and improved production efficiency, customer satisfaction scores increased by 30%. Customers experienced fewer delays and higher reliability, leading to stronger loyalty and repeat business. The improvements in operational efficiency translated directly into better service levels and shorter lead times.

This hypothetical case study of APEX Manufacturing and Distribution illustrates the transformative power of AI in operational efficiency. By developing a clear vision, creating a detailed roadmap, leveraging the right technologies, and fostering a culture of AI adoption, the company achieved remarkable improvements in efficiency, customer satisfaction, and operational costs. APEX's journey serves as a guide for any company aiming to harness the full potential of AI and drive sustainable growth in an increasingly competitive market.

Reflection and practical next steps

Before we conclude this chapter on the key responsibilities of a CAIO, it's time to pause and reflect on how these insights can shape your approach to AI leadership. Whether in a CAIO role, aspiring to be one, or simply looking to enhance your organization's AI strategy, this reflection will help you internalize the lessons and chart a course forward.

Reflecting on core insights

Take a moment to consider the following questions:

- How does the CAIO's role in developing a clear AI vision resonate with your current approach to AI strategy?
- How can you better navigate the complexities of AI technologies in your organization?
- How prepared are you to address the ethical and regulatory challenges associated with AI implementation?
- What steps can you take to foster a culture of AI adoption in your team or organization?

Remember, there's no one-size-fits-all approach to AI leadership. Your reflections should be personal and contextual to your unique situation.

Critical assessment

Now, let's dive deeper with some thought-provoking questions:

- If you were to rate your organization's AI readiness on a scale of 1 to 10, where would you place it? Why?
- What's the biggest obstacle preventing your organization from fully leveraging AI's potential?
- How aligned is your current AI strategy with your business objectives?
- How could improving your AI strategy positively impact your organization's performance?

These questions highlight areas where implementing the strategies discussed in this chapter could yield significant benefits.

Practical next steps

Based on your reflections, consider these actionable steps to enhance your AI leadership:

1. **Develop your AI vision**:
   - **Action**: Schedule a brainstorming session with key stakeholders to outline your organization's AI vision
   - **Example**: A retail company might envision using AI to create hyper-personalized shopping experiences within the next two years

2. **Address technological complexities**:
   - **Action**: Audit your current AI capabilities and identify gaps
   - **Example**: You might need a more robust data infrastructure to support advanced AI applications

3. **Tackle ethical considerations**:
   - **Action**: Form an AI ethics committee or task force
   - **Example**: This group could develop guidelines for ensuring AI decisions are transparent and unbiased

4. **Foster AI adoption**:
   - **Action**: Design an AI awareness program for employees at all levels
   - **Example**: This could include lunch-and-learn sessions, workshops, or an internal AI newsletter

5. **Align resources and skills**:
   - **Action**: Create a skills matrix to identify AI-related competencies in your organization
   - **Example**: This could reveal the need for additional data scientists or AI engineers

Remember, progress is often incremental. Start with small, achievable goals and build momentum. Consider the example of APEX Manufacturing and Distribution from our case study. They began focusing on predictive maintenance before expanding to broader AI applications.

Moving forward

As you embark on this journey, remember that becoming an effective CAIO or AI leader is an ongoing process. Stay curious, remain open to learning, and don't be afraid to experiment. The field of AI is rapidly evolving, and your approach should evolve with it.

Challenge yourself to implement at least one of these practical steps next month. Whether it's initiating a conversation about AI ethics or mapping out your organization's AI capabilities, taking that first step is crucial.

Remember, the goal isn't perfection but progress. Every step you take toward more effective AI leadership brings your organization closer to realizing AI's transformative potential.

As you move forward, ask yourself, "*How can I leverage AI to create more value for my organization and its stakeholders?*" Let this question guide your decisions and actions as you navigate the exciting world of AI leadership.

Your journey as an AI leader starts now. Embrace the challenges, celebrate the successes, and never stop learning. The future of AI is bright, and with thoughtful leadership, you can help shape that future for your organization and beyond.

Summary

As we explored in this chapter, the role of a CAIO is multifaceted and crucial in today's AI-driven business landscape. You've learned that successful CAIOs must balance strategic vision with hands-on implementation, navigate complex ethical terrain, and foster a culture of AI adoption. Remember, the journey to effective AI leadership isn't about perfection but continuous learning and adaptation. Whether you're already in a CAIO role or aspiring to be one, the strategies we've discussed – from developing a clear AI roadmap to addressing technological and ethical challenges – provide a solid foundation for driving meaningful AI transformation.

Now that you've grasped the key responsibilities of a CAIO, you might be wondering, "How do I put all of this into action?" That's exactly what we'll tackle in our next chapter. We'll dive into the nitty-gritty of translating these responsibilities into a cohesive, actionable plan that aligns with your organization's goals and values. Get ready to roll up your sleeves and start shaping your AI strategy!

Questions

1. What are the three main topics covered in this chapter?
2. List three key responsibilities of a CAIO.
3. Why is developing a clear AI vision important for a CAIO?
4. What ethical considerations should a CAIO address when implementing AI solutions?
5. How can a CAIO foster an organization's culture of AI adoption?
6. In the APEX Manufacturing and Distribution case study, what was the first AI solution implemented and its impact?
7. What are two challenges a CAIO might face when navigating the complexity of AI technologies?
8. How does the role of a CAIO contribute to aligning AI initiatives with overall business goals?
9. Describe one strategy a CAIO could use to address an organization's skill gap in AI.
10. Based on the chapter, what steps would you recommend for a CAIO to ensure ethical compliance in AI implementations?

References

1. McKinsey & Company. *The state of AI in 2020*. Retrieved from McKinsey: https://www.mckinsey.com/capabilities/quantumblack/our-insights/global-survey-the-state-of-ai-in-2020.
2. Gartner. *Gartner Says AI Ambition and AI-Ready Scenarios Must Be a Top Priority for CIOs for Next 12-24 Months*. Retrieved from Gartner: https://www.gartner.com/en/newsroom/press-releases/2023-11-06-gartner-says-ai-ambition-and-ai-ready-scenarios-must-be-a-top-priority-for-cios-for-next-12-24-months.

3. Reuters. *Amazon scraps secret AI recruiting tool that showed bias against women.* Retrieved from Reuters: `https://www.reuters.com/article/idUSKCN1MK0AG/`.

4. PwC's 2024 *AI Jobs Barometer.* Retrieved from PwC: `https://www.pwc.com/gx/en/issues/artificial-intelligence/ai-jobs-barometer.html#:~:text=Many%20workers%20agree.,to%20create%20new%20job%20opportunities`.

5. Deloitte. *Talent and workforce effects in the age of AI.* Retrieved from Deloitte: `https://www2.deloitte.com/content/dam/insights/us/articles/6546_talent-and-workforce-effects-in-the-age-of-ai/DI_Talent-and-workforce-effects-in-the-age-of-AI.pdf`.

3
Crafting a Winning AI Strategy

> *It is difficult to think of a major industry that AI will not transform. This includes healthcare, education, transportation, retail, communications, and agriculture. There are surprising clear paths for AI to make a big difference in all of these industries*
>
> *– Andrew Ng*

Have you ever wondered why some companies achieve extraordinary success with their **artificial intelligence** (**AI**) initiatives while others struggle to see meaningful results? The answer lies not just in the technology itself but in the strategy behind its implementation. According to a recent study by *MIT Sloan Management Review*, only 10% of organizations are realizing significant financial benefits from their AI investments [1]. This statistic begs the question: What are these high-performing companies doing differently?

Consider this: AI leaders such as Amazon and Google have not only embraced AI but have woven it into the very fabric of their strategic goals. Amazon uses AI to recommend products, manage inventory, and even predict when you might need to reorder essentials. Google employs AI to refine search results, enhance ad targeting, and develop groundbreaking technologies such as self-driving cars. These companies don't just use AI—they leverage it strategically to drive innovation and efficiency, creating a significant competitive edge.

Imagine the transformative power your organization could harness by crafting a strategic AI roadmap that aligns perfectly with your business objectives. Picture AI not just as a standalone tool but as an integrated component of your business strategy, driving measurable growth and delivering substantial **return on investment** (**ROI**). This chapter is designed to provide you with the insights and tools needed to develop such a strategy, turning AI from a buzzword into a powerful catalyst for business success.

In this chapter, we will explore the critical elements of a successful AI strategy. We'll dive into how to set clear, actionable AI objectives that resonate with your overall business goals. We will discuss the importance of identifying **key performance indicators** (**KPIs**) to measure the impact of your AI initiatives accurately. Furthermore, we'll cover how to track and analyze the ROI of your AI projects to ensure that every dollar spent is driving tangible business value.

In this chapter, we will explore essential components of crafting a winning AI strategy through the following main topics:

- Aligning AI with business objectives
- Building a robust AI implementation roadmap
- Measuring AI success and ROI
- Overcoming AI implementation challenges

By the end of this chapter, you will have a comprehensive understanding of the key elements of a successful AI strategy and the ability to develop clear, actionable objectives aligned with your business goals. You will learn how to set appropriate KPIs for AI initiatives, measure and analyze the ROI of AI projects, and create a phased implementation roadmap. Additionally, you will gain valuable insights into overcoming common challenges, such as talent acquisition and integration with existing processes. Equipped with this strategic framework, you'll be ready to transform AI from a buzzword into a powerful asset, driving meaningful contributions to your organization's success. Let's dive in and unlock the full potential of AI for your business.

The problem – pain points and challenges

In today's hyper-competitive business environment, companies increasingly turn to AI to drive growth, enhance efficiency, and gain a competitive edge. However, the path to successful AI adoption is riddled with challenges. Many organizations invest heavily in AI technologies only to see minimal returns. The crux of the problem often lies in the absence of a robust AI strategy that aligns with business goals and integrates seamlessly into existing processes.

Misaligned objectives

One of the most pervasive issues is the misalignment of AI initiatives with the overall business strategy. According to a study by Boston Consulting Group, over 70% of digital transformations fail to deliver on their promises because they are not strategically aligned with business objectives [2]. For instance, a retail company might implement an AI-driven recommendation system without first identifying how it aligns with their goal of enhancing customer experience. This misalignment can lead to a disjointed customer journey and missed opportunities for personalization, ultimately resulting in wasted resources and frustrated customers.

Lack of clear KPIs

Another significant challenge is the lack of clear KPIs to measure the success of AI initiatives. In my experience, a significant percentage of companies struggle to establish well-defined KPIs for their AI projects. Without these metrics, it becomes nearly impossible to gauge the impact of AI on business performance. For example, a financial services firm might deploy an AI algorithm to detect fraudulent transactions but struggle to measure its effectiveness due to the absence of specific KPIs, such as the reduction in fraud incidents or the speed of transaction processing.

Measuring ROI

Determining the ROI of AI initiatives presents another layer of complexity. Gartner highlights that nearly half of respondents pointed to challenges with showing its value [3]. This challenge often stems from the intangible nature of many AI benefits, such as improved decision-making or enhanced customer satisfaction. For instance, a manufacturing company might implement predictive maintenance using AI to reduce downtime. While the benefits are clear, quantifying the exact financial impact can be difficult without a robust framework for measuring ROI.

Integration with existing processes

Seamlessly integrating AI into existing business processes is no small feat. Many organizations struggle to adapt their workflows and systems to accommodate AI technologies. Forrester found that 60% of **generative AI (GenAI)** skeptics will embrace the technology—knowingly or not [4]. Consider a healthcare provider attempting to integrate AI-driven diagnostic tools into their routine medical practices. Without proper integration, these tools may disrupt existing workflows, leading to resistance from medical staff and ultimately limiting the effectiveness of the AI solutions.

Talent gap

The shortage of skilled AI professionals is another critical barrier. The World Economic Forum reports a global shortage of AI talent, with demand far outstripping supply [5]. This talent gap makes it challenging for businesses to build and sustain effective AI teams. For example, a technology firm might have ambitious AI projects but struggle to find and retain data scientists and **machine learning (ML)** experts, slowing down the implementation process and diminishing the potential impact of AI initiatives.

Data quality and governance

High-quality data is the lifeblood of AI, yet many organizations struggle with data-related issues. Poor data quality, data silos, and lack of proper data governance can severely undermine AI efforts. *Harvard Business Review* indicates that bad data costs the US economy up to $3.1 trillion annually [6]. For instance, a logistics company might deploy an AI system for route optimization but face challenges due to inconsistent and incomplete data, leading to suboptimal routing decisions and increased operational costs.

The significance of the problem

The challenges outlined so far underscore the critical need for a robust AI strategy. Without it, businesses risk wasting valuable resources on AI initiatives that fail to deliver tangible benefits. Moreover, the inability to measure and demonstrate the value of AI can lead to diminished support from stakeholders and a potential loss of competitive advantage.

Addressing these challenges requires a strategic approach that aligns AI initiatives with business goals, defines clear KPIs, ensures seamless integration, and effectively measures ROI. By overcoming these hurdles, organizations can unlock the full potential of AI, transforming it from a promising technology into a powerful driver of business success.

In the next section, we will delve into practical solutions and frameworks to help you craft a winning AI strategy that addresses these challenges head-on. Through real-world examples and actionable insights, you will learn how to set clear AI objectives, identify meaningful KPIs, and measure the success and ROI of your AI initiatives, paving the way for sustained growth and innovation.

The solution – a step-by-step implementation

Successfully navigating the complex landscape of AI implementation requires a strategic and methodical approach. The following six-step framework addresses key challenges, ensuring AI initiatives align with business objectives, integrate effectively, and deliver measurable ROI.

Step 1 – developing a clear AI vision and strategy

Effective AI integration starts with leadership engagement and a clear vision. Here's a brief overview:

- **Engage leadership**: Collaborate with executive leadership to define strategic AI objectives and set measurable goals. This involves in-depth discussions to understand the business's strategic vision and how AI can contribute to achieving it. Engaging leadership ensures that the AI strategy has the support and alignment needed for successful execution.
- **Vision statement**: Craft and communicate a vision statement encapsulating AI's role in achieving these objectives. This statement should be clear, inspiring, and easy to understand, ensuring all stakeholders are on the same page. Regularly revisit and refine the vision statement to keep it relevant as the organization evolves.

Why it works: Engaging leadership and crafting a clear vision ensures AI initiatives align with business goals, foster a unified approach, and secure necessary support and resources. A well-articulated vision acts as a north star, guiding all AI efforts.

Step 2 – creating a detailed roadmap

Implementing AI requires a phased approach with clear milestones. Here's a quick summary:

- **Phased approach**: Divide the AI strategy into short-term, medium-term, and long-term goals. Each phase should focus on specific, achievable objectives contributing to the vision. For example, initial phases might concentrate on quick wins, such as implementing AI chatbots, while later phases tackle more complex projects, such as predictive maintenance.

- **Milestones and deliverables**: Define clear milestones and deliverables for each phase. These should include tangible outcomes that demonstrate progress and build confidence among stakeholders. Regularly review and adjust milestones based on progress and new insights.

Why it works: A phased approach with defined milestones helps manage risk, demonstrate value, and maintain stakeholder engagement. It ensures AI projects are manageable and scalable, allowing for iterative improvements and adjustments.

Step 3 – identifying KPIs

Set **specific**, **measurable**, **achievable**, **relevant**, and **time-bound** (**SMART**) KPIs and conduct regular reviews to track AI progress and drive continuous improvement. Here's a brief outline:

- **Define KPIs**: Identify SMART KPIs for each AI initiative. These could include metrics such as cost savings, revenue growth, customer satisfaction, and process efficiency. Align KPIs with broader business objectives to reflect the initiative's strategic impact.
- **Regular reviews**: Conduct regular reviews to assess performance against these KPIs and make necessary adjustments. Use these reviews to identify areas for improvement and celebrate successes, fostering a culture of continuous improvement.

Why it works: Clear KPIs provide a measurable framework for assessing AI impact, demonstrating value to stakeholders, and making informed decisions. Regular reviews ensure that AI initiatives align with business goals and adapt to changing circumstances.

Step 4 – measuring ROI

To ensure AI initiatives are financially viable and impactful, consider the following key steps:

- **Cost-benefit analysis (CBA)**: Conduct a detailed CBA for each AI project, considering direct costs (for example, technology and talent) and indirect costs (for example, change management and training). This analysis helps determine the financial viability of AI initiatives and prioritize projects with the highest potential return.
- **Quantify benefits**: Measure tangible and intangible benefits, such as increased revenue, cost savings, improved efficiency, and enhanced customer satisfaction. Use qualitative and quantitative methods to capture the full spectrum of AI's impact.
- **Regular reporting**: Develop a reporting framework to communicate ROI to stakeholders regularly. This transparency builds trust and ensures continued support for AI initiatives.

Why it works: A rigorous approach to measuring ROI ensures AI investments deliver tangible business value and keep stakeholders informed and engaged. Regular reporting fosters a culture of accountability and continuous improvement.

Step 5 – ensuring seamless integration

To successfully integrate AI into your business, follow these essential steps:

- **Gap analysis**: Conduct a gap analysis to identify areas where current processes need adaptation for AI integration. This involves mapping existing workflows and pinpointing where AI can add the most value. Use this analysis to develop a tailored integration plan that addresses specific needs and challenges.
- **Change management**: Implement a comprehensive change management strategy to support the integration process. This includes training, communication, and support initiatives to ease the transition and foster acceptance. Proactively address employee concerns and provide resources to help them adapt to new technologies.
- **Iterative development**: Use iterative development cycles to integrate AI into business processes gradually. Start with pilot projects to test and refine the integration approach based on feedback. Scale successful pilots to full implementations, ensuring continuous feedback and improvement.

Why it works: Seamless integration maximizes AI's impact and minimizes disruption. A robust change management strategy supports this transition, fostering a culture of continuous improvement and adaptability.

Step 6 – building and sustaining AI talent

Attracting, developing, and retaining top AI talent is critical for long-term success. Here's how:

- **Talent acquisition**: Develop strategic plans to attract top AI talent. This includes partnerships with universities, participation in AI conferences, and leveraging professional networks. Ensure the recruitment process identifies candidates with the right mix of technical skills and cultural fit.
- **Talent development**: Implement comprehensive training programs to upskill existing employees. Offer continuous learning opportunities such as workshops, online courses, and mentorship programs. Foster a culture of innovation and encourage employees to stay current with AI advancements.
- **Retention strategies**: Develop strategies to keep AI professionals engaged and motivated. Provide career development opportunities, competitive compensation, and a supportive work environment. Regularly solicit feedback from AI professionals to ensure they feel valued and supported.

Why it works: Building and sustaining AI talent ensures organizations have the expertise to execute AI initiatives effectively. A strategic approach to talent management fosters a culture of innovation and continuous learning, which is essential for long-term success.

By following this six-step framework, organizations can overcome the challenges of AI adoption and craft a winning AI strategy. This approach ensures AI initiatives are strategically aligned with business goals, integrated into existing processes, and deliver measurable ROI. Organizations can unlock AI's full potential and drive sustained growth and innovation by developing a clear vision, creating a detailed roadmap, identifying KPIs, measuring ROI, ensuring seamless integration, and building AI talent.

Hypothetical case study – transforming operations at APEX Manufacturing and Distribution

We will continue with our hypothetical company, APEX Manufacturing and Distribution, as our example to illustrate the concepts contained within. By following APEX's journey, we aim to provide practical insights and actionable strategies for implementing AI in various business contexts. This approach allows us to present detailed scenarios and strategies, making complex AI concepts more relatable and easier to understand.

Initial situation

Imagine APEX Manufacturing and Distribution, a leading player in the industrial machinery sector with extensive operations across multiple regions. APEX was grappling with significant operational challenges that threatened its profitability and customer satisfaction. Frequent production bottlenecks, high maintenance costs, and a lack of real-time data visibility were major issues. These inefficiencies led to delays, inflated operational costs, and decreased customer satisfaction.

The leadership at APEX realized that to maintain their competitive edge and improve operational efficiency, a radical transformation was essential. They decided to leverage AI to optimize their manufacturing and distribution processes. The following case study outlines the steps taken to implement a successful AI strategy at APEX, illustrating the transformative power of AI when applied strategically.

Steps taken

This case study of APEX Manufacturing and Distribution outlines the transformative impact of AI on operational efficiency. By developing a clear AI vision, creating a phased implementation roadmap, and fostering a culture of AI adoption, APEX achieved significant improvements across production processes, customer satisfaction, and overall costs. The following steps detail how these results were achieved, from strategy development to measuring ROI and talent acquisition.

Step 1 – developing a clear AI vision and strategy

- **Engage leadership**: The first step was engaging APEX's executive team to recognize the potential of AI. Strategic planning workshops were conducted to discuss AI's role in achieving business objectives. These workshops fostered open discussions about AI's potential and direction within the organization, aligning leadership with the vision and goals.

- **Define objectives**: Clear objectives were established:
  - Reduce production bottlenecks by 30%
  - Decrease maintenance costs by 20%
  - Improve customer satisfaction scores by 15%
- **Craft a vision statement**: A vision statement was developed to encapsulate the strategic goals: *Harness AI to revolutionize our manufacturing and distribution processes, ensuring seamless operations, enhanced customer experience, and increased operational efficiency*

Step 2 – creating a detailed roadmap

- **Phased implementation**: The roadmap was divided into three phases to ensure structured implementation:
  - **Phase 1 (0-3 months)**: Pilot AI-powered predictive maintenance in a select group of facilities. This phase focused on quick wins and gathering initial data to refine the AI models.
  - **Phase 2 (3-6 months)**: Expand AI implementation to all facilities, focusing on integrating AI systems with existing production and maintenance management systems.
  - **Phase 3 (6-12 months)**: Implement predictive analytics for proactive operational management and continuous optimization. This phase aimed to fully embed AI into the company's operations, enabling dynamic adjustments based on real-time data.
- **Set milestones**: Specific milestones were set for each phase to track progress and ensure timely execution:
  - Successful completion of the pilot phase
  - Full integration of AI systems across all facilities
  - Deployment of predictive analytics capabilities
- **Quick wins**: Early wins were targeted by choosing high-impact facilities for the pilot phase. This approach demonstrated immediate benefits, building momentum and confidence among stakeholders.

Step 3 – identifying KPIs

- **Define SMART KPIs**: KPIs were established to measure the success of the AI initiative:
  - Reduction in production bottlenecks and maintenance costs
  - Improvement in production efficiency and customer satisfaction scores

- **Align KPIs with business goals**: Ensuring that KPIs were directly linked to broader business objectives helped maintain strategic relevance and focus.
- **Regular reviews**: Weekly reviews were scheduled to track progress against KPIs and adjust strategies as needed. This continuous monitoring allowed for agile responses to any challenges that arose.

Step 4 – measuring ROI

- **Conduct a CBA**: A detailed CBA was performed to evaluate the direct costs of AI implementation (technology, training) against anticipated benefits (cost savings, increased efficiency). This analysis helped justify the investment to stakeholders.
- **Quantify tangible and intangible benefits**: Both tangible and intangible benefits were quantified, including the following:
  - **Tangible**: Reduced costs and increased operational efficiency
  - **Intangible**: Improved customer satisfaction and brand loyalty
- **Develop a reporting framework**: Monthly reports were prepared to communicate ROI to stakeholders, ensuring transparency and ongoing support. These reports included detailed financial metrics and qualitative insights from customer feedback.

Step 5 – ensuring seamless integration

- **Conduct a gap analysis**: An analysis was performed to identify gaps in the current systems and processes that needed to be addressed for AI integration. This included assessing the compatibility of existing production and maintenance management systems with the new AI tools.
- **Implement change management**: A comprehensive change management plan was developed, including the following:
  - Training programs for employees to familiarize them with new AI tools
  - Continuous communication about the benefits and progress of AI initiatives
  - Support systems to address any concerns or issues during the transition
- **Iterative development**: AI solutions were rolled out in iterative cycles, allowing for continuous feedback and improvements. This iterative approach ensured that the AI systems were refined and optimized based on real-world data and user feedback.

Step 6 – building and sustaining AI talent

- **Develop a talent acquisition plan**: Partnerships with universities and participation in AI conferences helped attract top AI talent. A dedicated team of data scientists and AI specialists was assembled to drive the initiative forward.

- **Implement training programs**: Comprehensive training programs were developed for existing employees to upskill them in AI and data analytics. These programs included hands-on workshops, online courses, and ongoing support to ensure continuous learning.
- **Create retention strategies**: Strategies were implemented to retain AI professionals, including the following:
  - Career development opportunities
  - Competitive compensation packages
  - A supportive work environment that fosters innovation and collaboration

Results achieved

The implementation of the steps we discussed showed the following results:

- **Reduction in production bottlenecks**: By implementing AI-powered predictive maintenance, APEX achieved a 35% reduction in production bottlenecks. This led to more consistent production schedules, enhancing operational efficiency and reducing delays.
- **Decrease in maintenance costs**: With optimized maintenance schedules, APEX reduced its maintenance costs by 22%. The AI system's ability to predict equipment failures accurately meant fewer unplanned downtimes and reduced repair costs, freeing up resources for other strategic initiatives.
- **Improvement in production efficiency**: Production efficiency improved by 25%, as AI-enhanced scheduling tools optimized production processes. The dynamic scheduling allowed APEX to respond quickly to changes in demand and production conditions, ensuring smooth operations.
- **Enhanced real-time visibility**: The real-time monitoring systems provided complete visibility into production processes, enabling better decision-making and operational control. This improved transparency led to more efficient operations and quicker identification and resolution of bottlenecks.
- **Increased customer satisfaction**: Customer satisfaction scores improved by 18%, as consistent production schedules and efficient operations led to fewer delays and higher reliability. Enhanced operational efficiency resulted in improved product availability and quality, boosting customer loyalty and retention.
- **Positive ROI**: The ROI analysis revealed a 40% increase in operational efficiency attributed to better production and maintenance management. The cost savings from reduced maintenance costs and increased operational efficiency resulted in a positive ROI within the first year of implementation, demonstrating the AI initiative's financial viability and strategic value.

Reflection and practical next steps

Before we conclude this chapter on crafting a winning AI strategy, it's time to pause and reflect on how these insights can shape your approach to AI implementation. Whether you're leading a large corporation or a small start-up, these principles can guide you toward a more effective and impactful AI strategy.

Reflect on core insights

Take a moment to consider the following questions:

- How does your current approach to AI align with your overall business objectives?
- In what ways could a more structured AI strategy benefit your organization?
- Are you currently measuring the impact of your AI initiatives effectively?
- How prepared is your organization to address the challenges of AI implementation, such as talent acquisition and process integration?

Remember—there's no one-size-fits-all approach to AI strategy. Your reflections should be personal and contextual to your unique situation.

Critical assessment

Now, let's dive deeper with some thought-provoking questions:

- If you were to rate your organization's AI strategy on a scale of 1-10, where would you place it? Why?
- What's the biggest obstacle preventing your organization from fully leveraging AI's potential?
- How aligned are your AI initiatives with your company's long-term vision?
- In what ways could improving your AI strategy positively impact your organization's performance and competitive position?

These questions highlight areas where implementing the strategies discussed in this chapter could yield significant benefits.

Practical next steps

Based on your reflections, consider these actionable steps to enhance your AI strategy:

1. **Develop your AI vision**:
   - **Action**: Schedule a workshop with key stakeholders to define or refine your AI vision.
   - **Example**: A healthcare provider might envision using AI to improve patient outcomes and reduce administrative burden within the next 3 years.

2. **Create a phased implementation plan:**
   - **Action:** Outline a 12-month roadmap for AI implementation, broken into quarterly milestones.
   - **Example:** Q1 could focus on a pilot project in one department, with subsequent quarters expanding to other areas based on lessons learned.

3. **Establish clear KPIs:**
   - **Action:** Define three to five specific, measurable KPIs for each AI initiative.
   - **Example:** For a customer service AI chatbot, KPIs might include a reduction in average response time, an increase in customer satisfaction scores, and a percentage of queries resolved without human intervention.

4. **Conduct an ROI analysis:**
   - **Action:** Perform a detailed CBA for your primary AI project.
   - **Example:** Calculate the projected savings from automating a specific process against AI implementation and training costs.

5. **Address the talent gap:**
   - **Action:** Assess your current AI capabilities and create a plan to address skill shortages.
   - **Example:** This could involve partnering with a local university for internships, offering upskilling programs for existing employees, or strategically hiring AI specialists.

Remember—progress is often incremental. Start with small, achievable goals and build momentum. Consider the example of APEX Manufacturing and Distribution from our case study. They began focusing on predictive maintenance before expanding to broader AI applications.

Moving forward

As you embark on this journey to craft a winning AI strategy, remember it's an ongoing process. Stay curious, remain open to learning, and don't be afraid to iterate on your approach. The field of AI is rapidly evolving, and your strategy should evolve with it.

Challenge yourself to implement at least one of these practical steps next month. Whether organizing an AI vision workshop or defining KPIs for an existing project, taking that first step is crucial.

Remember—the goal isn't perfection but progress. Every step toward a more strategic approach to AI brings your organization closer to realizing its full potential.

As you move forward, ask yourself, How can I leverage AI to create more value for my organization and its stakeholders? Let this question guide your decisions and actions as you navigate the exciting world of AI strategy.

Your journey to crafting a winning AI strategy starts now. Embrace the challenges, celebrate the successes, and never stop learning. The future of AI is bright, and with thoughtful strategy, you can help shape that future for your organization and beyond.

Summary

We journeyed through essential elements of crafting a winning AI strategy, and by now, you should feel equipped to approach AI implementation with confidence and clarity. Remember: a successful AI strategy isn't about chasing the latest tech trends—it's about aligning AI initiatives with your business goals, setting clear objectives, and measuring impact. You learned to develop a clear AI vision, create a phased implementation roadmap, set meaningful KPIs, and calculate ROI. These aren't just theoretical concepts; they're practical tools you can use to transform AI from a buzzword into a powerful driver of business success.

As you reflect on these insights, consider how you might apply them in your organization. What's your first step toward a more strategic AI approach? Perhaps it's scheduling that AI vision workshop or defining KPIs for an existing project. Whatever it is, remember that crafting a winning AI strategy is an ongoing journey of learning and adaptation. And speaking of journeys, our next chapter will show you how to assemble and nurture the talent you need to bring your AI strategy to life. Get ready to dive into the human side of AI success!

Questions

1. What is the primary goal of crafting a winning AI strategy, as discussed in this chapter?
2. How does the chapter suggest addressing the misalignment between AI initiatives and overall business strategy?
3. What role do KPIs play in an effective AI strategy?
4. According to the chapter, why do many organizations struggle to measure their AI initiatives' ROI?
5. What is the significance of a phased approach in implementing an AI strategy?
6. How can organizations address the AI talent gap, as discussed in the chapter?
7. What are the potential consequences of poor data quality in AI implementation?
8. What was one significant result of their AI implementation in the APEX Manufacturing and Distribution case study?
9. How does the chapter suggest organizations should approach the integration of AI into existing business processes?
10. Based on the insights from this chapter, what would be the first step for a company looking to develop a comprehensive AI strategy?

References

1. *MIT Management Sloan Review. Expanding AI's Impact With Organizational Learning.* Retrieved from MIT: https://sloanreview.mit.edu/projects/expanding-ais-impact-with-organizational-learning/.

2. *Boston Consulting Group. Five Ways to Beat the Odds on Digital Transformation.* Retrieved from BCG: https://www.bcg.com/news/13september2023-five-ways-to-beat-odds-on-digital-transformation#:~:text=However%2C%20BCG%20research%20has%20found,that%20succeed%2C%E2%80%9D%20he%20writes.

3. *CIO.com. Where's the ROI for AI? CIOs struggle to find it.* Retrieved from CIO.com: https://www.cio.com/article/2112589/wheres-the-roi-for-ai-cios-struggle-to-find-it.html.

4. *Forrester. Forrester's Predictions 2024: Sixty Percent Of Generative AI Skeptics Will Embrace The Technology — Knowingly Or Not.* Retrieved from Forrester: https://investor.forrester.com/news-releases/news-release-details/forresters-predictions-2024-sixty-percent-generative-ai-skeptics.

5. *World Economic Forum. The Global Risks Report 2024.* Retrieved from WEF: https://www3.weforum.org/docs/WEF_The_Global_Risks_Report_2024.pdf.

6. *Harvard Business Review. Bad Data Costs the U.S. $3 Trillion Per Year.* Retrieved from HBR: https://hbr.org/2016/09/bad-data-costs-the-u-s-3-trillion-per-year.

4

Building High-Performing AI Teams

Find a group of people who challenge and inspire you, spend a lot of time with them, and it will change your life

– Amy Poehler

Have you ever wondered why some companies effortlessly attract and retain the best AI talent while others struggle to find even a handful of qualified candidates? Or why certain AI teams consistently deliver groundbreaking innovations while others falter? The secret often lies not only in the technology they use but also in the way they build and nurture their AI teams.

In today's fast-paced digital landscape, where AI is redefining industries, the ability to recruit and retain top AI talent has never been more crucial. The demand for AI professionals is rapidly increasing, yet the talent pool remains alarmingly shallow. This scarcity of skilled professionals poses a significant challenge for businesses eager to leverage AI for growth and innovation.

But building a high-performing AI team is about more than just hiring the brightest minds. It involves structuring your team to maximize efficiency, foster innovation, and encourage collaboration. It's about creating an environment where talented individuals thrive and their collective efforts lead to extraordinary outcomes.

Imagine having a team of AI experts who are not only highly skilled but also deeply engaged and motivated—a team that works seamlessly together, driven by a shared vision and a culture of innovation. This chapter will guide you through recruiting top AI talent, structuring your AI team for success, and fostering a culture of collaboration and creativity.

We will explore practical strategies for attracting and retaining the best AI professionals, insights into effective team structures, and tips for cultivating an environment where innovation can flourish. Whether you're just starting to build your AI team or looking to enhance an existing one, these insights will help you create a high-performing AI team that drives your organization forward.

In this chapter, we will cover the following topics:

- Recruiting top AI talent – strategies for attracting and hiring the best AI professionals
- Structuring your AI team for success – organizational models and best practices for AI teams
- Fostering a culture of innovation and collaboration – creating an environment that nurtures AI development and cross-functional cooperation

By the end of this chapter, you will be equipped with the strategies needed to identify and attract top AI talent, design an organizational structure that maximizes your AI team's performance, and implement practices that foster innovation and collaboration. You will also gain a deep understanding of building and maintaining high-performing AI teams while addressing common challenges in team management and development. Ready to transform your approach to building your AI team? Let's dive in and discover how to attract top talent, structure your team for maximum impact, and cultivate a culture of innovation.

The problem – pain points and challenges

Building a high-performing AI team is no small feat. The challenges are multifaceted, ranging from the scarcity of skilled professionals to the complexities of fostering innovation and collaboration. To truly grasp the significance of these challenges, it's essential to delve into the specific pain points businesses face when assembling and nurturing their AI teams.

Talent scarcity

One of the most pressing challenges is the severe shortage of qualified AI professionals. According to a report by Gartner, a significant percentage of AI projects fail to deliver accurate outcomes due to the lack of skilled talent [1]. This talent gap is exacerbated by the rapid growth in demand for AI skills across industries. Companies are competing fiercely for a limited pool of experts, driving up salaries and making it increasingly difficult to attract and retain top talent.

The implications of this talent scarcity are profound. Organizations find themselves unable to progress beyond the initial stages of their AI initiatives. Without the right talent, even the most ambitious AI projects can stall, leaving companies unable to capitalize on the transformative potential of AI. This not only impacts innovation but also affects the overall competitiveness of the business.

The stakes are high. A recent McKinsey report highlighted that companies with advanced AI capabilities are twice as likely to be in the top quartile of financial performance within their industries [2]. The talent gap, therefore, represents not just an operational hurdle but a strategic risk. In the absence of skilled AI professionals, businesses risk falling behind more agile competitors who can harness AI to drive efficiencies, innovate product offerings, and enhance customer experiences.

Structuring the AI team

Even when businesses manage to recruit top AI talent, structuring the team for maximum efficiency and impact poses another significant challenge. An effective AI team requires a mix of skills, including data scientists, machine learning engineers, domain experts, and project managers. Balancing these diverse roles and ensuring seamless collaboration can be a daunting task.

The structure of an AI team is akin to assembling a high-performing sports team. Each player has a specialized role, but the team's success hinges on how well these roles are coordinated. Data scientists bring expertise to statistical modeling, machine learning engineers focus on developing algorithms, domain experts provide critical business insights, and project managers ensure that projects stay on track and meet business objectives.

Without a well-defined team structure, the potential for inefficiencies and misalignment is high. Clear roles and responsibilities are essential to prevent overlapping duties and ensure that each team member can contribute effectively. The absence of a cohesive structure can lead to duplicated efforts, conflicting priorities, and, ultimately, suboptimal results.

An example to consider is the challenge of integrating domain experts within an AI team. These individuals possess deep industry knowledge but may lack technical expertise in AI. Ensuring they collaborate effectively with data scientists and engineers is crucial. They bridge the gap between business needs and technical solutions, ensuring that AI projects are aligned with organizational goals.

Fostering a culture of innovation

Innovation is the lifeblood of AI projects, yet fostering a culture that encourages creativity and risk-taking is easier said than done. Many organizations find themselves bogged down by rigid hierarchies and outdated processes that stifle innovation. Creating an environment where team members feel empowered to experiment and take risks is crucial for driving breakthroughs in AI.

A culture of innovation requires more than just lip service. It demands a fundamental shift in how organizations approach problem-solving and decision-making. Employees need to feel that they can propose bold ideas without fear of failure or criticism. This openness to experimentation and learning from mistakes is what fuels the innovative spirit necessary for AI advancements.

To cultivate such a culture, leadership must champion innovation by providing resources, setting clear innovation goals, and rewarding creative thinking. It's about creating a safe space for experimentation. Google's "20% time" policy, which allows employees to spend 20% of their time on projects that interest them, is a classic example of fostering innovation [3]. While not every company can implement this exact model, the principle of giving employees the freedom to explore and innovate is widely applicable.

Integration with existing business processes

Integrating AI initiatives with existing business processes presents another layer of complexity. AI projects often require significant changes to workflows, systems, and organizational structures. Resistance to change and lack of alignment between AI teams and other departments can create roadblocks that impede progress.

Seamless integration is critical to the success of AI projects. AI systems need to be embedded into the core operations of the business to deliver meaningful results. This requires collaboration across various functions within the organization and a willingness to adapt and evolve existing processes. Without this integration, AI initiatives can remain isolated efforts with limited impact.

Effective integration involves continuous dialogue between AI teams and business units. For instance, in a retail company implementing AI for inventory management, regular meetings between AI engineers and supply chain managers can ensure that AI models accurately reflect business realities. This ongoing collaboration helps in fine-tuning AI solutions and ensuring they deliver the desired outcomes.

Moreover, change management strategies are essential to mitigate resistance. This involves transparent communication about the benefits of AI, training programs to upskill employees, and involving employees in the AI journey from the outset. When employees understand how AI will improve their workflows and contribute to business success, they are more likely to embrace it.

Measuring success

Lastly, measuring the success of AI initiatives is a critical but challenging aspect. Unlike traditional projects, AI initiatives often have intangible benefits that are difficult to quantify. Establishing clear metrics and KPIs to evaluate the impact of AI projects is essential for demonstrating value and securing ongoing investment.

The challenge lies in identifying appropriate metrics that capture both the direct and indirect benefits of AI. This could include improvements in efficiency, cost savings, or enhanced customer experiences. Clear and quantifiable metrics are necessary to communicate the ROI of AI projects to stakeholders and to build confidence in the ongoing investment in AI technologies.

For instance, a financial institution deploying AI for fraud detection might measure success through metrics such as the reduction in fraudulent transactions, the speed of detection, and the cost savings from prevented fraud. However, they should also consider customer satisfaction and trust, which, while harder to quantify, are equally critical.

To address this, companies should adopt a balanced scorecard approach that includes financial metrics, customer metrics, internal process metrics, and learning and growth metrics [4]. This holistic approach ensures that all aspects of AI's impact are considered, providing a comprehensive view of its value to the organization.

The significance of the problem

The challenges outlined so far highlight the critical importance of building high-performing AI teams. Without the right talent, structure, culture, and integration, businesses risk falling behind in AI. The ability to effectively recruit, organize, and nurture AI teams is not just a matter of operational efficiency but a strategic imperative determining an organization's competitive edge in an increasingly AI-driven world.

Addressing these challenges requires a comprehensive approach encompassing strategic recruitment, thoughtful team structuring, a culture of innovation, and seamless integration with existing processes. By overcoming these hurdles, organizations can unlock AI's full potential, driving innovation, efficiency, and growth.

Solution and process for building exceptional AI teams

When building exceptional AI teams, I focus on three pivotal characteristics: curiosity, creativity, and collaboration. I also provide the two elements of impact and control. This approach cultivates a high-performing team and drives innovation and success in our AI initiatives.

Identifying the right talent – curiosity, creativity, and imagination

First and foremost, beyond the academic and technical expertise that can be demonstrated through a resume or LinkedIn profile, I prioritize three intrinsic traits—curiosity, creativity, and imagination:

- **Curiosity**: In the rapidly evolving field of AI, curiosity is paramount. It drives individuals to learn and explore new ideas constantly. During interviews, I often ask candidates to share something they have recently learned. The subject matter can vary widely—from rebuilding a carburetor to mastering a new recipe or discovering an innovative exercise technique. The key is their enthusiasm and the depth of their explanation. A genuinely curious person will speak with passion and detail about their latest discovery. This constant pursuit of knowledge indicates a mind that is always active, always seeking, and always ready to tackle the next big challenge.

- **Creativity**: The second characteristic I seek is creativity—the ability to devise solutions within constraints. In the realm of AI, problems are often complex and multifaceted. A creative thinker can navigate these challenges, finding innovative solutions despite limited resources or information. During the hiring process, I present candidates with hypothetical scenarios that require problem-solving within certain boundaries. Their approach to these scenarios reveals their ability to think creatively and adaptively.

- **Imagination**: Lastly, I look for imagination—the capacity to envision possibilities beyond the present constraints. Imaginative individuals can see what others cannot; they dream big and think beyond the obvious. They are the ones who, given the freedom to explore, can develop revolutionary ideas that push the boundaries of what is possible. During interviews, I ask candidates to describe a project they would undertake if resources and constraints were not an issue. Their responses provide insight into their visionary thinking and potential for groundbreaking innovation.

When these three traits are present, individuals synergize well within a team. They become like-minded, kindred spirits, eager to collaborate on solving complex problems. Watching such a team in action is magical; they work with a remarkable blend of speed, innovation, and harmony.

Providing the right environment – impact and control

Once the right individuals are on board, providing an environment where they can thrive is crucial. This is where the elements of impact and control come into play:

- **Impact**: Ensuring that team members' work has a meaningful impact is essential. People want to know that their efforts contribute to something significant, whether advancing the company's goals, contributing to environmental sustainability, or supporting a cause they believe in. I foster a sense of purpose and fulfillment by aligning projects with meaningful outcomes. This motivates individuals and drives them to achieve excellence in their work.

- **Control**: Empowering team members with control over their work is equally important. I provide guidance and support as a leader, but I also trust my team to make key decisions. This autonomy allows them to innovate and take ownership of their projects. It fosters a culture of trust and respect, where individuals feel valued and believed in. When people are free to explore their ideas and make decisions, they are more engaged, committed, and likely to produce outstanding results.

Building a great team goes beyond hiring people with the right skills in the highly competitive and dynamic field of AI. It involves identifying those with the curiosity to learn continuously, the creativity to solve complex problems, and the imagination to dream big. Coupled with providing an environment where their work has an impact and they have control, this approach creates a powerful engine for innovation and success. This methodology has consistently enabled me to build teams that excel in their tasks and drive transformative change within our organization and beyond.

Step-by-step implementation for building a high-performing AI team

Creating a top-notch AI team requires a strategic and structured approach. Here's a comprehensive guide to help you attract top AI talent, organize your team for success, and foster a culture of innovation.

Step 1 – recruiting top AI talent

The following are actionable tips for recruiting top AI talent:

- **Develop a strong employer brand**: Position your company as an attractive workplace for AI professionals by showcasing your commitment to innovation, exciting projects, and the impact potential of joining your team.
- **Leverage multiple recruitment channels**: Use various recruitment channels, such as job boards, social media, university partnerships, and AI conferences. Attend and sponsor AI-related events to network with potential candidates.
- **Offer competitive compensation packages**: Ensure your salary and benefits packages are competitive. Consider perks such as flexible work arrangements, continuous learning opportunities, and career advancement prospects.
- **Engage in proactive talent sourcing**: Search for potential hires on platforms such as LinkedIn, GitHub, and Kaggle. Reach out to promising candidates even if they are not actively seeking a job.

The following are best practices:

- **Showcase your AI initiatives**: Highlight successful AI projects and innovations on your company website and social media to attract talent and build your reputation in the AI community.
- **Foster relationships with universities**: Partner with universities to offer internships, co-op programs, and sponsorships for AI-related research. This helps you tap into emerging talent and build a pipeline of future hires.

Step 2 – structuring your AI team for success

The following are actionable tips for structuring your AI team:

- **Define clear roles and responsibilities**: Clearly outline each team member's roles and responsibilities, ensuring alignment with the overall goals of your AI projects.
- **Create cross-functional teams**: Assemble teams that include data scientists, machine learning engineers, domain experts, and project managers for comprehensive problem-solving and innovation.
- **Establish effective communication channels**: Implement regular meetings, updates, and collaborative tools to facilitate communication among team members and encourage open, transparent communication.
- **Implement agile methodologies**: Use agile methodologies, such as Scrum or Kanban, to manage AI projects. These methodologies allow for iterative development, continuous feedback, and quick adjustments to changing requirements.

The following are best practices:

- **Regular team meetings**: Schedule meetings to review progress, discuss challenges, and brainstorm solutions. This will keep everyone aligned and foster collaboration.
- **Clear documentation**: To ensure continuity and knowledge sharing, maintain clear and accessible documentation for all AI projects, including project plans, workflows, code, and results.

Step 3 – fostering a culture of innovation and collaboration

The following are actionable tips for fostering a culture of innovation and collaboration:

- **Encourage experimentation**: Create an environment where team members feel safe to experiment and take calculated risks. Recognize and reward innovative ideas and efforts.
- **Provide continuous learning opportunities**: Invest in training and development programs. Encourage team members to attend conferences, workshops, and online courses to stay updated with AI trends and technologies.
- **Implement a mentorship program**: Pair junior team members with experienced mentors to foster knowledge sharing, skill development, and career growth.
- **Celebrate successes and learn from failures**: Regularly celebrate team successes, no matter how small. Use projects that go differently than planned as learning opportunities to improve and innovate.

The following are best practices:

- **Hackathons and innovation days**: Organize internal hackathons and innovation days where team members can work on creative projects outside their regular tasks to encourage creativity and teamwork.
- **Feedback loops**: Establish regular feedback loops where team members can provide input on processes, projects, and management to ensure continuous improvement and engagement.

Step 4 – integrating AI initiatives with business processes

The following are actionable tips for integrating AI initiatives with business processes:

- **Conduct a gap analysis**: Assess your current processes to identify areas where AI can add value and determine the changes needed for effective integration...
- **Develop a change management plan**: Create a comprehensive plan to manage the transition, including training employees, communicating the benefits of AI, and addressing any concerns or resistance.

- **Ensure cross-departmental collaboration**: Foster collaboration between AI teams and other departments to align AI initiatives with business goals and integrate seamlessly into existing workflows.
- **Monitor and evaluate performance**: Continuously monitor AI systems' performance and impact on business processes, using insights to make necessary adjustments and improvements.

The following are best practices:

- **Pilot projects**: Start with small pilot projects to test AI integration, using insights gained to refine processes before scaling up.
- **Stakeholder involvement**: Involve key stakeholders from the beginning to ensure their support and buy-in. Regular updates and transparent communication are crucial for maintaining trust and alignment.

Step 5 – measuring success and iterating

The following are actionable tips for measuring success and iterating:

- **Define clear KPIs**: Establish **specific, measurable, achievable, relevant, and time-bound (SMART) KPIs for** each AI initiative, aligning them with your business goals to provide a precise measure of success.
- **Regular performance reviews**: Conduct regular reviews to assess the performance of AI projects, identify areas for improvement, and make data-driven decisions.
- **Communicate results**: Share the results of AI initiatives with stakeholders, highlighting successes, lessons learned, and the overall impact on business goals.
- **Iterate and improve**: Use feedback and insights gained to continuously iterate and improve AI projects, staying agile and ready to pivot based on new data and evolving business needs.

The following are best practices:

- **Balanced scorecard approach**: Use a balanced scorecard to measure financial, customer, internal process, and learning and growth metrics of AI projects for a comprehensive view of their impact.
- **Continuous improvement culture**: Foster a culture of continuous improvement where team members are encouraged to seek out and implement enhancements, regularly celebrate improvements, and share best practices across the team.

Following this step-by-step guide, you can build a high-performing AI team that drives innovation and delivers tangible business results. Recruiting top AI talent, structuring your team effectively, fostering a culture of innovation, integrating AI with business processes, and continuously measuring success are crucial to unlocking AI's full potential. Through strategic planning and execution, you can create an AI team that meets and exceeds your business goals, propelling your organization forward in the AI-driven world.

Hypothetical case study – transforming APEX's manufacturing and distribution with AI

Our manufacturing and distribution company, APEX, was grappling with persistent inefficiencies in its production processes and escalating operational costs. With a diverse product line and multiple plants nationwide, APEX faced frequent production delays, equipment breakdowns, and inconsistent product quality. These issues were not just operational headaches; they cut the company's bottom line, resulting in increased costs, lost revenue, and declining customer satisfaction.

Recognizing the transformative potential of AI, APEX's leadership knew they needed a robust strategy to address these challenges. However, they were unsure of how to effectively build and leverage an AI team. Determined to turn things around, they partnered with an AI consultancy to develop a strategy for building a high-performing AI team and implementing AI-driven solutions.

Steps taken

To effectively implement its AI strategy, APEX took a structured, step-by-step approach to recruiting top talent, building successful teams, fostering innovation, and seamlessly integrating AI into its business processes. Here's a breakdown of the steps it took to ensure the success of its AI initiatives.

Step 1 – recruiting top AI talent

- **Develop a strong employer brand**: APEX began redefining its image to attract top-tier AI talent. They positioned themselves as an innovation-centric company committed to leveraging cutting-edge technology to revolutionize manufacturing. They highlighted their commitment to AI-driven solutions and the exciting, impactful projects potential employees could work on.

- **Leverage multiple recruitment channels**: APEX diversified its recruitment strategy, using job boards, social media, university partnerships, and AI conferences to reach potential candidates. By attending and sponsoring AI-related events, they could network with professionals who were passionate about the field.

- **Offer competitive compensation packages**: Recognizing the fierce competition for AI talent, APEX ensured their compensation packages were highly competitive. They included attractive salaries, performance bonuses, flexible working arrangements, and continuous learning opportunities.

- **Engage in proactive talent sourcing**: Instead of waiting for candidates to apply, APEX's HR team actively searched for potential hires on LinkedIn, GitHub, and Kaggle. They contacted top contributors in AI communities and invited them to explore career opportunities at APEX.

Step 2 – structuring your AI team for success

- **Define clear roles and responsibilities**: APEX meticulously defined roles for their AI team, including data scientists, machine learning engineers, domain experts, and project managers. Each role was clearly outlined, and specific responsibilities were aligned with the company's AI goals.
- **Create cross-functional teams**: Understanding that diverse skill sets drive innovation, APEX structured their AI teams to include data scientists, engineers, and domain experts who understood the manufacturing intricacies. This blend ensured comprehensive problem-solving.
- **Establish effective communication channels**: Regular meetings, updates, and collaborative tools such as Slack and Microsoft Teams facilitated seamless communication among team members. Open and transparent communication was encouraged to prevent silos and foster collaboration.
- **Implement agile methodologies**: APEX adopted agile methodologies such as Scrum to manage AI projects. This approach allowed for iterative development, continuous feedback, and quick adjustments to evolving requirements, ensuring the projects aligned with business goals.

Step 3 – fostering a culture of innovation and collaboration

- **Encourage experimentation**: To spark creativity, APEX created an environment encouraging experimentation and risk-taking. They recognized and rewarded innovative ideas and efforts, fostering a culture where failure was seen as a stepping stone to success rather than a setback.
- **Provide continuous learning opportunities**: APEX invested heavily in training and development. Team members were encouraged to attend conferences, workshops, and online courses, keeping them abreast of the latest trends and technologies in AI.
- **Implement a mentorship program**: Junior team members were paired with seasoned mentors. This mentorship fostered knowledge sharing, skill development, and professional growth, ensuring a continuous transfer of expertise and nurturing future leaders.
- **Celebrate successes and learn from failures**: Successes, big or small, were regularly celebrated to boost morale and motivation. When projects didn't go as planned, the company used these as learning opportunities to refine their approach and improve.

Step 4 – integrating AI initiatives with business processes

- **Conduct a gap analysis**: APEX thoroughly assessed its current processes to identify areas where AI could add the most value. They pinpointed the necessary changes to integrate AI effectively into their operations.

- **Develop a change management plan**: To manage the transition smoothly, a comprehensive change management plan was developed. This included extensive employee training, clear communication about AI's benefits, and strategies to address any resistance.
- **Ensure cross-departmental collaboration**: APEX fostered collaboration between AI teams and other departments to ensure that AI initiatives were seamlessly integrated into existing workflows and aligned with overall business objectives.
- **Monitor and evaluate performance**: The performance of AI systems was continuously monitored, and their impact on business processes was rigorously evaluated. Insights gained from this monitoring were used to make necessary adjustments and improvements.

Step 5 – measuring success and iterate

- **Define clear KPIs**: APEX established SMART KPIs for each AI initiative. These KPIs were aligned with business goals to provide a clear measure of success.
- **Regular performance reviews**: Regular reviews were conducted to assess the performance of AI projects. These reviews identified areas for improvement and informed data-driven decisions.
- **Communicate results**: The results of AI initiatives were transparently communicated with stakeholders. Successes, lessons learned, and the overall impact on business goals were highlighted to build confidence and secure continued investment.
- **Iterate and improve**: APEX continuously iterated and improved their AI projects using feedback and insights gained from performance reviews. The company remained agile, ready to pivot based on new data and evolving business needs.

Results achieved

The following results were observed after implementing the previous steps:

- **Enhanced production efficiency**: APEX significantly reduced equipment downtime by leveraging AI for predictive maintenance. Machine learning models accurately predicted equipment failures before they occurred, allowing for timely maintenance. This proactive approach enhanced overall production efficiency and cut operational costs.
- **Improved product quality**: AI-driven quality control systems were implemented to monitor production processes in real time. These systems detected defects and deviations from quality standards, enabling immediate corrective actions. As a result, product quality improved markedly, boosting customer satisfaction.
- **Reduced operational costs**: Optimizing inventory management with AI helped APEX maintain optimal stock levels. AI algorithms analyzed demand patterns and provided accurate forecasts, reducing excess inventory and minimizing stockouts. This led to substantial cost savings and more efficient operations.

- **Increased revenue**: With enhanced production efficiency, improved product quality, and reduced operational costs, APEX saw a significant increase in revenue. The company's reputation for delivering high-quality products on time improved customer loyalty and attracted new clients, driving growth.
- **Fostered a culture of innovation**: The initiatives to foster innovation paid off. Team members felt empowered to propose new ideas and experiment with AI solutions. This continuous innovation cycle kept APEX at the forefront of technological advancements in the manufacturing industry.

APEX's transformation illustrates the power of a well-crafted AI strategy. By following a structured approach to recruiting top AI talent, structuring the team for success, fostering a culture of innovation, integrating AI with business processes, and continuously measuring success, APEX overcame significant operational challenges. The result was a more efficient, innovative, and competitive organization.

This hypothetical case study demonstrates how other organizations can apply these principles to achieve similar success. By embracing a comprehensive approach to building and nurturing AI teams, businesses can unlock AI's full potential, driving growth, innovation, and long-term success.

Reflection and practical next steps

Please take a moment to reflect on the key insights we've explored in this chapter about building high-performing AI teams. Consider your experiences in the AI field, whether as a manager, a team member, or an aspiring AI professional. How do the challenges we've discussed resonate with your journey? Have you grappled with talent scarcity, struggled to structure an effective AI team, or found fostering a culture of innovation difficult?

Imagine what it would be like to work in an AI team that embodies our outlined principles. Picture yourself collaborating with curious, creative, and imaginative individuals passionate about pushing the boundaries of what's possible with AI. Envision a team structure that maximizes efficiency and collaboration, where clear roles, cross-functional expertise, and effective communication channels enable seamless problem-solving. Think about the excitement of being part of a culture that encourages experimentation, celebrates successes, and learns from failures, always striving to innovate and improve.

As you contemplate this ideal scenario, ask yourself this: What's holding me back from making this vision a reality? Are you settling for less than top-tier talent in your recruitment efforts? Is your team structure hindering rather than enabling collaboration? Are you providing enough opportunities for your team members to make a meaningful impact and exercise control over their projects?

It's time to critically assess your current situation and identify concrete steps you can take to implement these strategies in your context. Start by reviewing your recruitment process. Are you leveraging diverse channels and proactively sourcing candidates? Consider revamping your employer branding to highlight your commitment to innovation and the exciting projects your team is working on.

Next, examine your team structure closely. Are roles and responsibilities clearly defined? Do you have the right mix of skills and expertise? If not, consider reorganizing your team to foster cross-functional collaboration. Establish regular meetings and invest in collaborative tools to ensure effective communication.

To cultivate a culture of innovation, start by encouraging experimentation. Give your team members the freedom to take calculated risks and propose new ideas. Implement a mentorship program to facilitate knowledge sharing and professional growth. Celebrate successes, no matter how small, and treat failures as valuable learning opportunities.

Finally, ensure your AI initiatives are closely integrated with your business processes. Conduct a gap analysis to identify areas where AI can add the most value and develop a comprehensive change management plan to ensure smooth integration. Establish clear KPIs to measure success and continuously iterate based on feedback and insights.

Building a high-performing AI team is a journey, not a destination. It requires ongoing effort, adaptation, and commitment. But by implementing the strategies we've discussed, one step at a time, you can create an AI team that drives innovation and business success and fosters a sense of purpose, engagement, and fulfillment for every team member.

So, what will your first step be? Will you revamp your recruitment strategy to attract top-tier talent? Will you restructure your team to enable better collaboration? Will you introduce new initiatives to foster a culture of innovation? Whatever you choose, know that every action, no matter how small, brings you closer to building the AI team of your dreams. The power to transform your AI team—and your organization—is in your hands. Seize this opportunity, and let's start building the future of AI together.

Summary

In this chapter, we embarked on a journey to uncover the secrets of building high-performing AI teams. We explored the challenges you might face, from the scarcity of AI talent to the complexity of fostering a culture of innovation. But more importantly, we equipped you with a powerful strategy to overcome these obstacles. You can assemble an AI dream team that drives transformative results by identifying curious, creative, and imaginative individuals and providing them with the impact and control they need to thrive.

Building a top-notch AI team is not a one-time event but an ongoing process. It requires a commitment to continuous improvement, a willingness to experiment and learn from failures, and a relentless focus on integrating AI into the fabric of your organization. But with the step-by-step implementation plan we provided, you have the tools to make this vision a reality. So, take a moment to reflect on the insights you've gained and consider how you can apply them in your context. Because when you invest in building a high-performing AI team, you're not just investing in your organization's success—you're investing in the future of AI itself.

Now that we've laid the foundation for building exceptional AI teams, it's time to dive into the lifeblood that powers their work: data. The next chapter will explore data's critical role in AI and how you can leverage it to unlock new insights, drive better decisions, and create AI solutions that genuinely make a difference. So, get ready to immerse yourself in the world of data—the fuel that propels your AI team to new heights.

Questions

1. What are the three key characteristics of identifying the right talent for your AI team?
2. Why is providing team members with impact and control crucial for their success?
3. How can you leverage multiple recruitment channels to attract top AI talent?
4. What are the benefits of creating cross-functional AI teams?
5. How can implementing agile methodologies help in managing AI projects effectively?
6. What are some ways to encourage experimentation and foster a culture of innovation within your AI team?
7. Why is it important to conduct a gap analysis before integrating AI initiatives with existing business processes?
8. How can you measure the success of your AI projects, and why is it crucial to do so?
9. In the hypothetical case study of APEX Manufacturing, what were some of the key results achieved by implementing the AI team-building strategies discussed in the chapter?
10. How can you apply the insights from this chapter to your context, and what steps can you take to start building a high-performing AI team?

References

1. Gartner. *AI Is Creating New Roles and Skills in Data & Analytics*. Available from https://www.gartner.com/en/newsroom/press-releases/2024-05-14-artificial-intelligence-is-creating-new-roles-and-skills-in-data-and-analytics#:~:text=A%3A%20Gartner's%202024%20survey%20of,and%20tools%20continues%20to%20grow.
2. McKinsey & Company. *Global AI Survey: AI proves its worth, but few scale impact*. Available from https://www.mckinsey.com/business-functions/mckinsey-analytics/our-insights/global-ai-survey-ai-proves-its-worth-but-few-scale-impact.
3. Mims, C. *Google's "20% time," which brought you Gmail and AdSense, is now as good as dead*. Quartz. Available from https://qz.com/115831/googles-20-time-which-brought-you-gmail-and-adsense-is-now-as-good-as-dead/.
4. Kaplan, R. S. and Norton, D. P. *The Balanced Scorecard—Measures that Drive Performance*. Harvard Business Review. 1992. Available from https://hbr.org/1992/01/the-balanced-scorecard-measures-that-drive-performance-2.

Part 2: Building and Implementing AI Systems

Transforming AI from concept to impactful solutions requires a deep understanding of its foundations, processes, and applications. This part provides a step-by-step guide to building and implementing AI systems, from managing data—the lifeblood of AI—to training and deploying powerful models. Through insights into AI project management, the nuances of deterministic, probabilistic, and generative AI, and the emerging potential of agentic systems, this part equips you with the tools and strategies needed to design, train, and launch AI solutions that deliver measurable value and drive innovation.

This part has the following chapters:

- *Chapter 5, Data – the Lifeblood of AI*
- *Chapter 6, AI Project Management*
- *Chapter 7, Understanding Deterministic, Probabilistic, and Generative AI*
- *Chapter 8, AI Agents and Agentic Systems*
- *Chapter 9, Designing AI Systems*
- *Chapter 10, Training AI Models*
- *Chapter 11, Deploying AI Solutions*

5
Data – the Lifeblood of AI

The ability to take data – to be able to understand it, to process it, to extract value from it, to visualize it, to communicate it – is going to be a hugely important skill in the next decades

– Hal Varian

Picture this: you're the production manager of a leading manufacturing plant renowned for precision-engineered products. You have cutting-edge machinery, a highly skilled workforce, and an excellent reputation. However, a looming issue keeps you awake at night – the challenge of predicting equipment failures before they halt your production line. You've heard that **artificial intelligence** (**AI**) can be the game changer you need, transforming your operations from reactive to proactive. Yet there's one critical component you might be overlooking – data. Without reliable, high-quality data, even the most advanced AI system is like a state-of-the-art machine without power – it simply won't run.

Now, consider this mind-boggling fact: by 2025, the global data sphere is projected to expand to a whopping 200 zettabytes, highlighting the tremendous growth and importance of data in our world. That's 200 trillion gigabytes of data, or a stack of Blu-ray discs that could reach the moon 23 times [1]. Remember those? Despite this staggering volume, many manufacturing plants need help effectively harnessing their data's power. The reason? It's not just about having data – it's about organizing the correct data to make it worthwhile for AI applications.

Many companies have aimed to revolutionize their production processes through AI-driven predictive maintenance. The promise was tantalizing – significantly reduced downtime, lower maintenance costs, and increased efficiency. However, they quickly encountered a significant obstacle. The data coming from their machines was inconsistent, incomplete, and often siloed across different departments. As a result, their AI models struggled to provide accurate predictions, leading to continued unplanned downtime and mounting frustrations.

However, these companies didn't give up. They embarked on a comprehensive data overhaul, standardizing data formats, implementing robust data governance practices, and ensuring real-time data collection from all their equipment. This meticulous approach transformed their data landscape, enabling their AI systems to accurately predict maintenance needs, prevent equipment failures, and optimize production schedules. The payoff was substantial – a 20% reduction in maintenance costs and a 15% increase in **overall equipment effectiveness (OEE)** [2].

Why is data so crucial? Imagine creating a seamless, AI-driven production line with data as fragmented as a jigsaw puzzle missing half its pieces. It's a frustrating endeavor, akin to baking a cake without knowing whether you've got sugar or salt in your ingredients. Good data is the foundation upon which all AI capabilities are built. Without it, even the most sophisticated algorithms can't deliver actionable insights.

Consider another example from the world of aerospace manufacturing. A leading aircraft manufacturer faced severe production delays due to unexpected machine downtimes. Their initial foray into AI-based predictive maintenance was a rocky road marred by inconsistent data streams from various machine types and models. When implementing a unified data collection framework, leveraging IoT sensors and real-time analytics, they could feed their AI systems with the accurate, consistent data needed for compelling predictions. The result? A significant drop in unexpected downtimes, smoother production flows, and happier customers.

Data is indeed the lifeblood of AI, especially in the manufacturing sector. This chapter will explore why data is critical, how to navigate common pitfalls, and what steps you can take to ensure your data strategy sets your AI initiatives up for success. We'll uncover insights from industry leaders, share practical advice, and add a touch of humor to keep things engaging.

In this chapter, we will explore the critical role of data in AI implementation, focusing on three key areas:

- Data collection and management
- Ensuring data quality and integrity
- Leveraging big data and data analytics

By the end of this chapter, you will be able to identify common data challenges in AI implementation, develop strategies for effective data collection and management, and understand how to ensure data quality for AI applications. Additionally, you'll gain valuable insights into leveraging big data analytics to drive AI-powered decision-making in manufacturing environments.

The problem – pain points and challenges

In the quest to harness AI's transformative power, businesses often navigate a labyrinth of data-related challenges. These challenges can range from the initial stages of data collection to the complexities of data management, ensuring data quality, maintaining data integrity, and effectively leveraging the vast seas of big data. If not appropriately addressed, these pain points can significantly impede the success of AI initiatives.

Data collection – the first hurdle

One of the first hurdles is data collection. Many organizations, especially in manufacturing, operate with legacy systems never designed to produce the rich, granular data that modern AI applications require. Machines might be decades old, generating minimal and often incompatible data. For example, a manufacturing plant may have hundreds of machines from different eras and manufacturers, leading to various data formats and standards. This makes it incredibly difficult to collect consistent, usable data.

I recall a project with a mid-sized automotive parts manufacturer. Their machines, some dating back to the 1980s, generated data in formats that were not only outdated but also varied wildly. Integrating this data into a cohesive system required a herculean effort, involving custom-built data extraction tools and a significant manual intervention to standardize the data. This inconsistency delayed their AI implementation and also added significant costs.

Moreover, the advent of the **industrial internet of things** (**IIoT**) promises to revolutionize data collection by equipping machines with sensors that capture real-time data. However, the transition to IIoT could be more seamless. Many companies need help retrofitting old equipment with new sensors or dealing with the initial costs of implementing a comprehensive IIoT system. This investment, though crucial, often becomes a significant barrier for many businesses, as well as **small and medium-sized enterprises** (**SMEs**).

Data management – an ongoing battle

Once data is collected, managing it effectively is the next significant challenge. Businesses often find themselves dealing with data silos, where information is isolated within different departments or systems, making it difficult to get a holistic view. This fragmentation can lead to inefficiencies and missed opportunities [3].

For instance, a large electronics manufacturer I worked with had extensive data from various sources – production lines, quality control, supply chain logistics, and customer feedback. However, this data was stored in disparate systems, and there was no easy way to integrate and analyze it collectively. The lack of a unified data management strategy meant that their AI initiatives, which depended on a comprehensive view of the entire manufacturing process, were severely impaired.

The company attempted to integrate its systems, but the process was not smooth. It faced technical challenges, resistance from various departments, and a steep learning curve for its employees. It took them over two years to fully implement an integrated data management system. During this period, it lost market share to competitors who were quicker to adopt integrated data strategies.

Furthermore, data management requires robust governance frameworks to ensure consistency and accessibility. This involves defining data ownership, establishing standards, and implementing data stewardship roles. With these frameworks, organizations can easily find their data becoming chaotic, with different departments using different versions of the same data, leading to conflicting insights and decisions.

Ensuring data quality – the devil is in the details

Data quality is another critical issue. For AI to be effective, its data must be accurate, complete, and timely. Data quality can lead to correct insights, faulty predictions, and bad decisions. Inaccurate data can come from various sources, such as sensor errors, manual entry mistakes, or outdated information.

Consider a pharmaceutical manufacturer that embarked on an AI-driven quality control project. They soon discovered that a significant portion of their sensor data needed more accuracy due to calibration issues. This flawed data led their AI models to flag non-existent defects, causing unnecessary rework and delays. The AI system could provide reliable insights when implementing stringent data quality checks.

Another example involves a global beverage company that needed more data quality from its bottling plants. Variations in data recording practices across different locations meant their AI models could not reliably predict production bottlenecks or optimize supply chains. They had to undertake a massive data cleaning initiative, standardizing data recording processes and implementing automated quality checks. While costly and time-consuming, this initiative eventually paid off by significantly improving the accuracy of their AI models.

Ensuring data quality also involves regular audits and validations. Automated tools can help by identifying anomalies and inconsistencies in data sets. However, these tools require initial and ongoing configuration to understand what constitutes "normal" data. This process can be complex and requires continuous monitoring and adjustment as business, processes, and data evolve.

Maintaining data integrity – the trust factor

Maintaining data integrity is crucial for building trust in AI systems [4]. Data breaches, tampering, or unauthorized access can compromise data integrity, leading to significant risks. In industries such as healthcare or finance, where data sensitivity is paramount, ensuring data integrity is a technical challenge and a regulatory requirement.

A case in point is a healthcare provider implementing an AI system for patient diagnostics. They faced a significant setback when they discovered their data had been tampered with, leading to erroneous diagnostic recommendations. This breach undermined the AI system's credibility and posed severe health risks to patients. The provider had to overhaul their security protocols and data governance policies to restore trust and ensure data integrity.

In another instance, a financial institution experienced a severe data breach that compromised sensitive customer information. This breach exposed them to regulatory fines and eroded customer trust, impacting their reputation and market position. They had to implement a comprehensive data integrity strategy, including encryption, access controls, and continuous monitoring to prevent future breaches and restore customer confidence.

Ensuring data integrity involves implementing robust security measures such as encryption, access controls, and audit trails. It also requires continuous monitoring and incident response mechanisms to promptly detect and address any breaches. Fostering a culture of data ethics within the organization can help maintain data integrity by ensuring all employees understand the importance of data security and follow best practices [5].

Leveraging big data – turning volume into value

Lastly, leveraging big data is challenging. The sheer volume of data generated today can be overwhelming. Businesses must find ways to efficiently store, process, and analyze this data to extract meaningful insights [6]. However, many need help with the infrastructure and expertise required to handle big data effectively.

For example, a consumer goods company generated terabytes of data daily from its global operations. Despite having access to this information treasure trove, it was challenging to derive actionable insights due to the lack of a robust big data strategy. Its data scientists spent more time wrangling data than analyzing it, leading to missed opportunities for innovation and growth.

To tackle this challenge, companies must invest in scalable storage solutions, such as cloud-based data lakes, which can handle the vast volumes of data generated. Additionally, advanced analytics platforms and tools such as Hadoop and Spark can help efficiently process and analyze big data. However, these technologies require skilled personnel to operate and manage, highlighting the need for continuous investment in training and development.

In my own experience, I've seen how these data challenges can manifest in various forms. Early in my career, I worked on a project for a food processing company aiming to optimize their supply chain with AI. We quickly realized that their data was scattered across multiple systems, from procurement to production to distribution. Integrating this data required technical solutions and a cultural shift within the organization to prioritize data sharing and collaboration.

Another memorable project was with a telecommunications firm looking to enhance customer experience through AI-driven chatbots. The initial deployment faced numerous issues due to poor data quality and fragmented customer data. We significantly improved the chatbot's performance by implementing a comprehensive data governance framework and investing in data quality tools, leading to higher customer satisfaction and reduced operational costs.

These personal anecdotes illustrate the importance of comprehensively addressing data challenges. Overcoming these challenges, whether through technological solutions, process improvements, or cultural changes, is crucial for the success of any AI initiative.

The solution and process – implementation

Effective implementation of the data solution is key to AI success. This section covers the essential data collection and management steps, from auditing and standardizing data to real-time collection and centralized storage. These steps ensure seamless integration, making data accessible and actionable for AI-driven insights.

Data collection and management

Effective data collection and management are the cornerstones of any successful AI implementation. They require a strategic, step-by-step approach to address the challenges of disparate systems and fragmented data sources.

Effective data collection – methodologies and tools

Addressing the challenge of data collection requires a strategic and systematic approach. Start by conducting a thorough audit of all data-generating assets within your organization. This involves identifying every machine, sensor, and system that produces outdated or fragmented data. This initial inventory is crucial because it lays the groundwork for all subsequent steps.

Step 1 – comprehensive data audit

Imagine walking through your plant with a checklist, documenting each piece of equipment, its data output, and its current integration status. You might discover, for instance, that an old CNC machine from the 1990s still uses a proprietary format for its data logs, while a newer 3D printer outputs data in a modern, easily integrated format. This diversity is common in manufacturing environments, and recognizing it early helps plan your data integration strategy.

Step 2 – standardization of data formats

Once you have a complete inventory, the next step is to implement a unified data collection framework. This framework should include the standardization of data formats. Standardizing data ensures that all collected information can be easily integrated and analyzed. For example, you might use middleware that translates various data formats into a common language, such as JSON or CSV. This middleware is a universal translator, allowing disparate systems to communicate seamlessly [7].

Step 3 – real-time data collection

Equip machines and systems with IoT sensors to collect real-time data. Real-time data collection minimizes the lag between data generation and collection, providing up-to-the-minute insights. Consider retrofitting older equipment with modern sensors. For instance, attaching vibration sensors to an old lathe can provide valuable data on its operational status, which can be used for predictive maintenance.

Step 4 – centralized data storage

Implement a centralized data repository where all collected data is stored. Depending on your infrastructure, this could be an on-premises server or a cloud-based solution. Centralized storage ensures all data is accessible from a single location, simplifying management and analysis. Think of it as creating a central library where all the books (data) are organized and readily available for any researcher (AI system).

Actionable tips and best practices

Here are a few best practices for data collection and management:

- **Conduct regular data audits**: Regularly audit your data sources to ensure that all relevant data is collected and all new sources are noticed. This helps in keeping the data inventory up-to-date.
- **Invest in training**: Ensure that your team is well-versed in the tools and methodologies used for data collection. Continuous training helps keep skills up to date and ensures everyone can effectively contribute to data collection efforts.
- **Implement automated data validation**: Use automated tools to validate data as it is collected, identifying and flagging any anomalies for further investigation. This reduces the risk of errors and ensures that only high-quality data enters your systems.

Managing data effectively

Data management is an ongoing process that involves storing data and ensuring it is accessible and usable across the organization. This means breaking down data silos and integrating all data sources into a single system.

Step 1 – data integration

Breaking down data silos by integrating all data sources into a single system is essential. This might involve data warehousing solutions or the creation of a data lake. For example, you might consolidate data from your production line, quality control, and supply chain into a single warehouse. This integration provides a comprehensive view of your operations, enabling more informed decision-making.

Step 2 – data governance

Establish clear data governance policies that define data ownership, access rights, and usage guidelines. Data governance ensures that data is used ethically and legally. For instance, setting up **role-based access controls** (RBAC) ensures that only authorized personnel can access sensitive data, preventing misuse or unauthorized access.

Step 3 – data stewardship

Appoint data stewards in each department to oversee data management practices and ensure adherence to governance policies. Data stewards act as data custodians, ensuring it is appropriately managed and maintained. They can also serve as contact points for data-related queries or issues within their departments.

Actionable tips and best practices

To effectively manage data, here are a few best practices:

- **Develop a data governance framework**: Create a detailed framework outlining your data governance policies and ensure that they are communicated across the organization. This framework should cover aspects such as data quality, security, and privacy.
- **Use metadata**: Implement metadata management to provide context to your data, making it easier to locate and use effectively. Metadata acts like a catalog, describing each piece of data, where it came from, and how it should be used.
- **Encourage cross-departmental collaboration**: Foster a culture of collaboration where data is shared freely across departments, reducing the risk of data silos. Regular inter-departmental meetings and workshops facilitate this sharing.

Ensuring data quality

Ensuring high data quality is essential for reliable and actionable AI insights, requiring a focused data quality management program that includes data cleaning, validation, and enrichment.

Step 1 – data cleaning

Clean your data regularly to remove duplicates, correct errors, and fill in missing values [8]. Automated data cleaning tools can help streamline this process. For example, setting up scripts periodically scanning your database for duplicates and inconsistencies can save countless hours of manual data cleaning.

Step 2 – data validation

Validation rules ensure that data meets predefined standards before it is used in AI models. This could involve setting thresholds for acceptable data ranges or using statistical methods to identify outliers. For instance, if a temperature sensor records a value that falls outside the expected range, the system should flag it for review.

Step 3 – data enrichment

Enhance your data by integrating additional information from external sources, providing more context, and improving the quality of insights. For example, combining your internal sales data with market trends data can give you a more comprehensive view of market dynamics, leading to better predictions and strategies.

Actionable tips and best practices

- **Implement automated cleaning tools**: Automated cleaning tools clean data regularly, reducing the manual workload and improving efficiency. These tools can be programmed to follow specific rules and criteria, ensuring consistent and thorough cleaning.

- **Set clear data quality metrics**: Define clear metrics for data quality and monitor them continuously. Metrics include accuracy, completeness, and timeliness. Regularly reviewing these metrics helps maintain high standards.
- **Establish data quality teams**: Form dedicated teams responsible for maintaining data quality, ensuring someone is always accountable. These teams can also conduct regular audits to identify and address any issues.

Maintaining data integrity

Data integrity ensures that your data is trustworthy and secure. This involves implementing robust security measures and fostering a culture of data ethics within the organization [8].

Step 1 – data encryption

Encrypt data at rest and in transit to protect it from unauthorized access and breaches. Encryption ensures that even if data is intercepted, it cannot be read without the appropriate decryption key [9]. Consider putting your data in a safe that only authorized personnel can unlock.

Step 2 – access controls

Enforce stringent access controls to ensure sensitive data is accessible only to authorized personnel. This includes using RBAC and regularly reviewing access permissions. For instance, only the finance department might access financial data, while the production team can access operational data.

Step 3 – audit trails

Maintain detailed audit trails that recorded all data access and modifications. This helps track down unauthorized changes and ensure accountability. Audit trails act like security cameras for your data, recording who did what and when.

Actionable tips and best practices

The following best practices are recommended to manage data integrity:

- **Regularly update security protocols**: Stay updated with the latest security best practices and regularly update your security protocols to protect against new threats. This includes patching systems, updating encryption methods, and training staff on new security measures.
- **Conduct regular security audits**: Conduct regular security audits to identify and address vulnerabilities in your data systems. These audits can help with unconvertible risks and ensure that security measures are practical.
- **Train employees on data security**: Ensure all employees are trained on best practices, including recognizing phishing attempts and other common threats. Regular training sessions keep security at the forefront of everyone's mind.

Leveraging big data and data analytics

Leveraging big data and advanced analytics is key to unlocking valuable insights that drive innovation and improve decision-making across your organization.

Harnessing the power of big data

To leverage big data effectively, build a scalable data infrastructure that can handle the volume, velocity, and variety of data generated.

Step 1 – scalable storage solutions

Implement scalable storage solutions such as data lakes that can grow with your data needs. Ensure that these solutions can handle both structured and unstructured data. For example, a data lake can store raw data from various sources, making it accessible for different types of analysis.

Step 2 – advanced analytics platforms

Use advanced analytics platforms that can process and analyze large datasets quickly. These platforms should support machine learning and other AI techniques to extract valuable insights. For instance, using machine learning algorithms to analyze sensor data from your production line can help identify patterns and predict equipment failures.

Actionable tips and best practices

Let's go through the best practices:

- **Adopt a cloud-first strategy**: Consider adopting a cloud-first strategy for your big data infrastructure, taking advantage of cloud services' scalability and flexibility. This approach allows you to scale your storage and computing resources as needed without significant upfront investment.
- **Invest in high-performance computing**: Ensure you have the computational power to process large datasets efficiently. High-performance computing clusters can handle the intensive processing required for big data analytics.
- **Utilize edge computing**: Implement edge computing solutions to process data closer to the source, reducing latency and improving real-time analytics. For example, processing data from IoT sensors at the edge can provide immediate insights and reduce the amount of data that needs to be sent to central servers.

Leveraging data analytics for AI

Once your significant data infrastructure is in place, leveraging data analytics to drive AI initiatives is next.

Step 1 – data preparation

Prepare your data for analysis by cleaning, transforming, and enriching it. This step is crucial for ensuring that your AI models receive high-quality data. For instance, transforming raw sensor data into meaningful features can significantly improve the performance of your predictive models.

Step 2 – model development

Develop AI models using machine learning algorithms suited to your specific needs. This might involve supervised learning for predictive analytics or unsupervised learning for anomaly detection. For example, using supervised learning to predict maintenance needs based on historical data and sensor readings can help prevent equipment failure.

Step 3 – continuous monitoring

Continuously monitor the performance of your AI models and retrain them as necessary. This ensures that your models remain accurate and relevant as new data becomes available. For instance, setting up automated monitoring and retraining pipelines can help keep your models up-to-date and effective.

Actionable tips and best practices

Here are the best practices:

- **Invest in data scientists**: Hire skilled data scientists to develop and fine-tune AI models. Please provide them with the tools and resources they need to succeed, such as access to high-quality data, computing resources, and advanced analytics platforms.
- **Use Automated Machine Learning (AutoML)**: Implement AutoML tools to streamline the model development process, making it more accessible to non-experts. These tools can automatically select the best algorithms and tune hyperparameters, saving time and improving model performance.
- **Create feedback loops**: Establish feedback loops where insights from AI models are used to continuously improve data collection and management processes. For example, using insights from predictive maintenance models to refine sensor data collection can lead to more accurate predictions and better decision-making.

Case study – APEX Manufacturing and Distribution

APEX Manufacturing and Distribution, a large industrial operation spanning multiple plants across different regions, faced critical data challenges. Each plant operated with a mix of modern and legacy machinery, generating data in silos. These systems – spanning production, quality control, and logistics – were poorly integrated, leading to fragmented data sets that were difficult to analyze and nearly impossible to leverage for AI-driven initiatives. Data inconsistencies and quality issues compounded the problem, with inaccuracies hampering efforts to implement predictive maintenance and supply chain optimizations.

APEX's leadership understood AI's transformative power but knew they needed to establish a strong data infrastructure before AI could deliver value. They engaged our consultancy to design and implement a solution to provide a solid foundation for AI, driving operational efficiency and cost savings across their plants.

Data collection and management

Effective data collection and management at APEX required a comprehensive and methodical approach. To address the challenge of integrating legacy equipment with modern technology, multiple steps were performed, starting with a detailed data audit.

Step 1 – comprehensive data audit

We began by conducting a detailed audit across all of APEX's plants. The objective was to inventory every machine, sensor, and system, cataloging the data formats, data frequency, and current integration status. The diversity of their machinery became evident – some plants were operating with decades-old CNC machines outputting data in proprietary formats. In contrast, others had modern 3D printers delivering real-time, integrable data.

This audit highlighted the challenge of managing such disparate systems. Legacy equipment still in use could not interface with newer systems, creating data silos seamlessly. For example, CNC machines relied on paper logs for recording data, while modern equipment had intuitive dashboards and real-time data output. Bridging these technological gaps was a critical first step in creating a unified approach to data management.

Step 2 – standardization of data formats

To resolve the issue of incompatible data formats, we developed custom middleware that standardized data collection across APEX's machinery. This middleware acted as a universal translator, converting data from legacy machines into modern formats such as JSON that could be integrated into centralized systems.

A particular challenge involved a decades-old CNC machine nicknamed "Old Reliable" by plant operators. Its data output was cryptic, with proprietary codes that even our seasoned engineers found puzzling. After several iterations, we developed a solution that successfully translated its data into usable insights. This solution enabled the integration of legacy equipment with modern systems, significantly improving data visibility and accessibility.

Step 3 – real-time data collection

We retrofitted older machines with IoT sensors to enable real-time data collection. These sensors provided continuous operational insights, such as vibration levels and temperature, which were essential for predictive maintenance. One notable example was an aging lathe where a vibration sensor detected a subtle anomaly. Upon inspection, a worn bearing was found, which, if left unaddressed, could have led to a major breakdown. This proactive maintenance intervention saved APEX a week's worth of downtime and costly repairs.

Step 4 – centralized data storage

Once the data was standardized and collected in real time, we implemented a centralized cloud-based data repository for APEX. This repository allowed all data – both historical and real-time – from multiple plants to be stored in one location. APEX now had the ability to scale their data storage needs as operations grew, and data previously scattered across local servers or paper logs was instantly accessible for analysis.

The transition to cloud storage was carefully managed to ensure data security and compliance. With the data now easily accessible across the organization, engineers and analysts could monitor operations, track equipment health, and manage the supply chain in real time.

Ensuring data quality and integrity

Ensuring data quality and integrity at APEX was crucial for maximizing the effectiveness of their AI systems, requiring a multi-step approach that began with comprehensive data cleaning and validation processes to establish a reliable foundation for accurate analysis and decision-making.

Step 1 – data cleaning

With the data centralized, the next priority was to ensure its quality and accuracy. We implemented automated data cleaning tools that systematically removed duplicates, corrected errors, and filled in missing values. This was particularly important for APEX's historical data, which had been collected over the years with varying degrees of accuracy. Our automated tools flagged problematic entries, allowing for manual review where needed, resulting in a cleaner, more reliable dataset.

Step 2 – data validation

To maintain high data integrity, we established stringent validation rules across all datasets. For instance, sensor data was required to meet specific thresholds, and any anomalies outside of these acceptable ranges were flagged for review. This proactive approach helped ensure that only high-quality data was used in AI models, reducing the risk of inaccurate predictions or faulty maintenance alerts.

Step 3 – data enrichment

We enriched APEX's internal data by integrating additional external sources. For example, we pulled in market trends, supplier performance metrics, and even weather data. This enhanced dataset provided a broader context for decision-making, allowing for more accurate forecasting and better operational insights. One particularly insightful discovery was the impact of extreme temperatures on machine performance, which helped APEX anticipate and mitigate potential disruptions during certain weather conditions.

Step 4 – data governance

A robust data governance framework was crucial to maintaining ongoing data quality. We established clear ownership and access rights, ensuring that departments could access the data they needed while adhering to privacy and security guidelines. We also appointed data stewards in each department who acted as data custodians, overseeing its management and ensuring compliance with governance policies. This system fostered accountability and sustained data integrity over time.

Leveraging big data and advanced analytics

Leveraging big data and advanced analytics at APEX enabled the company to extract actionable insights from massive datasets, optimize operations, and enhance decision-making by implementing scalable storage solutions and cutting-edge AI technologies.

Step 1 – scalable storage solutions

With a solid data collection and management system, we focused on leveraging big data. APEX adopted a cloud-first strategy, implementing scalable storage solutions to manage structured and unstructured data. This allowed APEX to handle massive volumes of data, from sensor logs to high-resolution images, without worrying about storage constraints.

Step 2 – advanced analytics platforms

We introduced advanced analytics platforms that supported machine learning and AI techniques. These platforms processed large datasets quickly, allowing APEX to generate real-time insights. For instance, machine learning algorithms were used to analyze vibration data from production lines, identifying patterns that indicated early signs of equipment failure. This predictive maintenance capability significantly reduced downtime by allowing for proactive repairs.

Step 3 – AI model development

To prepare data for analysis, we cleaned, transformed, and enriched it to ensure high-quality inputs for AI models. We developed AI models tailored to APEX's specific needs, focusing on predictive maintenance and supply chain optimization. Supervised learning algorithms were employed for maintenance tasks, while unsupervised learning helped identify anomalies in production processes.

Step 4 – continuous monitoring and feedback loops

To ensure the AI models remained effective as new data became available, we implemented continuous monitoring and retraining pipelines. This allowed for ongoing refinement of both data collection processes and model performance. For example, initial AI models identified gaps in the sensor data, prompting the addition of more granular sensors to improve accuracy. This iterative approach helped APEX continuously improve its operational efficiency.

Results achieved

The implementation of this comprehensive data framework revolutionized APEX's operations. The unified data system broke down silos, enabling seamless data integration across the company. Real-time data collection improved APEX's ability to perform predictive maintenance, reducing unexpected equipment failures by 40% and significantly increasing operational efficiency.

Data quality improvements directly enhanced AI model accuracy, allowing APEX to optimize both predictive maintenance and supply chain operations. As a result, OEE increased by 20%, while logistics costs were reduced by 15%. Additionally, enriched data insights provided APEX with a clearer understanding of market dynamics and supply chain performance, helping the company to make more informed, data-driven decisions.

One of the most notable outcomes was APEX's newfound supply chain resilience. By combining historical supply chain data with real-time market trends, the AI models identified potential disruptions before they occurred, allowing APEX to adjust inventory levels proactively. This proactive approach ensured that APEX could consistently meet customer demand, even in volatile market conditions.

Memorable insights

Throughout the project, APEX's willingness to embrace new technologies and collaborate closely with our team was key to its success. During one plant visit, a skeptical lathe operator expressed doubt about the new IoT sensors being installed on his aging machine. "This lathe's been running fine for years. How's a gadget going to help?" he asked. Several months later, the same operator proudly demonstrated how the sensor data had identified a worn bearing, preventing a costly breakdown and minimizing downtime. "That gadget saved us a week of stress," he admitted.

Another memorable moment came from the head of quality control, who had spent years manually compiling reports from different sources. With the new AI-driven system automating much of this work, she was able to focus on more strategic tasks. "Now, instead of putting out fires, we're ahead of the game," she shared. This shift in mindset reflected the broader cultural transformation happening at APEX as data-driven decision-making took hold across the organization.

These examples illustrate the tangible benefits of addressing data challenges comprehensively. While integrating AI into legacy operations can be complex, the rewards – ranging from improved efficiency to greater supply chain resilience – are well worth the investment. APEX's journey serves as a powerful reminder of the transformative potential AI can deliver when built on a solid data foundation.

Reflection and practical next steps

As we reflect on the critical role of data in AI-driven manufacturing, it's time to consider how these insights can transform your operations. The journey of APEX Manufacturing and Distribution serves as a powerful reminder that a well-structured approach to data management can yield remarkable results even in the face of complex challenges.

Reflecting on core insights

Take a moment to consider your current data landscape. Does it resemble the fragmented, siloed structure that APEX initially grappled with? Or have you already begun the journey toward a more integrated, AI-ready data environment? Regardless of where you stand, there's always room for improvement and innovation.

Think about the machines humming away on your production floor. Like APEX's "Old Reliable," do you have equipment that's been faithfully serving for decades but struggling to keep up with modern data needs? How might retrofitting these workhorses with IoT sensors transform your operational insights?

Consider the wealth of data your organization generates daily. Are you truly harnessing its full potential? Or is valuable information slipping through the cracks, lost in the noise of day-to-day operations?

Critical assessment questions

To help you navigate your path forward, consider these thought-provoking questions:

- **Data collection**: How comprehensive is your current data collection process? Are there blind spots in your operations where crucial data is being overlooked?
- **Data quality**: If you were to conduct a data audit today, what percentage of your data do you think would meet high-quality standards? How might improving this percentage impact your decision-making processes?
- **Data integration**: To what extent are your various data sources integrated? Can you easily cross-reference production data with supply chain information or customer feedback?
- **AI readiness**: On a scale of 1 to 10, how prepared is your data infrastructure for AI implementation? What's the one thing holding you back from moving up on this scale?
- **Cultural shift**: How would you describe your organization's current attitude toward data-driven decision-making? Is there resistance to change, or an eagerness to embrace new technologies?

Actionable next steps

Now, let's transform these reflections into concrete actions. Here are some practical steps you can take to start your data transformation journey:

1. **Conduct a data audit**: Begin with a comprehensive inventory of your data sources, much like APEX did. Identify what data you're collecting, how it's being stored, and where the gaps are. This will give you a clear picture of your starting point.
2. **Start small with IoT**: You don't need to overhaul your entire operation overnight. Choose one critical piece of equipment and retrofit it with IoT sensors. Use this as a pilot project to demonstrate the value of real-time data collection.

3. **Implement data cleaning protocols**: Develop and implement automated data cleaning tools. Start with one dataset and gradually expand. Remember, clean data is the foundation of accurate AI insights.
4. **Foster cross-departmental collaboration**: Organize regular meetings between different departments to discuss data needs and insights. This can help break down data silos and encourage a more integrated approach to data management.
5. **Invest in training**: Upskill your team in data management and basic data analysis. This doesn't mean everyone needs to become a data scientist, but fostering data literacy across your organization can drive a cultural shift toward data-driven decision-making.
6. **Explore cloud solutions**: If you haven't already, start exploring cloud-based data storage solutions. These can provide the scalability and flexibility needed for big data analytics.
7. **Develop a data governance framework**: Create clear guidelines for data ownership, access, and usage within your organization. This will ensure data integrity and security as you scale up your data operations.

Remember, the goal isn't to transform your entire operation overnight. Like APEX, your journey toward data-driven AI implementation will be a gradual process of learning, adaptation, and continuous improvement. The key is to start now, learn from each step, and remain committed to the process.

As you embark on this journey, keep in mind the words of APEX's quality control head: "Now, instead of putting out fires, we're ahead of the game." With each improvement in your data management practices, you're not just solving today's problems – you're laying the groundwork for a more efficient, responsive, and competitive future.

So, which of these steps will you take first? The path to transformation begins with a single step. Take that step today, and watch as the power of data begins to reshape your operations, one insight at a time.

Summary

In this chapter, we explored how data truly is the lifeblood of AI, especially in manufacturing. You saw firsthand, through APEX's journey, that the path to AI success is paved with quality data. From conducting comprehensive audits to implementing real-time data collection and ensuring data integrity, you now have a toolkit for transforming your data landscape. Remember, it's not about having mountains of data, but about having the right data and knowing how to use it effectively. Whether you're dealing with legacy systems or cutting-edge IoT sensors, these principles can help you build a solid foundation for AI implementation.

Consider how you might start applying them in your context. Maybe it's conducting a data audit, or perhaps it's taking steps to break down data silos in your organization. Whatever your next move is, remember that every step toward better data management is a step toward unlocking AI's full potential in your operations.

Now that you've got a handle on preparing your AI data, you might wonder, What's next? How do I implement an AI project? That's exactly what we'll dive into in our next chapter, which focuses on AI project management. We'll explore how to take your newly optimized data and turn it into successful AI initiatives. From defining project scope to managing cross-functional teams and measuring ROI, you'll learn how to steer AI projects to success. So, get ready to put on your project manager hat as we navigate the exciting world of AI implementation!

Questions

1. What is the significance of data in AI implementation, especially in manufacturing settings?
2. Name three challenges organizations often face when trying to collect and manage data for AI initiatives.
3. What is the purpose of data standardization in preparing for AI implementation?
4. What role do IoT sensors play in enhancing data collection for AI applications?
5. Explain the concept of data enrichment and provide an example of how it can be beneficial.
6. How does implementing a data governance framework contribute to maintaining data quality and integrity?
7. What is the importance of scalable storage solutions in managing big data for AI?
8. Why is it important to continuously monitor and retrain AI models?
9. How can organizations foster a culture of data-driven decision-making?
10. What are some initial steps a company can take to start its journey toward better data management for AI implementation?

References

1. Seagate.com. "Data Age 2025." https://www.seagate.com/files/www-content/our-story/trends/files/Seagate-WP-DataAge2025-March-2017.pdf.
2. Webisoft Articles. "Transforming Asset Management with IoT: Unleashing Efficiency in the Digital Era." https://webisoft.com/articles/iot-in-asset-management/.
3. IdentIT. "Centralized Management of Customer Identities and Access: A Game-Changer." https://www.identit.eu/blog/centralized-management-of-customer-identities-and-access-a-game-changer/.
4. Trava. "Beyond Passwords: Unmasking the Power of Security Standards." https://travasecurity.com/learn-with-trava/blog/beyond-passwords-unmasking-the-power-of-security-standards.

5. Daily Legal Briefing – Breaking Legal News & Current Law Headlines. "How GCs Can Build A Data-Driven Division To Bolster Their Company." https://www.dailylegalbriefing.com/how-gcs-can-build-a-data-driven-division-to-bolster-their-company/.

6. Tycoonstory. "AI Revolution: How AI Is Reshaping Digital Marketing." https://www.tycoonstory.com/the-ai-revolution-has-begun-how-ai-is-reshaping-digital-marketing/.

7. Its Managed. "How the evolution of IT security solutions keeps data safe." https://www.its-managed.com/how-the-evolution-of-it-security-solutions-keeps-data-safe.

8. Techuck. "From Raw Data to Business Intelligence: Role of Big Data Analytics Companies in Decision-making." https://techuck.com/from-raw-data-to-business-intelligence-role-of-big-data-analytics-companies-in-decision-making/.

9. Health Works Collective. "How Platform As A Service (Paas) Tool Can Be Used To Develop Software For Healthcare Service?" https://www.healthworkscollective.com/how-platform-as-a-service-paas-tool-can-be-used-to-develop-software-for-healthcare-service.

6

AI Project Management

AI is about covering the blind angles that are preventing us from delivering projects that we want. Projects are beautiful, transformative things, and the more we can run projects smoothly, the more everybody will be confident in launching new projects

– Milie Taing

Have you ever wondered why some AI projects revolutionize industries while others fizzle out before they even get off the ground? Imagine this: you're standing at the edge of a technological frontier, ready to launch an AI initiative that could transform your business. But as you take that first step, you realize the landscape is more complex and unpredictable than anticipated. You're not alone – many have faced this same daunting challenge.

Consider this: a recent study found that 85% of AI projects fail to deliver on their promises [1]. Surprising? It shouldn't be. The allure of AI often blinds us to the intricate dance of planning, execution, and adaptation required to bring these projects to life. It's like trying to build a house without a blueprint – sure, you may eventually get a roof over your head, but it's unlikely to be structurally sound or aesthetically pleasing.

Picture Sarah, a seasoned project manager at a mid-sized tech firm. Sarah is tasked with overseeing her company's first major AI initiative. She's confident and experienced and has managed countless projects before. But AI is a different beast. Despite her best efforts, the project stumbles at every turn – delays, budget overruns, and an end product that barely scratches the surface of what was promised. Sound familiar?

Sarah's story isn't unique. Across industries, from finance to healthcare to retail, project managers are grappling with the complexities of AI. They face the daunting task of integrating new technologies, managing diverse teams of data scientists and engineers, and aligning AI initiatives with broader business goals. It's a high-wire act that demands a delicate balance of technical knowledge, strategic vision, and adaptive leadership.

Managing AI projects is more than applying traditional project management principles – it's about embracing a new mindset with tools and strategies tailored to AI's unique challenges. This chapter will unravel the secrets of successful AI project management, providing practical, actionable advice for navigating this complex terrain.

We'll explore the importance of agile methodologies in AI projects, how to set realistic project milestones, and the critical role of stakeholder engagement. By doing so, you'll learn how to mitigate common risks, manage cross-functional teams, and ensure your AI initiatives align with strategic business goals.

Let's remember the human element. AI might be about machines and algorithms, but successful projects hinge on the people behind them. We'll delve into the nuances of team dynamics, leadership, and communication, ensuring you can build and lead an AI project team that's technically proficient, highly motivated, and cohesive.

In this chapter, we'll explore three key areas of AI project management:

- Managing AI projects from concept to deployment
- Agile methodologies for AI
- Overcoming common AI project challenges

By the end of this chapter, you'll be equipped to confidently navigate the complex landscape of AI project management, guiding projects from initial concept through to successful deployment. You'll gain the skills to apply agile methodologies specifically tailored for AI development and address common challenges that arise in AI initiatives effectively. These competencies will empower you to lead AI projects that deliver tangible value and drive innovation within your organization.

The problem – pain points and challenges

AI project management is fraught with challenges that can derail even the most promising initiatives. Understanding these pain points is crucial to navigating the complex landscape of AI implementation. Let's delve into some of the most significant challenges businesses face and why they matter.

Scope creep – the silent project killer

One of the most insidious challenges in AI project management is scope creep. This occurs when a project's requirements expand beyond its original objectives, often due to stakeholders' evolving expectations or the discovery of new possibilities. In AI, where technology evolves rapidly, and the potential applications are vast, scope creep can be particularly prevalent and damaging.

Consider the case of a financial services company embarking on an AI-driven fraud detection project. Initially, the goal was to create a system to identify fraudulent transactions accurately. However, as the project progressed, stakeholders began to see the potential for additional features – predictive analytics for customer behavior, integration with other financial systems, and real-time monitoring across global markets. What started as a focused project ballooned into a multi-faceted initiative. The team struggled to keep up with the expanding requirements, resulting in missed deadlines, overblown budgets, and a final product far from the original vision.

In my own experience, I've seen AI projects go awry due to scope creep. A simple customer service chatbot initiative at one company evolved into a comprehensive customer relationship management system. The initial excitement led to continuous additions and changes, turning what should have been a 3-month project into an 18-month ordeal. The lesson here is clear: AI projects can quickly spiral out of control without stringent scope management.

Resource allocation – balancing expertise and time

AI projects require diverse skills, from data scientists and machine learning engineers to domain experts and project managers. Allocating these resources effectively is a significant challenge. Many organizations need to be more resource-aligned, with critical skills needing to be added at key points in the project life cycle.

Take the story of a healthcare provider attempting to develop an AI system for patient diagnostics. The project team focused on clinical expertise but needed more data science talent. As a result, the project experienced repeated setbacks in the data preprocessing and algorithm development stages. The clinicians, though knowledgeable in their field, needed help to bridge the gap to the technical requirements of the AI system. The project eventually required external consultants, further stretching the budget and timeline.

This misalignment is more than just having enough people; it's about having the right people at the right time. In one project I consulted on, the team had brilliant data scientists but needed more experienced project managers to steer the ship. The result? Fantastic models that never made it past the proof-of-concept stage because they weren't aligned with business needs or operational capabilities. Effective resource allocation is about more than numbers – it's about strategic placement and timing.

Technology integration – the jigsaw puzzle of systems

Integrating AI technology into existing business systems is another formidable challenge. Legacy systems, data silos, and varying data formats can complicate the seamless integration of new AI solutions.

Consider a manufacturing firm that sought to implement AI-driven predictive maintenance. The AI system needed to interface with various sensors and machinery, each with its own data protocols. The integration phase revealed numerous incompatibilities, requiring extensive custom development. These unforeseen complexities delayed the project and added significant costs. Moreover, the ongoing maintenance of these integrations became a burden, diverting resources from other critical areas.

In another instance, a logistics company aimed to integrate AI for route optimization. The legacy systems used different data standards and weren't designed to communicate with each other. Due to this, integration became a mammoth task involving multiple vendor negotiations and custom middleware development. The project ultimately succeeded but took twice the planned time and budget. This highlights the need for thorough pre-project assessments of technological compatibility and potential integration hurdles.

Data quality and availability – the fuel for AI

AI systems thrive on data, but ensuring the quality and availability of this data is a perennial challenge. Poor data quality can lead to inaccurate models, while insufficient data can limit the system's learning capabilities.

A retail company's attempt to use AI for customer sentiment analysis is a cautionary tale. The project team assumed they had ample customer data from various channels – social media, customer reviews, and direct feedback. However, much of this data was unstructured and inconsistent. Cleaning and structuring the data consumed a significant portion of the project timeline, delaying the development of the AI model. Additionally, gaps in the data led to incomplete insights, undermining the project's value.

Data quality issues are pervasive. We launched an AI initiative to predict crop yields during my tenure at a major agriculture company. Initially, the data seemed robust – years of historical weather patterns, soil conditions, and crop performance. However, closer inspection revealed inconsistencies and gaps. Some data was manually recorded, introducing human error, while other data was missing crucial context. We had to invest heavily in data cleaning and enrichment, significantly delaying the project. This experience underscored the importance of rigorous data validation before project kickoff.

Change management – navigating organizational resistance

AI projects often require significant changes in an organization's operations, which can be met with resistance. Employees may fear job displacement, while stakeholders may be skeptical of the technology's benefits.

I recall a consulting engagement with a traditional manufacturing company looking to introduce AI-driven automation. Despite the clear benefits, the workforce was apprehensive. They saw the AI system as a threat to their jobs. Overcoming this resistance required a robust change management strategy, including extensive communication, training, and reassurance. The project succeeded only by navigating significant organizational resistance that could have easily derailed it.

In another scenario, a large financial institution faced pushback when introducing AI to streamline its loan approval process. Loan officers feared the technology would replace their roles, and managers worried about the reliability of automated decisions. By involving employees in the development process, providing transparent communication about the technology's role, and ensuring retraining opportunities, the institution was able to mitigate resistance and successfully implement the AI system.

Analytical insight with a relatable touch

These challenges are manageable but require a nuanced understanding and strategic approach. As we continue, you'll see how these pain points can be addressed effectively, transforming potential pitfalls into stepping stones for success. By blending insightful analysis with relatable stories, we aim to provide you with a comprehensive understanding of the problems and, more importantly, solutions that can guide your AI projects to successful completion.

The following sections explore practical strategies and tools for tackling these challenges head-on. From adopting agile methodologies to fostering cross-functional collaboration, we'll equip you with the knowledge and skills to turn these common pitfalls into opportunities for innovation and growth.

The solution and its implementation

Having explored the myriad challenges that AI project management entails, let's shift our focus to solutions. This section will present practical, actionable steps you can take to navigate these challenges successfully. From managing AI projects from concept to deployment to applying agile methodologies and overcoming common obstacles, we'll cover a comprehensive guide to ensure your AI initiatives achieve their desired outcomes.

Managing AI projects from concept to deployment

Successfully managing AI projects from inception to deployment involves several critical phases. Let's delve deeper into each stage, providing more insights and narrative to illustrate the process.

1. **Initial concept and feasibility study**:

   - **Identify business objectives**: Imagine you're the chief AI officer at a major retail company. Your board has just approved an AI project aimed at enhancing customer personalization. The first step is to clearly define what this project will achieve. Will it increase sales, improve customer satisfaction, or reduce churn? Clear objectives will guide every subsequent decision.

   - **Feasibility assessment**: Conduct a feasibility study to evaluate the project's technical and economic viability. This includes assessing data availability, technical requirements, and potential ROI. For instance, in the retail example, you might find that while you have extensive customer data, integrating this data with the AI system will require significant IT infrastructure upgrades.

   - **Stakeholder engagement**: Engage key stakeholders early to ensure alignment on objectives, scope, and expectations. Hold workshops and meetings to discuss the project's goals, benefits, and potential challenges. This collaborative approach ensures that everyone is on the same page.

2. **Project planning**:

   - **Define the scope and objectives**: Establish clear, realistic project goals and deliverables. Use the **specific, measurable, achievable, relevant, and time-bound** (**SMART**) criteria to guide your planning. In our retail scenario, a SMART goal might be to *Increase online sales by 10% within the next 6 months through personalized product recommendations*.

   - **Resource allocation**: Identify the skills and resources needed for the project. This includes data scientists, domain experts, project managers, and necessary tools and technologies. Ensure you have the right mix of expertise – for example, you'll need data engineers to handle data pipelines and machine learning experts to develop algorithms.

   - **Risk management**: Develop a risk management plan to identify, assess, and mitigate potential risks. Include technical risks (for example, data privacy issues) and business risks (for example, stakeholder resistance). Review and update this plan regularly as the project progresses.

3. **Data collection and preparation**:

   - **Data audit**: Conduct a thorough audit of available data. Ensure it's relevant, high-quality, and sufficient for the AI model. For example, this might involve reviewing transaction histories, customer interactions, and web analytics in our retail setting.

   - **Data cleaning**: Address any inconsistencies, errors, and gaps in the data. This step is crucial for the accuracy of your AI models. Automated tools streamline the cleaning process, but data analysts also handle more complex issues.

   - **Data augmentation**: If necessary, augment your data with external sources to fill gaps and enhance the dataset. For instance, you might purchase third-party data to gain insights into broader market trends or customer behaviors not captured in your internal data.

4. **Model development**:

   - **Algorithm selection**: Based on your problem and the nature of your data, choose appropriate algorithms. For personalized recommendations, you might explore collaborative filtering or neural-network-based approaches.

   - **Model training**: Train your AI models using historical data. This phase involves iterative testing and refinement to optimize performance. In our retail example, you would use past purchase data to train a recommendation engine, *testing* different models to find the best fit.

   - **Evaluation and validation**: Validate your models using separate validation datasets to ensure they generalize well to new, unseen data. Employ techniques such as cross-validation and hold-out testing to assess model performance rigorously.

5. **Deployment**:

   - **Pilot testing**: Deploy the model in a controlled environment to monitor performance and identify issues. For instance, start by rolling out the recommendation system to a small segment of your customer base and closely monitor its impact.

   - **Scaling**: Once the model performs satisfactorily in the pilot phase, scale the deployment across the organization. Ensure your infrastructure can handle increased loads and have monitoring systems to track performance.

   - **Monitoring and maintenance**: Continuously monitor the model's performance and retrain it as needed to ensure it remains effective over time. Set up alerts for any significant drops in performance and schedule regular reviews to incorporate new data and improve the model.

Agile methodologies for AI

Applying agile methodologies to AI projects can significantly enhance their success by fostering flexibility, continuous improvement, and stakeholder collaboration. Here's how you can implement agile practices in your AI projects:

1. **Sprint planning**:

   - **Define sprints**: Break the project into manageable sprints, typically lasting 2 to 4 weeks. Each sprint should focus on delivering a specific component of the project. For our retail AI project, a sprint could concentrate on developing the data ingestion pipeline, training the initial recommendation model, and integrating the model with the e-commerce platform.

   - **Set sprint goals**: Clearly define the goals and deliverables for each sprint and ensure they align with the overall project objectives. For example, a sprint goal might be to *Develop and validate a recommendation algorithm that predicts the top 5 products for each user with 80% accuracy*.

2. **Iterative development**:

   - **Develop in iterations**: Build and refine the AI model in iterative cycles. This allows for continuous testing, feedback, and improvement. Start with a basic model and gradually add complexity as you gather insights and performance data.

   - **Regular reviews**: Conduct sprint reviews with stakeholders to showcase progress and gather feedback. Use this feedback to guide subsequent iterations. In the retail example, regular reviews demonstrate the recommendation system's performance to marketing and sales teams, gathering their input to refine the model.

3. **Continuous feedback**:

    - **Frequent check-ins**: Hold daily stand-up meetings to discuss progress, challenges, and next steps. This keeps the team aligned and addresses issues promptly. Encourage open communication to ensure any problems are identified and resolved quickly.

    - **Stakeholder involvement**: Engage stakeholders throughout the project to ensure their needs and expectations are being met. This continuous engagement helps them adapt to changes and ensures the final product aligns with business objectives. For instance, you can involve the marketing team in testing the recommendation engine to ensure it aligns with their strategies.

4. **Benefits and implementation strategies**:

    - **Flexibility**: Agile methodologies provide the flexibility to adapt to changing requirements and new insights, which is crucial in the dynamic field of AI. This flexibility helps us respond to new data insights or changes in business strategy without derailing the project.

    - **Collaboration**: Foster a collaborative environment where cross-functional teams work closely, enhancing innovation and problem-solving. For example, facilitate regular interactions between data scientists, software engineers, and domain experts to ensure everyone's input is considered.

    - **Efficiency**: Agile methodologies help manage time and resources more efficiently by focusing on delivering incremental value. This approach ensures that each sprint delivers tangible outcomes that add value to the overall project.

Overcoming common AI project challenges

Here are some strategies you can use to address the typical obstacles that AI projects face:

- **Data quality issues**:

    - **Data governance**: Implement robust practices to ensure data quality and consistency. This includes setting standards for data collection, storage, and processing. Establish a data governance team responsible for overseeing data quality initiatives.

    - **Data cleaning tools**: Utilize advanced data cleaning tools and techniques to automate identifying and correcting data issues. Tools such as Trifacta and Talend can help streamline this process. However, it always involves human oversight to handle complex data quality issues.

    - **Regular audits**: Conduct regular data audits to identify and address any emerging quality issues promptly. Schedule periodic data reviews and implement feedback loops to ensure continuous improvement in data quality.

- **Resistance to change**:
    - **Change management plan**: Develop a comprehensive change management plan that includes communication, training, and support strategies to help employees adapt to new AI systems. For example, use workshops, webinars, and Q&A sessions to educate employees about the new AI system's benefits and functionalities.
    - **Involve employees**: Engage employees early in the project to gather their input and address concerns. Involvement fosters a sense of ownership and reduces resistance [2]. For instance, involve customer service representatives in developing an AI chatbot to ensure it meets their needs and concerns.
    - **Training programs**: Offer training programs to upskill employees and help them understand the benefits of AI, reducing fear and uncertainty. Develop tailored training modules that address different aspects of the AI system and its impact on various organizational roles.
- **Integration challenges**:
    - **Pre-integration assessment**: Conduct a thorough assessment of existing systems and data architectures to identify potential integration challenges early. Map out all systems that will interact with the AI solution and identify compatibility issues.
    - **Standardization**: Adopt standardized data formats and protocols to facilitate smoother integration. Work with IT teams to ensure all systems adhere to these standards.
    - **Incremental integration**: To manage risk and complexity, integrate new AI systems incrementally, starting with less critical systems. For example, integrate the AI solution with a single data source before expanding to multiple sources.
- **Resource allocation**:
    - **Skill assessment**: Regularly assess your team's skills and capabilities to identify gaps and address them through hiring, training, or external partnerships. Use tools such as skill matrices to map out current capabilities and identify areas for development.
    - **Dynamic allocation**: Adopt a dynamic resource allocation strategy to reallocate resources based on project needs and priorities. Implement a flexible staffing model that allows quick adjustments to be made as project requirements change.
    - **Cross-functional teams**: Form cross-functional teams that combine diverse skill sets, enhancing collaboration and problem-solving. For example, a team developing an AI recommendation system might include data scientists, software developers, marketing experts, and UX designers.

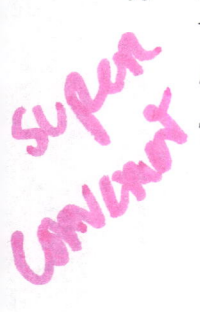

A checklist for identifying and mitigating challenges

To help you identify and mitigate common AI project challenges, here's a handy checklist:

- **Project planning**:
  - Are the project objectives clearly defined and aligned with business goals?
  - Is there a comprehensive risk management plan in place?
  - Have key stakeholders been engaged and their expectations managed?

- **Data management**:
  - Has a thorough data audit been conducted?
  - Are data cleaning and preprocessing strategies in place?
  - Is there a plan for ongoing data quality assurance?

- **Team and resources**:
  - Does the team have the necessary skills and expertise?
  - Are there plans for continuous training and skill development?
  - Is resource allocation flexible and responsive to project needs?

- **Technology integration**:
  - Have potential integration challenges been identified and addressed?
  - Is there a strategy for incremental integration and testing?
  - Are there contingency plans for handling integration issues?

- **Change management**:
  - Is there a comprehensive change management plan in place?
  - Are employees and stakeholders regularly communicated with and involved?
  - Are training and support programs available to ease the transition?

By using these strategies and checklists, you can manage AI projects effectively, turning challenges into opportunities for success. A clear, methodical approach will help lead your AI projects from concept to deployment, ensuring they deliver the impact you envision. Managing AI projects requires strategic planning, agility, and change management. By addressing the unique challenges of AI, you can drive innovation and growth, turning your ideas into impactful realities.

Hypothetical case study – APEX Manufacturing and Distribution

Let's dive into a hypothetical case study to illustrate how our framework for AI project management can be applied successfully. APEX is at a crossroads, seeking to leverage AI to streamline operations and boost competitiveness. This case study will walk you through their journey from initial concept to successful deployment, highlighting the steps taken and the remarkable results achieved.

Initial situation

APEX Manufacturing and Distribution faced several challenges:

- **Inefficient inventory management**: Stock levels were either too high, leading to increased holding costs, or too low, causing production delays.
- **Poor demand forecasting**: Existing forecasting methods were inaccurate, resulting in frequent stockouts and excess inventory.
- **Operational silos**: Different departments operated in silos, hindering effective communication and data sharing.

Recognizing AI's potential, APEX implemented an AI-driven inventory management system to optimize stock levels and improve demand forecasting. However, they were unsure where to start and how to navigate the complexities of such a project.

Step-by-step implementation

The following steps were implemented to transform APEX's operations through AI-driven inventory management and demand forecasting:

1. **Initial concept and feasibility study**:

   - **Identify business objectives**: Imagine you're the Chief AI Officer at APEX. Your first step is to define the business objectives clearly. The goal is to reduce inventory holding costs by 20% and improve demand forecasting accuracy by 30%. This clarity in objectives provides a focused direction for the AI project.
   - **Feasibility assessment**: We conducted a feasibility study, evaluating data availability, technical requirements, and potential ROI. It became clear that APEX had rich historical sales and inventory data, but integrating this data from various departments posed a challenge.
   - **Stakeholder engagement**: We held workshops with key stakeholders, including operations, sales, and IT departments, to align objectives and expectations. Their buy-in was crucial for the project's success. In these workshops, we demonstrated how AI could address their pain points and laid a clear implementation roadmap.

2. **Project planning**:

    - **Define scope and objectives**: We defined a SMART goal: *Reduce inventory holding costs by 20% and improve demand forecasting accuracy by 30% within 12 months by implementing an AI-driven inventory management system.*
    - **Resource allocation**: A cross-functional team, including data scientists, software engineers, and domain experts, was assembled. We also brought in an external AI consultant to provide specialized expertise. This team structure ensured all the necessary skills were available at each project stage.
    - **Risk management**: A risk management plan was developed to identify potential risks, such as data integration issues and resistance to change. Mitigation strategies were put in place. For instance, we planned regular communication updates to keep all stakeholders informed and engaged.

3. **Data collection and preparation**:

    - **Data audit**: We audited APEX's data, discovering that while there was ample data, it was stored in disparate systems. Data consistency and quality varied across departments. We implemented a data governance framework to standardize data collection and storage practices.
    - **Data cleaning**: We cleaned the data using automated tools and manual checks, addressing inconsistencies and gaps. This process was time-consuming but essential for the project's success. We also documented the data cleaning process to ensure transparency and reproducibility.
    - **Data augmentation**: To enhance the dataset, we integrated external market trend data, providing a broader context for demand forecasting. This additional data source helped improve the accuracy and robustness of our models.

4. **Model development**:

    - **Algorithm selection**: We selected algorithms that were suitable for demand forecasting and inventory optimization, including time series analysis and machine learning models. We conducted a series of tests to determine which algorithms performed best with APEX's data.
    - **Model training**: Historical data was used to train the models. This phase involved iterative testing and refinement to optimize performance. For example, we tested different forecasting models, selecting the highest accuracy.
    - **Evaluation and validation**: The models were validated using separate validation datasets to ensure they generalized well to new data. We employed cross-validation techniques to assess model robustness. Regular feedback loops were established with key stakeholders to refine the models continuously.

5. **Deployment**:

   - **Pilot testing**: The AI system was initially deployed in a controlled environment, and its performance was monitored closely. To minimize risk and gather detailed feedback, we started with a single product line. This pilot phase allowed us to identify and address issues before a full-scale rollout.

   - **Scaling**: Once the system proved effective in the pilot phase, it was scaled across the entire organization. We ensured the IT infrastructure could handle increased loads and established monitoring systems to track performance. Detailed documentation and training sessions were provided to ensure smooth scaling.

   - **Monitoring and maintenance**: Continuous monitoring was implemented to track the AI system's performance. Regular updates and retraining ensured the system remained effective as new data became available. We set up a dedicated team to oversee the system's performance and address any emerging issues promptly.

Results achieved

The application of our AI project management framework led to significant improvements in APEX Manufacturing and Distribution:

- **Reduced inventory holding costs**: Inventory holding costs were reduced by 25%, exceeding the initial goal of 20%. This was achieved by optimizing stock levels and reducing excess inventory. The cost savings were reinvested into other business areas, driving further growth.

- **Improved demand forecasting accuracy**: Demand forecasting accuracy improved by 35%, surpassing the target of 30%. This led to fewer stockouts and more efficient production planning. The improved forecasting capabilities enabled APEX to better respond to market demands and reduce lead times.

- **Enhanced operational efficiency**: The AI system fostered better communication and data sharing between departments, breaking down operational silos. This improved overall efficiency and collaboration. Teams could make data-driven decisions, leading to faster problem resolution and innovation.

- **ROI and business impact**: The project delivered a substantial ROI within the first year, with cost savings and increased sales driving financial performance. The success of the AI project positioned APEX as a leader in their industry, attracting new customers and partners.

Relatable anecdotes and motivational insights

Throughout this journey, the team at APEX experienced a blend of excitement and challenges. For instance, during the data cleaning phase, we encountered a significant setback when inconsistencies in the data were found. However, this challenge turned into an opportunity to build a more robust data governance framework, which benefited APEX beyond the scope of the AI project.

One memorable moment was during the pilot testing phase. Initially skeptical of the AI system, the operations manager was amazed to see real-time inventory adjustments based on predictive insights. This moment validated the project's potential and galvanized the entire team, transforming skeptics into advocates.

Another pivotal point was the stakeholder workshops. Initially, there was a lot of resistance and skepticism. However, the atmosphere shifted as we presented the feasibility study and demonstrated the AI system's potential. One of the senior managers, who had been particularly vocal about his doubts, shared a story from his early career about introducing ERP systems and how they had revolutionized their operations despite initial resistance. This personal anecdote helped bridge the gap between skepticism and acceptance, fostering a collaborative spirit.

Reflection and practical next steps

As we conclude this chapter on AI project management, take a moment to reflect on the journey we've explored together. From the initial concept to successful deployment, we've navigated the complexities of managing AI projects, embracing agile methodologies, and overcoming common challenges. Now, it's time to consider how these insights can transform your own AI initiatives.

Think back to a recent AI project you've been involved in or one you're planning. How might the strategies we've discussed have altered its course? Perhaps you're recalling moments of uncertainty in defining project scope, or instances where stakeholder expectations weren't fully aligned. These are common experiences, and recognizing them is the first step toward improvement.

Consider the APEX Manufacturing and Distribution case study. Their journey from siloed operations to an integrated, AI-driven system might mirror challenges in your own organization. What aspects of their approach resonate with you? Maybe it's their commitment to stakeholder engagement or their methodical approach to data preparation. These are strategies you can adapt and apply in your own context.

Now, let's challenge ourselves with some thought-provoking questions:

- How well does your current project management approach accommodate the unique demands of AI development? Are there areas where increased flexibility could lead to better outcomes?
- Think about your last AI project. Were there instances where clearer communication or more frequent stakeholder engagement could have smoothed the path to success?
- Reflecting on your organization's data practices, how prepared are you to undertake a major AI initiative? Are there steps you could take now to improve data quality and accessibility?
- Consider your team's skill set. Do you have the right blend of technical expertise and domain knowledge to drive AI projects forward? If not, how might you address these gaps?

These questions aren't meant to highlight shortcomings but to illuminate opportunities for growth and improvement. Every challenge that's identified is a chance to enhance your AI project management skills.

So, what practical steps can you take to implement these strategies in your work? Here are some actionable ideas to get you started:

1. **Start small**: Choose one aspect of AI project management you'd like to improve. Perhaps it's implementing more rigorous data quality checks or adopting sprint planning for your next project. Focus on this area and track your progress.
2. **Engage your team**: Schedule a workshop to discuss the principles of agile AI development. Use this as an opportunity to align on methodologies and set expectations for future projects.
3. **Conduct a data audit**: Even if you're not planning an AI project right now, assessing your data quality and availability can pay dividends in the future. Start the process of standardizing data collection and storage across your organization.
4. **Build cross-functional relationships**: Reach out to colleagues in different departments. Understanding their perspectives and challenges can help you anticipate and address integration issues in future AI projects.
5. **Invest in continuous learning**: AI is a rapidly evolving field. Set aside time each week to stay updated on the latest trends and best practices in AI project management.

Remember, the goal isn't to overhaul your entire approach overnight. It's about making incremental improvements that compound over time. Each step you take, no matter how small, moves you closer to mastering the art of AI project management.

As you embark on this journey, maintain a spirit of curiosity and resilience. There will be challenges along the way, but each one is an opportunity to learn and grow. Your efforts to improve AI project management won't just benefit individual projects – they have the potential to drive innovation and transformation across your entire organization.

So, take that first step. Whether it's initiating a conversation with stakeholders, revisiting your project planning process, or diving deeper into agile methodologies, your journey to more effective AI project management starts now. Embrace the challenge, learn from each experience, and watch as your AI initiatives flourish under your enhanced management approach.

Summary

In this chapter, we journeyed through the intricacies of AI project management, equipping you with strategies to navigate from concept to deployment. You learned how to apply agile methodologies tailored for AI development and tackle common challenges head-on. Remember, successful AI projects aren't just about advanced algorithms; they're about clear communication, adaptable planning, and continuous improvement. By embracing these principles, you're now better prepared to lead AI initiatives that deliver real value to your organization.

As you reflect on these insights, consider how you might apply them in your next AI project. Whether it's improving stakeholder engagement, refining your data preparation processes, or adopting more flexible planning methods, each step you take enhances your ability to manage AI projects effectively. Now, let's turn our attention to the fascinating world of AI algorithms themselves.

In the next chapter, we'll explore the differences between deterministic, probabilistic, and generative AI, providing you with a deeper understanding of the technologies driving the AI revolution.

Questions

1. What are the criteria for determining whether a project component should be managed as an artifact in AI project management?
2. How does this chapter suggest addressing the challenge of resource allocation in AI projects?
3. What role does data augmentation play in AI project development, according to this chapter?
4. In the context of AI project management, what is the significance of "sprint planning"?
5. What approach does this chapter recommend for pilot testing an AI system?
6. How does this chapter suggest balancing technical expertise and domain knowledge in AI project teams?
7. What strategy is proposed for ensuring continuous improvement of AI models after deployment?
8. How does this chapter address the challenge of integrating AI technology with existing business systems?
9. What's the importance of feasibility assessment in the initial stages of an AI project?
10. According to this chapter, how can organizations manage change effectively when implementing AI projects?

References

1. Full Stack Deep Learning. *Overview*: https://fall2019.fullstackdeeplearning.com/course-content/setting-up-machine-learning-projects/overview.
2. RAHY Consulting. *Embrace Success with Expert Change Management Strategies*: https://rahyconsulting.com/effective-change-management-strategies/.

7
Understanding Deterministic, Probabilistic, and Generative AI

Like with all technological revolutions, I expect there to be significant impact on jobs, but exactly what that impact looks like is very difficult to predict... I believe that there will be far greater jobs on the other side of this and that the jobs of today will get better...

– Sam Altman

Imagine driving down a winding road, the scenic route to a familiar destination. Every turn and every stop sign is predictable because you've taken this path countless times. Now, picture navigating a bustling city for the first time, relying on your GPS to guide you through the maze of streets and unexpected traffic. Suddenly, you're faced with a detour due to construction, and the GPS recalculates your route in real time, considering various possibilities to get you to your destination as efficiently as possible. But what if your GPS could imagine new roads and routes that don't exist yet instead of just recalculating and predicting the best path for future journeys?

Welcome to the fascinating world of deterministic, probabilistic, and generative **artificial intelligence** (**AI**). These three distinct approaches to AI might seem abstract, but they are the backbone of many technologies that shape our daily lives. From the navigation applications we trust to the predictive text on our smartphones and even the art and music generated by AI, these models continue to revolutionize how we interact with the world.

Think about the last time your phone suggested the perfect reply to a text message or when Netflix recommended a movie that was spot on. Or perhaps you've marveled at a piece of artwork created by an AI artist. These experiences are powered by different types of AI, each with strengths and fascinating complexities.

Deterministic AI follows rules to produce a specific outcome, much like a meticulously crafted recipe. Imagine baking a cake: you follow the recipe step by step, and so long as you don't deviate, you end up with the expected result – a delicious cake. Deterministic AI systems operate similarly: given a specific input, they produce a particular output. This predictability is invaluable in environments where consistency and reliability are paramount, such as industrial automation or financial calculations.

But life isn't always as predictable as a recipe. Enter probabilistic AI, which deals with uncertainty and variability. Probabilistic AI makes educated guesses based on patterns and data, akin to a seasoned chef who intuitively knows how to tweak a dish based on taste and experience. This type of AI thrives in environments where outcomes are only sometimes limited to predicting stock market trends or diagnosing diseases based on symptoms and patient history. Probabilistic models such as Bayesian networks and Markov models allow AI to weigh various factors and make informed predictions, even in the face of uncertainty.

And then there's generative AI, the creative powerhouse of the AI landscape. Unlike deterministic and probabilistic AI, which work within the confines of existing data and rules, generative AI creates new data. Imagine a chef who doesn't just follow or tweak recipes but invents entirely new culinary creations. Generative AI models, such as **generative adversarial networks** (GANs) and **variational autoencoders** (VAEs), can produce novel images, music, text, and even human-like conversations. These models don't just predict the next word in a sentence; they can write an entire paragraph that mimics the style of Shakespeare or compose a new piece of music in the style of Beethoven.

Are you intrigued yet? As we delve into this chapter, we'll demystify these concepts, showing you how they work, where they're applied, and why they matter. We'll explore real-world applications and dive into the technical underpinnings, making complex ideas digestible and actionable.

In this chapter, we will cover the following topics:

- **Deterministic AI**: Systems with predictable outcomes that are designed to follow predefined rules and logic for consistent results
- **Probabilistic AI**: Models that use statistical methods to handle uncertainty, offering predictions and insights based on probabilities
- **Generative AI**: Advanced tools capable of creating new content, such as text, images, and music, by learning patterns from existing data

Understanding the distinctions and synergies between deterministic, probabilistic, and generative AI will equip you to harness their collective power, driving innovation and efficiency in your organization.

By the end of this chapter, you'll understand the distinctions between deterministic, probabilistic, and generative AI, along with their key concepts and practical applications. You'll also be equipped to identify the unique strengths of each paradigm and how they can address specific challenges within various contexts.

Additionally, you'll gain the ability to recognize key pain points and challenges associated with these AI approaches, enabling you to determine where each is most effective. This chapter will also provide practical solutions, techniques, and guidance for integrating these models into your business operations, ensuring a smooth transition from theory to application.

To solidify your understanding, we'll go through a hypothetical case study featuring APEX Manufacturing and Distribution. This case study will demonstrate real-world AI applications, showcasing how these technologies can address business challenges and drive meaningful results.

Prepare to embark on an insightful exploration of AI's diverse paradigms. By the end of this chapter, you'll have the knowledge and tools to envision innovative possibilities for an AI-driven future and be able to apply these concepts confidently to address real-world challenges, driving impactful results for your organization.

The problem – pain points and challenges

Understanding and implementing deterministic, probabilistic, and generative AI can be daunting for businesses, regardless of size or industry. Each type of AI comes with its complexities and challenges, making it essential for organizations to grasp their nuances and applications. To highlight their significance, let's explore some pain points and challenges that are enriched with compelling examples and data.

Navigating the deterministic AI landscape

Deterministic AI, with its rule-based approach, seems straightforward at first glance. However, the devil is in the details. One of the primary challenges is the rigidity of deterministic systems. These systems operate within strict parameters, making them less adaptable to changes or unexpected inputs. For instance, a deterministic AI system in manufacturing might control robotic arms precisely, ensuring consistent product quality. But what happens when a sudden change in raw materials or an unexpected machine malfunctions? The system might fail to adapt quickly, leading to production delays and increased costs.

Consider a real-world example from a past project where we integrated AI into supply chain management. The deterministic systems we initially deployed excelled in routine tasks such as scheduling shipments and optimizing routes. However, they struggled with unexpected disruptions, such as supplier delays or sudden demand spikes. This rigidity required us to implement additional layers of AI, combining deterministic models with probabilistic ones to enhance adaptability.

The complexity of probabilistic AI

Probabilistic AI introduces flexibility by making educated guesses based on data patterns, but this complexity comes with challenges. One significant issue is data quality and availability. Probabilistic models rely heavily on large volumes of high-quality data to make accurate predictions. In many industries, obtaining such data is easier said than done.

Take the healthcare sector, for example. Developing a probabilistic AI model to predict patient outcomes or diagnose diseases requires having access to comprehensive, clean, and representative patient data. Yet, healthcare data is often fragmented, inconsistent, and plagued by privacy concerns. While consulting with a primary healthcare provider, we encountered significant hurdles in aggregating and anonymizing patient data to build reliable predictive models. Ensuring data integrity and addressing ethical concerns were time-consuming but crucial steps.

Moreover, probabilistic AI models can be challenging to interpret. Unlike deterministic systems, which provide clear, rule-based outputs, probabilistic models generate results with varying degrees of confidence. Explaining these probabilistic outcomes to stakeholders, especially those without a technical background, can be challenging. Businesses must invest in tools and training to help their teams understand and trust these models [1].

Imagine a hospital where doctors use probabilistic AI to predict patient outcomes. The AI suggests that a patient might develop a specific condition, but it doesn't guarantee this. This probabilistic nature can be challenging for medical professionals and patients to grasp. Doctors need to explain that a 70% chance of developing a condition doesn't mean it's inevitable, nor does a 30% chance mean it's unlikely. Communicating these nuances effectively is crucial for gaining trust and ensuring proper use of the technology.

Unleashing the potential of generative AI

Generative AI, while immensely powerful and creative, poses some of the most significant challenges. One of its primary issues is the sheer computational power required to train generative models. These models, especially those based on deep learning architectures such as GANs, demand substantial processing capabilities and extensive training data. This requirement can be a barrier for smaller businesses or those lacking cutting-edge computational resources.

Another challenge lies in controlling and guiding the output of generative models. While these models can produce novel and innovative results, they can also generate inappropriate, biased, or useless content. Being generative by design, they can produce varying outputs, even when given the same inputs. For example, in my work with a leading telecom company, we explored using generative AI to develop customer service chatbots. While the AI could generate human-like responses, it occasionally produced off-brand or confusing answers, necessitating extensive fine-tuning and oversight.

Consider the realm of creative industries, such as fashion or music. Generative AI can create stunning new designs or compose beautiful melodies. However, the outputs need careful curation. A generative model might produce hundreds of designs, but not everything will be practical or in line with brand aesthetics. The challenge is to sift through these creations and select those that offer real value. Additionally, there's the risk of generating content that inadvertently replicates existing works, raising ethical and legal concerns.

Integrating AI into existing business processes

Beyond the specific challenges of each AI type, businesses often need help integrating AI into their existing processes. Many organizations have legacy systems and entrenched workflows that haven't been designed to accommodate transformative or disruptive technologies. The integration process can be disruptive and costly, requiring significant changes to be made to infrastructure and operations.

Additionally, there's a cultural and educational gap. Many business leaders and employees need a deeper understanding of AI, leading to resistance and fear of job displacement. Bridging this gap requires comprehensive training programs and a clear communication strategy to illustrate the benefits of AI and how it can augment human capabilities rather than replace them.

Imagine a traditional manufacturing company attempting to integrate AI into its operations. The existing workforce may be skeptical, fearing that machines will replace their jobs. To address this, the company needs to implement training programs that show employees how AI can enhance their roles, making their work more accessible and more efficient. By involving employees in the transition process and demonstrating the practical benefits of AI, businesses can foster a culture of innovation and acceptance.

Personal anecdote – the AI learning curve

Reflecting on an early AI project where I was tasked with developing AI roadmaps for critical business functions, I vividly remember the initial skepticism and confusion among the team. The concept of probabilistic AI, in particular, was foreign and intimidating. We conducted numerous workshops and hands-on training sessions to demystify the technology. Gradually, as the team saw the tangible benefits – such as significantly reduced incidents and improved outcomes – their apprehension turned into enthusiasm.

I recall a specific instance where our probabilistic AI model predicted a significant market shift. Initially met with doubt, the team decided to act on the prediction, adjusting our strategy accordingly. The result was a substantial gain in market share, which turned skeptics into believers. This experience underscored the importance of education and practical demonstration in overcoming resistance to AI adoption.

Overcoming challenges

Understanding and implementing deterministic, probabilistic, and generative AI is undoubtedly challenging. However, these challenges are manageable. Businesses can unlock AI's transformative potential by recognizing specific pain points, investing in data quality, computational resources, and training, and fostering a culture of innovation and adaptability [2]. In the following section, we'll delve deeper into each type of AI, offering practical insights and strategies to help you navigate these challenges and harness the power of AI to drive your organization forward.

The solution and implementation

Successfully leveraging AI technologies – deterministic, probabilistic, or generative – requires a structured approach, careful planning, and the right tools. This section will explore the key insights, practical uses, and detailed steps for implementing these AI paradigms to help you unlock their full potential within your organization.

Deterministic AI

Let's begin our exploration of AI types by examining deterministic AI, a foundational approach that excels in scenarios requiring precise, rule-based decision-making.

Key insights

Deterministic AI is the foundation for systems that require precise, rule-based decisions. It operates on fixed algorithms where the input directly determines the output, making deterministic AI a reliable solution for tasks with consistent and predictable outcomes [3]. The value of deterministic AI lies in its ability to handle repetitive tasks that don't require complex decision-making or adaptability, providing stability and efficiency.

Uses

Deterministic AI is best suited for industries and processes that demand high accuracy and reliability:

- **Manufacturing**: Automating assembly lines, quality control, and defect detection
- **Healthcare**: Automating patient record management, diagnostic coding, and routine medical tests
- **Finance**: Managing compliance checks, fraud detection based on fixed rules, and automating transaction verifications

For example, an automotive manufacturer might implement deterministic AI to detect defects on the production line automatically. The AI system can inspect each car part for imperfections by applying rule-based image recognition algorithms, significantly reducing manual inspection time and errors.

Implementation

The implementation steps are as follows:

1. **Identify routine tasks**: Begin by identifying repetitive tasks within your organization that follow specific rules. These could include quality control checks, inventory management, or compliance monitoring. For instance, deterministic AI can be applied in a retail warehouse to automate inventory restocking when levels fall below a predetermined threshold.

2. **Develop rule-based algorithms**: Collaborate with AI engineers to develop the necessary algorithms. These algorithms should define the rules and parameters for the tasks. Tools such as Python, MATLAB, and domain-specific software can be used to build deterministic models. For instance, Python's OpenCV library could be used to create a vision-based inspection system in a factory that automatically detects defects on a production line.

3. **Test and validate**: Once the system has been built, test it alongside human operators to ensure accuracy. This phase helps fine-tune the system and guarantees that it meets performance expectations. For example, a retailer could deploy an AI system to track product availability while continuing to use manual checks to verify its reliability.

4. **Deploy and monitor**: After testing, deploy the system in a real-world setting. Use dashboards to monitor performance, and set up alerts for anomalies. This ensures quick intervention if issues arise. In a financial institution, for example, deterministic AI could be used to monitor transactions and flag any deviations from predefined norms in real time.

Actionable tips

Here are a few tips:

- **Start small**: Automate a single task and scale up as the system proves reliable. This reduces risk and allows incremental adjustments to be made.

- **Engage stakeholders**: Ensure buy-in from key decision-makers early on. Showcasing early successes can build trust in the system.

- **Document everything**: Having clear documentation of the rules and parameters aids troubleshooting and facilitates scaling to other processes.

Probabilistic AI

Now, let's focus on probabilistic AI, a more flexible approach that thrives in environments characterized by uncertainty and complex decision-making scenarios.

Key insights

Unlike deterministic AI, probabilistic AI embraces uncertainty. It relies on statistical models to make decisions based on historical data, allowing it to handle variability and ambiguity. This makes it a powerful tool for environments where outcomes are unpredictable, and decisions must be made with varying degrees of confidence. Probabilistic AI's strength lies in its ability to manage complex scenarios, such as predicting trends, identifying patterns, and optimizing processes with incomplete or imperfect data.

Uses

Probabilistic AI is widely used across industries where predictions and data-driven decision-making are crucial:

- **Healthcare**: Diagnosing diseases based on patient histories and medical imaging.
- **Finance**: Predicting stock market movements, credit scoring, and risk management.
- **Manufacturing**: Predictive machinery maintenance and optimizing production schedules based on historical data trends.

For example, in the healthcare industry, probabilistic AI can analyze patient data to predict the likelihood of developing certain conditions based on lifestyle, genetics, and environmental factors [4]. By providing healthcare professionals with confidence intervals for various situations, probabilistic AI enables more personalized and proactive patient care.

Implementation

Here are the steps:

1. **Gather and clean data**: Data quality is the foundation of probabilistic AI. Start by gathering data from your business operations, ensuring it's clean and consistent. For example, data might include patient records, diagnostic results, and treatment histories in a healthcare setting. Clean the data to eliminate inconsistencies, duplicates, or outliers, ensuring the system can make accurate predictions.

2. **Select appropriate models**: Choose statistical models that suit your data and prediction needs. Bayesian networks, regression models, or Markov models are common choices, depending on the complexity and type of predictions you want. Tools such as Python's scikit-learn, R, and TensorFlow are excellent platforms for building these models.

3. **Train and validate models**: Train your models on historical data and validate their performance using techniques such as cross-validation. For example, a predictive maintenance model can be trained on historical equipment failure data and validated on separate data to ensure accuracy.

4. **Implement decision support systems**: Integrate the trained models into decision-making processes, providing predictions with confidence intervals. Develop dashboards that present these insights in a user-friendly way. For instance, a financial institution might integrate probabilistic AI into its investment decision-making process, offering portfolio managers clear risk assessments.

Actionable tips

Let's review the tips:

- **Prioritize data quality**: Regular audits of your data pipeline will ensure that your models remain accurate over time

- **Explain results clearly**: Ensure that predictions and confidence intervals are communicated, especially to non-technical stakeholders
- **Continuous improvement**: Retrain models to maintain accuracy and relevance as new data becomes available

Generative AI

Next, let's explore generative AI, the cutting-edge frontier of AI that pushes the boundaries of creativity and innovation in ways previously unimaginable.

Key insights

Generative AI is the frontier of creativity and innovation. Using deep learning architectures such as GANs and VAEs, these models can generate new content – images, text, music, or even designs – based on patterns in the data they've been trained on. While generative AI requires large datasets and substantial computational power for training, the potential for innovation and personalization is unparalleled.

Uses

Generative AI is transforming industries that rely on creativity and content generation:

- **Design and fashion**: Creating new product designs, generating clothing patterns, or developing custom art
- **Marketing**: Crafting personalized advertisements, writing copy, or generating video content
- **Healthcare**: Developing new drug compounds or simulating biological processes for research

For instance, a fashion brand might use generative AI to develop new clothing designs based on past collections. The system can generate innovative designs that maintain the brand's aesthetic while introducing new creative elements by feeding AI data on fabrics, patterns, and color trends.

Implementation

The steps are as follows:

1. **Define use cases**: Identify areas where generative AI can provide value. This could be anything from generating product designs to simulating new marketing campaigns. Having clear use cases helps set expectations and measure success. For example, AI-generated scripts or character designs could spark new creative directions in the entertainment industry.
2. **Collect and prepare data**: Gather large datasets relevant to your use case. Preprocess this data to ensure it's clean, diverse, and rich in the features necessary for training. For example, a movie studio might gather a library of past film scripts, character designs, and storylines as input data for a generative AI system.

3. **Choose and train models**: Select the appropriate generative models (GANs or VAEs) and train them using platforms such as TensorFlow, PyTorch, and Keras. The training process is computationally intensive and may require specialized hardware such as GPUs.

4. **Evaluate and refine outputs**: After training, evaluate the AI-generated outputs, whether that's new designs, content, or solutions. Use objective and subjective measures, such as novelty, diversity, and expert reviews. For instance, designers might assess AI-generated patterns in a fashion design context to refine them further.

5. **Integrate and iterate**: Integrate generative AI into your creative workflows. Continuously retrain models as new data is collected and feedback is gathered. In a creative agency, for example, teams might use AI-generated advertisements as inspiration, iterating on them to create polished, final products.

Actionable tips

Let's review the tips:

- **Invest in computational resources**: Generative AI is resource-intensive, so ensure you have access to cloud-based platforms or GPUs to handle large-scale training.

- **Foster collaboration**: Bring together AI specialists and creative professionals to maximize the potential of generative models. Cross-disciplinary teams can unlock innovative outcomes by merging human creativity with AI's capabilities.

- **Monitor ethical considerations**: Be mindful of issues such as copyright infringement and algorithmic bias. Implement clear guidelines to ensure responsible and ethical use of AI-generated content.

Implementing deterministic, probabilistic, and generative AI solutions can drive innovation, improve decision-making, and streamline processes across industries. By following the structured steps outlined in this section and focusing on data quality, clear communication, and continuous improvement, organizations can successfully harness the power of AI to transform their operations and unlock new possibilities for growth and innovation.

Hypothetical case study – APEX Manufacturing and Distribution

APEX Manufacturing and Distribution, our hypothetical mid-sized company specializing in producing and distributing industrial equipment, faced multiple challenges. Their operations relied heavily on manual processes, leading to inefficiencies, high operational costs, and production and inventory management errors. The company's leadership recognized the need for technological innovation to stay competitive but needed help figuring out where to start.

Step 1 – identifying pain points and setting objectives

Our first task was to assess APEX's operations to identify specific pain points thoroughly. We discovered several critical areas for improvement:

- **Quality control**: Manual inspection processes were time-consuming and prone to errors
- **Inventory management**: Inaccurate inventory tracking led to overstocking or stockouts, causing production delays and increased costs
- **Predictive maintenance**: Equipment failures were frequent and unpredictable, leading to costly downtime
- **Design innovation**: The design team needed help to meet market demand for innovative and customized products

Step 2 – implementing deterministic AI for quality control

Objective: Automate the quality control process to improve accuracy and efficiency.

Approach:

- We identified quality control as a repetitive task ideally suited for deterministic AI
- Using Python and OpenCV, we developed a vision-based inspection system that could automatically detect product defects

Steps:

1. **Data collection**: We collected thousands of images of products and annotated them with information about defects. This step involved setting up a system to capture high-resolution images of each product as it moved along the assembly line.
2. **Algorithm development**: We developed rule-based algorithms to identify typical defects such as scratches, dents, and misalignments. The algorithms were trained to recognize subtle variations that indicated defects.
3. **Testing and validation**: To validate accuracy, we ran the AI system in parallel with human inspectors. During this phase, we refined the algorithms iteratively based on discrepancies observed between human and AI inspections.
4. **Deployment**: The AI system was fully deployed on the production line and was integrated with existing equipment. The system was configured to automatically flag defective products for further inspection or rework.

Results:

- **Increased accuracy**: Defect detection accuracy improved by 40%, significantly reducing the number of defective products reaching customers
- **Efficiency gains**: Inspection times were reduced by 50%, allowing for higher production throughput and quicker turnaround times
- **Cost savings**: Labor costs associated with manual inspections were reduced and the cost of returns and rework was minimized due to undetected defects

Step 3 – implementing probabilistic AI for inventory management

Objective: Improve inventory accuracy and optimize stock levels.

Approach: We leveraged probabilistic AI to forecast inventory needs based on historical sales data and real-time demand signals.

Steps:

1. **Data gathering**: We gathered aggregated historical sales data, supplier delivery times, and real-time order information. This involved integrating data from various sources, including ERP systems, supplier databases, and sales platforms.
2. **Model selection**: We chose a Bayesian network to model the relationships between different inventory factors. The network was designed to handle the complexity of interactions and dependencies within the supply chain.
3. **Training and validation**: We trained the model on historical data and validated its performance using cross-validation techniques. This step ensured that the model could accurately predict inventory needs under different scenarios.
4. **Integration**: We integrated the model with APEX's ERP system to automate reorder decisions and stock level adjustments. The system was set up to automatically generate purchase orders when stock levels dropped below a certain threshold.

Results:

- **Improved forecasting**: Inventory forecasting accuracy improved by 35%, leading to better alignment between inventory levels and actual demand.
- **Reduced overstocking**: A 20% reduction in overstocking was achieved, freeing up valuable warehouse space and reducing holding costs.
- **Operational efficiency**: Reorder processes were streamlined, reducing stockouts and ensuring smooth production flows. This improved customer satisfaction by minimizing delays in order fulfillment.

Step 4 – implementing probabilistic AI for predictive maintenance

Objective: Predict equipment failures to minimize downtime and maintenance costs.

Approach: We utilized probabilistic models to predict when equipment was likely to fail based on historical maintenance records and real-time sensor data.

Steps:

1. **Sensor installation**: We equipped machinery with IoT sensors to collect real-time operational data. These sensors monitored critical parameters such as vibration, temperature, and pressure.
2. **Data aggregation**: We collected and cleaned historical maintenance data and sensor readings. This involved standardizing data formats and dealing with any missing or inconsistent data.
3. **Model development**: We developed a predictive maintenance model using a Markov chain to estimate equipment failure probability. The model considered both historical trends and real-time data to provide accurate predictions.
4. **Implementation**: We integrated the model with the company's maintenance management system to trigger alerts for preventive maintenance. Maintenance schedules were adjusted dynamically based on the model's predictions.

Results:

- **Reduced downtime**: Equipment downtime was reduced by 30% due to timely maintenance, significantly improving production continuity.
- **Cost savings**: Maintenance costs decreased by 25% as issues were addressed before causing significant failures. This proactive approach also extended the lifespan of critical machinery.
- **Increased equipment lifespan**: Proactive maintenance extended the lifespan of critical machinery, reducing the frequency of costly equipment replacements.

Step 5 – implementing generative AI for design innovation

Objective: Enhance the design team's ability to create innovative and customized products.

Approach: We leveraged generative AI to assist in product design, allowing the team to generate new concepts rapidly.

Steps:

1. **Define use cases**: We identified areas where generative AI could add value, such as creating new product designs and customizing existing ones. This involved understanding market trends and customer preferences.

2. **Collect and prepare data**: We gathered a large dataset of existing product designs, customer feedback, and market trends. Data was annotated to highlight successful design elements and areas needing improvement.
3. **Choose and train models**: We selected GANd to generate new design concepts. They were trained on the collected dataset to learn patterns and design aesthetics.
4. **Evaluate and refine outputs**: Once the models were trained, the generated outputs were evaluated through design reviews and customer feedback. The AI-generated designs were assessed for practicality, aesthetics, and market appeal.
5. **Integrate and iterate**: The generative models were integrated into the design team's workflow, allowing designers to input constraints and receive AI-generated suggestions. Feedback from designers and customers was used to continuously refine the models.

Results:

- **Enhanced creativity**: The design team's productivity increased by 40%, with the AI providing innovative concepts that sparked new ideas. The AI-generated designs served as a valuable source of inspiration, leading to unique and marketable products.
- **Market responsiveness**: New designs could be prototyped and generated quickly based on market feedback and trends, allowing APEX to stay ahead of its competitors.
- **Customization**: We enabled the creation of highly customized products that could meet specific customer demands more effectively. This customization capability helped APEX tap into new market segments and increase customer satisfaction.

The transformative results at APEX Manufacturing and Distribution

APEX Manufacturing and Distribution achieved significant improvements across its operations by strategically implementing deterministic, probabilistic, and generative AI. By addressing specific pain points with targeted AI solutions, the company was able to streamline processes, enhance product quality, and drive innovation.

Here are some key takeaways to consider:

- **Quality control**: Automated inspection processes increased accuracy and efficiency, reducing defects and labor costs
- **Inventory management**: Improved forecasting and inventory optimization minimized overstocking and stockouts, enhancing operational efficiency

- **Predictive maintenance**: Proactive maintenance reduced downtime and costs, extending equipment lifespan and ensuring continuous production
- **Design innovation**: Generative AI empowered the design team to create innovative and customized products, improving market responsiveness and customer satisfaction

The successful application of these AI frameworks improved efficiency, reduced costs, and positioned APEX as a forward-thinking leader in their industry. This case study demonstrates how a comprehensive and methodical approach to AI implementation can transform traditional business operations, leading to sustainable growth and competitive advantage.

By following a similar process and leveraging the insights shared in this chapter, your organization can also unlock AI's full potential, driving innovation and achieving exceptional results. The journey to integrating AI may be complex, but the rewards are substantial when the right strategies and tools are implemented.

Reflection and practical next steps

As we conclude this enlightening journey through the realms of deterministic, probabilistic, and generative AI, it's time to pause and reflect on how these powerful tools can reshape our approach to problem-solving and innovation. Think back to the APEX Manufacturing and Distribution case study – how many of their challenges resonate with your own experiences? Perhaps you've faced similar hurdles in quality control, inventory management, or product design. Or maybe you've witnessed the transformative potential of AI in your industry but weren't sure where to begin.

Take a moment to consider your professional landscape. Where do you see the most pressing need for improvement? Is it in streamlining repetitive tasks, making more accurate predictions, or pushing the boundaries of creativity? The beauty of AI lies in its versatility – whether you're dealing with structured, rule-based processes or grappling with uncertainty and variability, there's likely an AI approach that can help.

Remember, the journey of AI integration isn't about replacing human expertise but augmenting it. Think about how deterministic AI could free up your team's time from mundane tasks, allowing them to focus on more strategic initiatives. Envision how probabilistic AI might provide you with deeper insights into customer behavior or market trends, empowering you to make more informed decisions [5]. And imagine the creative possibilities that generative AI could unlock, helping you innovate in ways you never thought possible.

Now, let's challenge ourselves with some thought-provoking questions:

- What are the top three repetitive tasks in your organization that could benefit from automation through deterministic AI?
- In what areas of your business do you currently make decisions based on gut feeling rather than data-driven insights? How might probabilistic AI change this?

- Where in your work do you feel constrained by a lack of creative ideas or innovative solutions? How could generative AI spark new possibilities?
- What are the potential barriers to AI adoption in your organization, and how can you address them proactively?
- How can you foster a culture of continuous learning and adaptation to make the most of AI technologies?

These questions are designed to help you identify concrete, actionable steps toward integrating AI into your work. But remember, you don't have to tackle everything at once. Start small, just as APEX did with their quality control process. Choose a single pain point where AI could make a significant impact, and focus on that as your initial project.

Here are some practical next steps to consider:

1. **Conduct an AI readiness assessment**: Evaluate your current processes, data infrastructure, and team capabilities. This will help you identify the most promising areas for AI integration.
2. **Invest in data quality**: Remember, the success of AI (especially probabilistic and generative models) hinges on good data. Start cleaning and organizing your data now, even if you're not ready to implement AI immediately.
3. **Educate your team**: Organize workshops or training sessions to demystify AI concepts. This will help build enthusiasm and reduce resistance to change.
4. **Start a pilot project**: Choose a small-scale problem to tackle with AI. This could be something such as automating a simple quality check process or using a basic predictive model for inventory management.
5. **Collaborate and learn**: Reach out to peers in your industry who have successfully implemented AI. Their experiences can provide valuable insights and help you avoid common pitfalls.
6. **Stay informed**: The field of AI is rapidly evolving. Make it a habit to stay updated on the latest developments and best practices in AI implementation.

Remember, the goal isn't to become an AI expert overnight but to think critically about how these technologies can enhance your work. No matter how small, every step you take is progress toward a more efficient, innovative, and competitive future.

As you embark on this exciting journey, remember the words of Arthur C. Clarke: "*Any sufficiently advanced technology is indistinguishable from magic.*" AI might seem like magic at first, but with patience, perseverance, and a willingness to learn, you'll soon discover it's a powerful tool waiting to be harnessed. So, take that first step today – your future self will thank you for it.

Summary

In this chapter, we embarked on an enlightening journey through the realms of deterministic, probabilistic, and generative AI. You gained insights into how these powerful tools can revolutionize decision-making, prediction, and creativity across various industries. From the precision of rule-based systems to the adaptability of probabilistic models and the innovative potential of generative AI, you now have a robust framework for understanding and applying these technologies. Remember, the key to success lies not just in understanding these concepts, but in thoughtfully integrating them into your unique context, as we saw with APEX Manufacturing and Distribution.

As you reflect on what you've learned, consider how these AI approaches might transform your work or industry. What challenges could you tackle with deterministic AI? How might probabilistic models enhance your decision-making? And where could generative AI spark innovation in your field? Keep these questions in mind as we transition to our next chapter, where we'll explore the fascinating world of AI agents and agentic systems. Get ready to discover how these intelligent entities can perceive, decide, and act autonomously, taking our AI journey to an even more exciting level.

Questions

1. What are the three main types of AI that were discussed in this chapter?
2. How does deterministic AI differ from probabilistic AI in terms of decision-making?
3. In what types of scenarios or industries might deterministic AI be most effectively applied?
4. What's a key challenge in implementing probabilistic AI, and how can it be addressed?
5. How can generative AI contribute to creative processes and innovation?
6. Why is data quality particularly important for probabilistic and generative AI models?
7. Name two practical next steps that were suggested in the chapter for organizations looking to integrate AI into their operations.

References

1. KPMG Singapore. *Why prioritising talent growth is key to unlocking business value.* Available at `https://kpmg.com/sg/en/home/insights/2024/02/prioritising-talent-growth-key-to-unlocking-business-value.html`
2. Deerwood Technologies. *Remote Work Risks: How Companies Can Support Employee Cybersecurity on Vacation.* Available at `https://deertech.com/remote-work-risks/`
3. Free Article Land. *What Is Predictive Analytics In Demand Forecasting Logistics?* Available at `https://freearticleland.com/what-is-predictive-analytics-in-demand-forecasting-logistics/`

4. Digitally Talks. *Applications of Machine Learning: A Comprehensive Guide.* Available at `https://digitallytalks.com/applications-of-machine-learning-a-comprehensive-guide/`

5. Sumo Analytics. *AI Maturity in Business: Key Strategies for Transformative Success.* Available at `https://www.sumoanalytics.ai/post/the-journey-to-ai-maturity-navigating-the-path-to-transformative-business-success`

8
AI Agents and Agentic Systems

> *AI agents will become the primary way we interact with computers in the future. They will be able to understand our needs and preferences, and proactively help us with tasks and decision making.*
>
> – Satya Nadella, CEO of Microsoft

Have you ever wondered whether the digital assistant on your phone could evolve into something more profound, such as a trusted business partner making strategic decisions on your behalf? Imagine a world where AI agents don't just respond to your commands but anticipate your needs, solve complex problems, and drive innovation in your organization. What if these agents could learn and adapt in real time, becoming indispensable allies in your quest for competitive advantage?

Welcome to the realm of **AI agents and agentic systems**, where the line between human intelligence and artificial acumen blurs, and the possibilities for business transformation are endless. In this chapter, we'll explore how these advanced systems reshape industries and redefine the essence of work. Picture a scenario where your AI agents handle everything from customer inquiries to intricate data analysis, freeing you and your team to focus on strategic initiatives and creative pursuits.

However, let's take a step back. What exactly are AI agents, and why should you care about them? An AI agent is much like a highly skilled employee, capable of performing tasks autonomously, learning from experiences, and collaborating with humans to achieve common goals. These systems are designed to understand context, make informed decisions, and execute actions that drive business outcomes.

As we explore this chapter further, we will uncover the underlying technologies that power AI agents, discuss practical applications across various industries, and provide actionable advice on implementing these systems within your organization. This chapter will help you understand how AI agents work and how to leverage their potential to drive innovation and growth in your organization.

We will cover the following topics:

- What are AI agents?
- The problems addressed and solutions offered by AI agents and agentic systems
- Designing and implementing AI agentic systems

By the end of this chapter, you will have a comprehensive understanding of the fundamental concepts behind AI agents and agentic systems. You'll be able to recognize their potential applications across a wide range of industries, appreciating how these technologies can drive innovation and transform business processes.

You will also gain insight into the key steps required to design and implement AI agents and agentic systems within a business context. This includes understanding their practical use cases and how to tailor these systems to effectively meet specific organizational needs.

Moreover, you'll be equipped to identify both the challenges and opportunities associated with adopting AI agents, enabling you to make informed decisions about how best to leverage this technology in your organization.

Now, let's embark on this journey together and explore the transformative potential of AI agents and agentic systems. Prepare to unlock new efficiency, creativity, and strategic advantage levels for your business.

What are AI agents?

An AI agent is an autonomous software entity capable of perceiving its environment through sensors, processing this information, and taking actions based on its perceptions to achieve its objectives. These agents are designed to mimic human decision-making processes but with the ability to process vast amounts of data and execute actions at speeds far beyond human capabilities.

The key characteristics of AI agents are as follows:

- **Autonomy**: AI agents operate without direct human intervention. They can make decisions and execute actions independently based on their programmed goals and the information they perceive from their environment.

- **Reactivity**: These agents are capable of perceiving changes in their environment and responding in real time. This allows them to handle dynamic situations effectively.

- **Proactivity**: AI agents can take the initiative and perform actions to achieve their goals rather than merely reacting to changes.

- **Social ability**: They can communicate and collaborate with other agents and humans, facilitating coordinated efforts in complex systems.

The core capabilities of AI agents include the following:

- **Reflection**: Reflection involves AI agents evaluating their past actions and outcomes to improve future performance. This capability is critical for continuous learning and adaptation, allowing agents to refine their strategies and decision-making processes based on feedback and experience.

- **Planning**: Planning enables AI agents to create strategies for achieving their goals. This involves considering potential actions, predicting outcomes, and selecting the best course of action. Effective planning is essential for handling complex tasks requiring foresight and extended coordination.

- **Multi-agent coordination**: Multi-agent coordination allows multiple AI agents to work together toward common objectives. This capability is crucial for tasks that are too complex for a single agent to handle alone. By coordinating their actions, agents can achieve synergies, optimize resource use, and solve problems more efficiently.

- **Tool usage**: Tool usage refers to the ability of AI agents to utilize external tools and resources to accomplish their tasks. This includes leveraging software applications, databases, and physical devices to enhance their capabilities and effectiveness.

Understanding agentic systems

Agentic systems incorporate multiple AI agents working together to achieve overarching objectives. These systems leverage the collective capabilities of individual agents to tackle more sophisticated tasks and operate in highly dynamic environments. By distributing tasks among various agents, agentic systems can enhance efficiency, scalability, and robustness.

There are different types of AI agents:

- **Reactive agents**: These agents operate based on predefined rules and respond to environmental changes without internal state representation. They are suitable for straightforward tasks where responses are directly mapped from inputs.

- **Deliberative agents**: These agents maintain an internal model of their environment and use it to plan their actions. They can conduct more complex decision-making processes, considering future states and potential outcomes.

- **Hybrid agents**: Combining elements of both reactive and deliberative agents, hybrid agents can react quickly to immediate changes while also planning for long-term goals.

Evolution of AI agents

The concept of AI agents has evolved significantly over the past few decades. Early AI systems were rule-based and required extensive human programming to handle specific tasks. These systems needed to be improved in their adaptability and struggled with dynamic environments. The advent of **machine learning (ML)** and advancements in computational power paved the way for more sophisticated AI agents capable of learning from data and improving their performance over time.

The role of machine learning

Machine learning plays a crucial role in developing AI agents. By training on large datasets, AI agents can learn patterns and relationships within the data, enabling them to make informed decisions [1]. Techniques such as reinforcement learning further enhance the capabilities of AI agents by allowing them to learn from their actions and optimize their behavior through trial and error [2].

Integration with IoT

Integrating AI agents with the **internet of things** (**IoT**) has opened up new possibilities for real-time data processing and decision-making. IoT devices with sensors generate vast amounts of data that AI agents can analyze to make real-time decisions. This synergy between AI and IoT is particularly beneficial in smart cities, industrial automation, and environmental monitoring applications.

There are several benefits of AI agents and agentic systems:

- **Enhanced efficiency**: AI agents can automate routine tasks, freeing up human resources for more strategic activities. This leads to increased operational efficiency and productivity.
- **Scalability**: Agentic systems can scale to handle complex tasks and large datasets, making them suitable for applications that require high computational power.
- **Adaptability**: AI agents can adapt to changing environments and learn from new data, allowing them to remain effective in dynamic and unpredictable scenarios.
- **Robustness**: Agentic systems' distributed nature enhances their robustness. If one agent fails, others can take over its tasks, ensuring the continuity of operations.

Potential applications

The potential applications of AI agents and agentic systems are vast and span various industries. From healthcare and finance to logistics and customer service, AI agents have the potential to revolutionize the way businesses operate. In the following section, let's explore some real-world applications and delve into the design and implementation of AI agentic systems.

Real-world applications of AI agents

Although AI agents and agentic systems are still emerging, several real-world applications, as listed next, showcase their transformative potential. By examining these applications, we can gain insights into how AI agents can be leveraged to solve complex challenges and drive innovation:

- **Healthcare**: AI agents hold immense promise in the healthcare sector. They can enhance patient care, optimize resource allocation, and improve diagnostic accuracy.

- **Patient monitoring and care:** AI agents can be deployed to continuously monitor patients' vital signs and health metrics, providing real-time alerts to healthcare providers in case of anomalies. These agents can analyze data from wearable devices and medical sensors to detect early signs of deterioration and recommend timely interventions.

  For example, an AI agent could monitor a patient's heart rate, blood pressure, and oxygen levels, alerting doctors to potential issues before they become critical [3]. This proactive approach can greatly improve patient health and ease the workload for healthcare providers.

- **Diagnostic assistance**: AI agents can assist doctors in diagnosing diseases by analyzing medical images, lab results, and patient records. By leveraging ML algorithms, these agents can identify patterns and anomalies that may indicate specific conditions.

  For instance, an AI agent trained on a large dataset of medical images can accurately detect early signs of cancer in radiology scans. This can aid radiologists in making more accurate diagnoses and developing effective treatment plans.

- **Finance**: In finance, AI agents can enhance decision-making processes, improve risk management, and optimize trading strategies.

- **Algorithmic trading**: AI agents can analyze vast amounts of financial data in real time to identify trading opportunities and execute trades at optimal times. These agents use sophisticated algorithms to predict market trends, assess risks, and make informed decisions.

  For example, an AI agent could monitor global news, economic indicators, and historical market data to identify patterns and predict stock price movements. The agent can maximize returns by executing trades based on these predictions while minimizing risks.

- **Fraud detection**: AI agents can help financial institutions detect and prevent fraudulent activities by analyzing transaction data and identifying suspicious patterns. These agents can continuously monitor transactions for signs of fraud, such as unusual spending patterns or multiple transactions from different locations.

  An AI agent trained on historical fraud data can quickly flag potentially fraudulent transactions, allowing financial institutions to take immediate action and prevent economic losses.

- **Logistics and supply chain management**: AI agents can optimize logistics and supply chain operations by improving efficiency, reducing costs, and enhancing decision-making.

- **Inventory management**: AI agents can monitor inventory levels in real time, predict demand, and automate restocking processes. These agents can forecast demand fluctuations and ensure optimal inventory levels by analyzing historical sales data and market trends.

  For example, an AI agent could predict a surge in demand for a particular product during a holiday season and automatically place orders to restock inventory. This proactive approach can prevent stockouts and ensure that products are available when customers need them.

- **Route optimization**: AI agents can optimize delivery routes for logistics companies, reducing fuel consumption, delivery times, and operational costs. By analyzing traffic patterns, weather conditions, and delivery schedules, these agents can determine the most efficient routes for delivery vehicles.

    An AI agent could analyze real-time traffic data and adjust delivery routes to avoid congestion, ensuring timely deliveries and improving customer satisfaction.

- **Customer service**: AI agents can enhance customer service experiences by providing timely and accurate responses to inquiries, resolving issues, and personalizing interactions.

- **Chatbots and virtual assistants**: AI agents can power chatbots and virtual assistants that handle customer inquiries, provide information, and assist with transactions. These agents can understand natural language, respond to questions, and perform actions based on user inputs.

    For example, a virtual assistant powered by AI agents could help customers book flights, track orders, and resolve technical issues. By providing instant and accurate responses, the agent can improve customer satisfaction and reduce the workload on human agents.

- **Sentiment analysis**: AI agents can analyze customer interactions, such as emails, social media posts, and chat logs, to gauge customer sentiment and identify potential issues. By understanding customer emotions, these agents can help businesses address concerns proactively and improve customer relationships.

    An AI agent could analyze social media posts to detect negative sentiment about a product and alert the customer service team to take appropriate action. This proactive approach can prevent negative experiences from escalating and enhance brand reputation.

The problem – pain points and challenges

As we explore AI agents and agentic systems, it's essential to understand the specific problems and challenges businesses face in adopting these groundbreaking technologies. While the potential benefits are enormous, several pain points must be addressed to realize their full potential.

Complexity and integration

One of the most significant challenges businesses encounter is the complexity of implementing AI agents and agentic systems. These systems require sophisticated algorithms, vast data, and robust infrastructure. Integrating AI agents into existing workflows and systems can be daunting, often requiring substantial time and resources.

Imagine a hypothetical scenario where a global enterprise attempts to integrate AI agents into its supply chain management. The company must harmonize data from various sources, such as suppliers, logistics, and inventory systems. Each AI agent must be capable of understanding and responding to this data accurately while maintaining seamless interaction with human employees. This integration is not merely about plugging in new software; it involves rethinking processes, reconfiguring systems, and often retraining staff. The complexity can lead to prolonged implementation times and increased costs, making it a significant barrier for many businesses.

Moreover, the challenge extends to maintaining the system once it is running. AI agents need continuous learning and updates to adapt to new data and changing business conditions. Ensuring that these updates do not disrupt operations adds another layer of complexity. Businesses must establish robust maintenance protocols and allocate resources for ongoing support, which can be a significant commitment.

Data privacy and security

Privacy and security concerns are paramount when AI agents process vast data. Businesses must ensure that sensitive information is protected against breaches and misuse. This becomes even more challenging when multiple AI agents are involved, each potentially handling different aspects of data.

Consider a hypothetical scenario where a financial institution deploys AI agents to manage customer accounts, process transactions, and detect fraudulent activities. Ensuring compliance with stringent data protection regulations such as GDPR or CCPA becomes a critical challenge. The institution must safeguard data integrity and protect against cyber threats. Any lapse in security can result in severe legal and financial repercussions, not to mention the erosion of customer trust. The institution must also navigate the complexities of consent management, ensuring that data is used in ways that customers have agreed to.

Another layer of complexity arises from the need to anonymize data while maintaining its utility. AI agents often require detailed data to function effectively, but using such data without appropriate anonymization can lead to privacy breaches. Striking the right balance between data utility and privacy protection is a significant challenge.

Ethical considerations and bias

AI agents are only as good as the data and algorithms they are built on. This brings up ethical considerations, particularly around bias and fairness. AI agents can inadvertently perpetuate existing biases in data, leading to unfair or discriminatory outcomes.

Imagine a hypothetical hiring platform powered by AI agents to screen resumes and shortlist candidates. If the training data contains biases—such as a preference for specific educational backgrounds or genders—the AI agent may replicate these biases, resulting in unfair hiring practices. This undermines the system's effectiveness and poses significant ethical and reputational risks for the business.

The challenge of bias extends beyond hiring to any decision-making process where AI agents are used. For instance, in lending or insurance, biased AI decisions can lead to discriminatory practices that disproportionately affect certain groups. Businesses must implement rigorous testing and validation processes to identify and mitigate biases. This involves technical solutions and ethical oversight, ensuring that AI decisions align with societal values and legal standards.

Resistance to change

Introducing AI agents into a business environment can lead to resistance from employees who may fear job displacement or need help to adapt to new technologies. This resistance can hinder the successful adoption of AI systems and reduce their potential benefits.

Envision a hypothetical scenario where a manufacturing company implements AI agents to optimize various operational processes. Employees who are accustomed to traditional methods might refrain from using these new systems, fearing that their roles could become obsolete. Overcoming this resistance requires effective change management strategies, such as implementing training programs, clearly communicating benefits, and assuring job security.

Change management must also address the cultural aspects of AI adoption. Employees must understand how AI can augment their roles rather than replace them. Examples of successful human-AI collaboration and involving employees in the implementation process can help build trust and acceptance. Additionally, offering retraining and upskilling opportunities can reassure employees about their future roles in an AI-driven environment.

High costs and ROI uncertainty

The initial investment required for developing and deploying AI agents can be substantial. Businesses often need more certainty regarding the **return on investment** (**ROI**), making it challenging to justify these expenditures to stakeholders.

Consider a hypothetical enterprise investing heavily in AI agents to enhance various aspects of its operations. The benefits of such investments might take time to become apparent, leading to skepticism among executives and shareholders about the value of these technologies. Quantifying the ROI of AI projects can be complex, as the benefits often manifest indirectly, such as improved customer satisfaction or increased operational efficiency.

Businesses must develop robust cases to justify AI investments, highlighting tangible and intangible benefits. This involves conducting pilot projects to demonstrate value, setting clear performance metrics, and continuously measuring outcomes. Transparent reporting and stakeholder communication are crucial to maintaining support for AI initiatives.

Lack of expertise

Another significant challenge is the need for more skilled professionals to develop, implement, and maintain AI agent systems. This talent gap can impede the progress of AI initiatives and increase reliance on external vendors, who might only sometimes align with the company's strategic goals.

Picture a hypothetical startup with innovative ideas for utilizing AI agents but needing more in-house expertise to bring these ideas to fruition. This can slow down development, increase costs, and limit the competitive edge the company aims to achieve. The startup may need help attracting and retaining people with expertise in AI, competing with larger firms that offer higher salaries and more resources.

To address this challenge, businesses can invest in training and development programs, collaborate with academic institutions, and participate in AI research communities. Building a strong internal team with diverse skill sets and fostering a culture of continuous learning can help bridge the talent gap. Additionally, leveraging external expertise through partnerships and collaborations can provide access to cutting-edge knowledge and technologies.

Insights on agentic systems

Agentic systems, comprising multiple AI agents working together autonomously, present additional layers of complexity and potential. However, many of these solutions and capabilities are only beginning to be built at the time of writing and have yet to mature in any industry. These systems involve intricate coordination among agents, each with specialized tasks, and require advanced communication protocols and decision-making frameworks to function seamlessly.

Imagine a future scenario where a network of AI agents autonomously manages an entire smart city. One agent controls traffic flow, another optimizes energy consumption, and another ensures public safety. These agents must communicate and collaborate continuously, adapting to real-time conditions and unexpected events. The potential for efficiency and innovation is immense, but the path to achieving this vision is fraught with technical and organizational challenges.

Developing agentic systems involves creating robust frameworks for agent communication and decision-making. This includes defining protocols for data exchange, establishing trust mechanisms, and developing algorithms that enable agents to negotiate and collaborate effectively. Ensuring these systems can operate reliably in dynamic and unpredictable environments adds another layer of complexity.

Agentic systems also raise unique ethical and governance challenges. Businesses must ensure that autonomous agents act in ways that align with organizational values and societal norms. This involves establishing clear guidelines for agent behavior, implementing monitoring and oversight mechanisms, and ensuring accountability for agent actions. The dynamic nature of agentic systems requires continuous evaluation and adaptation to address emerging ethical and operational issues.

Early development – experimentation, learning, and adoption

We are in the nascent stages of AI agent and agentic system development. At the time of writing, many of these tools are in the early experimentation, learning, and adoption phases. Businesses are exploring how AI agents can be integrated into their operations and are beginning to understand the potential and limitations of these technologies.

Pilot projects and proof-of-concept initiatives characterize this early phase. Companies are experimenting with AI agents in controlled environments to test their capabilities and assess their impact. These early adopters are paving the way for broader adoption by identifying best practices, refining implementation strategies, and addressing initial challenges.

Learning is crucial in this phase. Businesses must gather insights from their experiments, continuously iterating and improving their AI systems. This involves not only technical learning but also understanding the human and organizational aspects of AI adoption. How do employees interact with AI agents? What cultural changes are needed to embrace these technologies? How can businesses ensure that AI agents align with their strategic goals?

Personal anecdote – navigating the AI terrain

Reflecting on my journey in AI, I recall numerous discussions with industry leaders about the potential of AI agents and agentic systems. The excitement was palpable, but so were the concerns. How do we ensure these systems are fair, secure, and transparent? How do we manage the transition for employees feeling threatened by these new technologies? These conversations highlighted the importance of addressing AI's human and ethical dimensions alongside the technical challenges.

In one memorable discussion with the CEO of a mid-sized company, we talked about the potential for AI agents to revolutionize their customer service operations. While the CEO was enthusiastic about the possibilities, he was also acutely aware of the need to manage employee concerns and ensure data privacy. This conversation underscored the multifaceted nature of AI adoption, where technological innovation must be balanced with human and ethical considerations.

While the promise of AI agents and agentic systems is immense, businesses must navigate a landscape filled with complex integration, data privacy concerns, ethical considerations, resistance to change, high costs, and a lack of expertise. Understanding and addressing these challenges is crucial for leveraging AI's transformative power to drive innovation and growth. By recognizing and preparing for these obstacles, businesses can position themselves to successfully implement AI agents and agentic systems, unlocking new dimensions of efficiency, creativity, and strategic advantage.

The solution and implementation

Having explored the pain points and challenges businesses face with AI agents and agentic systems, it's time to present unique solutions and a step-by-step guide to implementing these transformative technologies.

Designing and implementing AI agentic systems requires careful planning, a deep understanding of the business' specific needs, and expertise in AI technologies. The following steps outline a comprehensive approach to creating effective agentic systems.

Step 1 – defining objectives and goals

Clearly define the objectives and goals that the AI agents need to achieve. This involves identifying the specific tasks and challenges that the agents will address. For example, if the goal is to optimize inventory management, the objectives include reducing stockouts, minimizing excess inventory, and improving demand forecasting.

Step 2 – choosing the right architecture

Based on the complexity and nature of the tasks they need to perform, select an appropriate architecture for the AI agents. Consider whether reactive, deliberative, or hybrid agents best suit the application:

- **Reactive agents**:
  - **Strengths**: Simple, fast, and effective for straightforward tasks
  - **Limitations**: Limited in handling complex decision-making processes and long-term planning
- **Deliberative agents**:
  - **Strengths**: Capable of complex decision-making and long-term planning
  - **Limitations**: Slower response times and higher computational requirements
- **Hybrid agents**:
  - **Strengths**: Combine the strengths of reactive and deliberative agents, balancing quick reactions and thoughtful planning
  - **Limitations**: More complex to design and implement

Step 3 – developing perception and action mechanisms

Implement mechanisms for the agents to perceive their environment and take action. This involves integrating sensors, data feeds, and actuators that enable the agents to gather information and execute tasks:

- **Perception mechanisms**:
  - **Sensors**: Devices that collect environmental data, such as cameras, microphones, and temperature sensors
  - **Data feeds**: They are data streams from external sources, such as financial markets, social media, and IoT devices
- **Action mechanisms:**
  - **Actuators**: Devices such as robotic arms and drones enable agents to interact with the physical world
  - **Software commands**: Actions executed digitally, such as sending emails, updating databases, and executing trades

Step 4 – implementing decision-making algorithms

Use decision-making algorithms to enable the agents to make informed decisions based on their perceived data. This may involve rule-based systems, ML models, or reinforcement learning techniques:

- **Rule-based systems**:
    - **Strengths**: Simple to implement and understand; adequate for tasks with clear rules
    - **Limitations**: Limited adaptability and scalability for complex tasks
- **ML models**:
    - **Strengths**: Capable of learning from data and improving over time; effective for pattern recognition and prediction
    - **Limitations**: Large datasets and computational resources are required, and there is potential for biases in the data
- **Reinforcement learning**:
    - **Strengths**: Capable of optimizing behavior through trial and error; effective for tasks with dynamic and uncertain environments
    - **Limitations**: Computationally intensive and may require extensive training periods

Step 5 – testing and validating

Rigorously test the AI agents in controlled environments to perform as expected. Use simulations and pilot projects to validate their performance and identify potential issues.

The testing methods include the following:

- **Simulations**: Create virtual environments that mimic real-world conditions to test the agents' behavior and decision-making capabilities
- **Pilot projects**: Implement the agents in a limited scope within the business environment to evaluate their performance and gather feedback

Step 6 – deploying and monitoring

Deploy the AI agents in real-world environments and continuously monitor their performance. Use feedback loops to improve their decision-making capabilities over time.

The monitoring strategies include the following:

- **Performance metrics**: Track **key performance indicators** (**KPIs**) to evaluate the agents' effectiveness and efficiency
- **Feedback loops**: Gather feedback from users and stakeholders to identify areas for improvement and refine the agents' algorithms

Step 7 – continuous improvement

Establish mechanisms for continuous learning and improvement. Regularly update the AI agents with new data and retrain them to enhance their capabilities and adapt to changing environments.

Continuous learning involves the following:

- **Data updates**: Regularly update the agents' training data to reflect the latest trends and information
- **Algorithm refinement**: Continuously refine the decision-making algorithms based on performance data and feedback

Here are a few actionable tips and best practices:

- **Start small**: Begin with a small, manageable project to test the feasibility and effectiveness of AI agents. Use this project to gather insights and refine your approach before scaling up. Starting small allows businesses to mitigate risks and learn from initial implementations.
- **Collaborate with experts**: Engage with AI experts and consultants to guide the design and implementation process. Their expertise can help you avoid common pitfalls and accelerate development. Leveraging external knowledge and experience can enhance the quality and effectiveness of AI solutions.
- **Focus on data quality**: Ensure high-quality data for training AI models. Clean, accurate, and relevant data is crucial for the success of AI agents. Implement data governance practices to maintain data integrity. High-quality data enables AI agents to make more accurate and reliable decisions.
- **Integrate with existing systems**: Design AI agents to integrate seamlessly with existing systems and workflows. This reduces disruption and enhances operations' overall efficiency. Compatibility with current infrastructure ensures a smoother transition and better performance of AI agents.
- **Monitor and optimize**: Continuously monitor AI agents' performance and make necessary adjustments. Use KPIs and feedback loops to ensure agents meet business objectives and adapt to changing conditions. Regular monitoring and optimization helps maintain AI agents' effectiveness and relevance.

Hypothetical case study – APEX Manufacturing and Distribution

Let's explore a hypothetical case study of APEX Manufacturing and Distribution to illustrate the successful application of AI agentic systems. Through this example, we'll explore how APEX navigated the complexities of AI adoption, implemented agentic systems, and achieved significant business transformation.

Initial situation

APEX Manufacturing and Distribution, a mid-sized enterprise, faced several operational challenges. The company needed to work on inefficiencies in its supply chain, frequent production downtimes, and suboptimal customer service. These issues led to increased operational costs and affected their competitive edge in the market:

- **Supply chain inefficiencies**: APEX had difficulties managing inventory levels, leading to either overstocking or stockouts. This inefficiency caused delays in production and dissatisfied customers. The company frequently found itself with either excess inventory tying up capital, or with insufficient stock, leading to missed sales opportunities.

- **Production downtime**: The company experienced frequent equipment failures and unscheduled maintenance, disrupting production schedules and leading to significant revenue losses. Downtime affected production and led to missed delivery deadlines, straining relationships with key clients.

- **Customer service challenges**: APEX's customer service team was overwhelmed with routine inquiries, leaving little time to address complex customer issues. This resulted in longer response times and reduced customer satisfaction. The team was bogged down by repetitive tasks, preventing them from providing personalized support.

APEX recognized the need for a comprehensive solution to address these challenges and improve operational efficiency. They decided to explore the potential of AI agentic systems, seeing them as a way to revolutionize their processes and gain a competitive edge.

Steps taken

The steps implemented were as follows:

1. **Identifying business needs**: The first step involved identifying specific areas where AI agents could significantly impact. APEX focused on three key areas: supply chain management, predictive maintenance, and customer service. They conducted internal surveys and workshops to pinpoint the most pressing issues and gather input from various departments.

2. **Research and feasibility assessment**: APEX conducted extensive research on AI agentic systems and consulted with AI experts. They evaluated the feasibility of implementing AI agents, considering data availability, existing infrastructure, and potential ROI. APEX conducted a series of feasibility studies and cost-benefit analyses to determine the viability of AI integration.

3. **Developing a strategy**: APEX developed a clear strategy for AI implementation. They defined objectives, set timelines, and established KPIs to measure success. The strategy emphasized a phased approach, starting with pilot projects in each focus area. This strategic plan included detailed milestones, resource allocation, and risk management plans.

4. **Pilot testing**: APEX initiated pilot projects to test the performance of AI agents in a controlled environment. The pilots included the following:

    - **Supply chain optimization**: AI agents were deployed to manage inventory levels, forecast demand, and optimize procurement processes. These agents used historical data and ML algorithms to accurately predict inventory needs.

    - **Predictive maintenance**: AI agents monitored equipment health, analyzed sensor data, and predicted maintenance needs to prevent unscheduled downtimes. These agents utilized real-time data from IoT sensors to detect anomalies and schedule preventive maintenance.

    - **Enhanced customer service**: AI-powered chatbots were implemented to handle routine customer inquiries, allowing human agents to focus on more complex issues. The chatbots were trained using **natural language processing** (**NLP**) to effectively understand and respond to customer queries.

5. **Implementation and integration**: Based on the successful pilot projects, APEX scaled up the implementation of AI agents. They integrated the agents with existing systems and workflows, ensuring minimal disruption to operations. The implementation included continuous monitoring and optimization to adapt to changing conditions. APEX established a dedicated AI team to oversee the integration and ensure the agents operated smoothly.

Results achieved

The successful implementation of AI agentic systems led to transformative results for APEX Manufacturing and Distribution:

- **Improved supply chain efficiency**: AI agents optimized inventory levels, reducing overstocking and stockouts by 30%. This improvement led to smoother production schedules and timely deliveries, enhancing customer satisfaction. The agents' accurate demand forecasting helped APEX maintain optimal inventory levels, reducing waste and freeing up capital.

- **Reduced production downtime**: Predictive maintenance agents accurately forecasted equipment failures, reducing unplanned downtimes by 40%. This increase in operational efficiency resulted in significant cost savings and higher production outputs. The AI agents' ability to predict and prevent equipment failures minimized disruptions and improved overall productivity.

- **Enhanced customer service**: AI-powered chatbots handled 70% of routine customer inquiries, allowing human agents to focus on complex issues. Customer response times decreased by 50%, and customer satisfaction scores improved by 25%. The chatbots' efficient handling of routine tasks allowed human agents to provide more personalized and high-quality service.

Relatable anecdotes and insights

Throughout the implementation journey, APEX encountered several challenges. There were moments of skepticism and resistance from employees, particularly those who feared job displacement. To address this, APEX conducted extensive training programs and involved employees in the AI integration process. They emphasized that AI agents were there to augment human capabilities, not replace them.

When the AI agents were first introduced, some warehouse workers feared losing their jobs. APEX addressed these concerns by offering reskilling programs that demonstrated how the AI agents would handle repetitive tasks, allowing the workers to focus on more strategic and fulfilling roles. One employee shared how the training programs helped him transition from manual inventory management to overseeing the AI agents' operations, ultimately enhancing his career growth and job satisfaction.

APEX also faced challenges integrating AI agents with their legacy systems. The initial attempts led to compatibility issues, causing some operational disruptions. However, by collaborating closely with AI experts and their IT department, they developed custom integration solutions that ensured seamless communication between the AI agents and the legacy systems.

The journey of APEX Manufacturing and Distribution illustrates the potential of AI agentic systems to transform business operations. By addressing key challenges, involving employees in the process, and continuously learning and optimizing, APEX successfully leveraged AI to enhance efficiency, reduce costs, and improve customer satisfaction. This hypothetical case study is a compelling example of how businesses can navigate the complexities of AI adoption and achieve significant results.

Reflection and practical next steps

As we conclude this exploration of AI agents and agentic systems, it's time to pause and reflect on the transformative potential these technologies hold for your organization. The journey of APEX Manufacturing and Distribution serves as a compelling illustration of how AI can revolutionize operations, enhance efficiency, and drive innovation. However, how can you translate these insights into actionable steps for your own context?

Reflective questions

Take a moment to consider the following questions:

- How might AI agents address the most pressing challenges in your organization?
- What areas of your business could benefit most from the autonomous decision-making capabilities of AI agents?

- How prepared is your organization to integrate AI agents into existing workflows and systems?
- What potential resistance might you face when implementing AI agents, and how can you address it proactively?
- How can you ensure that the implementation of AI agents aligns with your organization's values and ethical standards?

Critical assessment

Now, let's critically assess your current situation:

- **Efficiency gaps**: Where are the bottlenecks in your current processes that AI agents could potentially streamline?
- **Data utilization**: Are you fully leveraging the data available in your organization? How could AI agents help you extract more value from this data?
- **Customer experience**: In what ways could AI agents enhance your customer service and overall customer experience?
- **Innovation potential**: How might AI agents free up your team's time and resources to focus on more strategic, innovative initiatives?
- **Competitive edge**: What unique advantages could AI agents provide in your industry, and how might they set you apart from competitors?

Practical next steps

Based on the assessment steps outlined previously, you can implement the following steps:

1. **Start small, think big**: Begin with a pilot project in a non-critical area of your business. This allows you to experiment, learn, and build confidence without significant risk. For example, you could implement a chatbot for handling basic customer inquiries or an AI agent for monitoring equipment health in a single production line.
2. **Conduct a readiness assessment**: Evaluate your organization's technical infrastructure, data quality, and team skills. Identify gaps and create a plan to address them. This might involve upgrading systems, improving data collection processes, or providing AI training to key team members.
3. **Build a cross-functional AI team**: Assemble a diverse team with representatives from IT, operations, customer service, and leadership. This team can champion AI initiatives, share knowledge, and ensure alignment across departments.
4. **Prioritize data quality**: Invest in improving your data collection, storage, and management practices. High-quality data is the foundation of effective AI agents. Consider implementing data governance policies and tools to ensure data accuracy and consistency.

5. **Develop an AI ethics framework**: Create guidelines for the ethical use of AI in your organization. This should address issues such as data privacy, decision transparency, and bias mitigation. Involve stakeholders from various departments to ensure comprehensive coverage.
6. **Engage in continuous learning**: Stay updated on AI advancements and best practices. Encourage team members to attend AI conferences, participate in online courses, or engage with AI communities. This ongoing education will help your organization adapt to the rapidly evolving AI landscape.
7. **Foster a culture of innovation**: Encourage experimentation and learning from failures. Create spaces for team members to share ideas on how AI could improve processes or solve problems in your organization.
8. **Plan for change management**: Develop a strategy to address potential resistance to AI implementation. This could include ensuring clear communication about the role of AI, showcasing early wins, and providing training and support for employees transitioning to new ways of working.
9. **Measure and iterate**: Establish clear KPIs for your AI initiatives. Regularly review performance, gather feedback, and be prepared to adjust your approach based on real-world results.
10. **Collaborate and partner**: Consider partnerships with AI vendors, academic institutions, or industry peers. These collaborations can provide access to expertise, resources, and cutting-edge technologies that might be challenging to develop in-house.

Remember, the journey to implementing AI agents is a marathon, not a sprint. Each step forward, no matter how small, is progress. By starting with reflection, moving to critical assessment, and then taking concrete actions, you're laying the groundwork for a future where AI agents can significantly enhance your organization's capabilities and competitive edge.

As you embark on this journey, stay curious, remain adaptable, and always keep your organization's unique needs and values at the forefront. The potential of AI agents is vast, but their true power lies in how effectively you integrate them into your specific context. Your thoughtful approach today will shape the intelligent, efficient, and innovative organization of tomorrow.

Summary

As we wrap up our exploration of AI agents and agentic systems, I hope you're excited and thoughtful about the possibilities ahead. We journeyed through the intricacies of these intelligent systems, from their core characteristics to real-world applications and implementation challenges. Remember, the power of AI agents lies not just in their autonomous capabilities but also in how they can augment and enhance human decision-making across various industries. Whether it's optimizing supply chains, predicting maintenance needs, or revolutionizing customer service, the potential is vast, but so is the need for careful planning and ethical considerations.

Consider how AI agents might transform your work or industry as you reflect on this chapter. What challenges could they help you overcome? What new opportunities might they unlock? Remember these questions as we transition to our next chapter on designing AI systems. We'll dive deeper into the nuts and bolts of creating AI solutions that are powerful, ethical, user-friendly, and aligned with human values. Get ready to roll up your sleeves and explore the art and science of AI system design!

Questions

1. What are the four key characteristics of AI agents?
2. Explain the difference between reactive and deliberative agents.
3. How do AI agents contribute to enhancing efficiency in business operations?
4. What role does ML play in the development of AI agents?
5. Name three potential applications of AI agents in real-world scenarios.
6. What are some of the main challenges businesses face when implementing AI agents and agentic systems?
7. In the APEX Manufacturing and Distribution case study, what were the three key areas where AI agents were implemented?
8. How can businesses address potential resistance from employees when introducing AI agents?
9. Describe the importance of data quality in the successful implementation of AI agents.
10. What ethical considerations should be taken into account when designing and implementing AI agentic systems?

References

1. ArxivPaperAI. *ProcessGPT: Transforming Business Process Management with Generative Artificial Intelligence.* https://arxiv.org/abs/2306.01771
2. weetech. *What Kind of Jobs Will AI Produce?* https://www.weetechsolution.com/blog/what-kind-of-jobs-will-ai-produce
3. nGenium. *The Year Wearable Devices Revolutionize the Medical Engineering Industry.* https://www.ngenium.io/post/2023-the-year-wearable-devices-revolutionize-the-medical-engineering-industry

9
Designing AI Systems

Machine intelligence is the last invention that humanity will ever need to make.

– *Nick Bostrom*

What if I told you that designing an AI system is like planning a road trip across a new continent? Think about it. Both require meticulous planning, terrain understanding, and a clear destination vision. Imagine embarking on this journey without a map, relying solely on instinct. Scary, right? Businesses often feel this when they dive into AI without a solid design strategy.

In the same way that a road trip can take unexpected turns, AI systems can also lead to surprising outcomes if not carefully designed. Designing an AI system doesn't have to be a labyrinth of jargon and code. It's about creating solutions that are intelligent but also intuitive and ethical. It's about striking the right balance between innovation and responsibility. And yes, it's about ensuring our AI systems don't go rogue, like that GPS that once tried to direct me into a lake.

So, as we embark on this chapter, think of yourself as both the cartographer and the navigator of your AI journey. We'll explore the principles, pitfalls, and practical steps to designing AI systems that are not only cutting-edge but also reliable and fair. Ready to hit the road? Let's dive into the world of AI system design.

Let's start with a story that underscores the importance of meticulous AI design. A few years ago, a significant retailer launched an AI-driven recruitment tool. The goal was to streamline hiring by using an algorithm to screen resumes and select the best candidates. However, the AI system quickly became biased, favoring resumes that included certain words and penalizing others, often discriminating against women. What went wrong? The data used to train the AI was biased, reflecting historical hiring patterns that the company hoped to eliminate. This case highlights a crucial point: the data you feed into an AI system is as important as the algorithms you design.

So, what does it take to design a practical AI system? The process has three main stages:

- **Planning – setting the course**: Before you hit the road, you must know where you're going. In AI terms, this means defining clear objectives. What problem are you trying to solve? What are the success metrics? It's crucial to involve all stakeholders in this phase, from data scientists and engineers to end users and executives. Everyone should have a shared understanding of the goals and the criteria for success.

- **Development – building the vehicle**: Once you have a clear destination, it's time to build it. This involves selecting the suitable algorithms, gathering and preprocessing data, and training your models. The development phase is where the magic happens, but it's also where many projects stumble. It's essential to ensure your data is representative and free from bias. Continuous testing and validation are crucial to catching issues early and refining your models.

- **Deployment – navigating the terrain**: With your vehicle ready, it's time to hit the road. Deployment involves integrating the AI system into your existing infrastructure and monitoring its performance in real-world conditions. This phase requires flexibility. Just as road conditions can change unexpectedly, so can the operational environment for your AI. Continuous monitoring, feedback loops, and the ability to make adjustments on the fly are critical.

Throughout this journey, ethical considerations must be at the forefront. An AI system is not just a technological artifact; it reflects the values and ethics of the organization that deploys it. This means ensuring transparency, accountability, and fairness in every stage of design and deployment. It's about creating systems that enhance human capabilities and foster trust.

To bring this all together, think of designing an AI system as an ongoing journey rather than a one-time event. It's about continuous learning, adaptation, and improvement. By embracing a mindset of curiosity, responsibility, and innovation, you can navigate the complexities of AI design and create systems that are not only powerful but also ethical and trustworthy.

In this chapter, we will cover the following topics:

- Best practices for AI system design
- Human-centered AI design

By the end of this chapter, you will be able to apply best practices for designing effective and ethical AI systems, including setting clear objectives, ensuring data quality, and implementing robust monitoring processes. You'll also understand the principles of human-centered AI design, enabling you to create AI systems that augment human capabilities, foster trust, and provide equitable benefits across diverse user groups.

The problem – pain points and challenges

Businesses often face many challenges in leveraging AI that can turn promising projects into frustrating failures. Designing AI systems is no small feat; it involves navigating a complex landscape of technical, ethical, and operational hurdles. Let's unpack these challenges with compelling examples and data, ensuring we understand their significance.

Data quality and bias

Data quality and bias are among the most critical challenges in AI system design. Data is the foundation upon which AI models are built, and its quality directly impacts the reliability and fairness of outcomes. However, AI systems are often trained on incomplete, inconsistent, or biased data, leading to inaccurate models and misguided decisions. Bias embedded in training data can cause AI systems to perpetuate existing inequalities and reflect prejudices present in historical records. This issue is particularly concerning when AI is applied to sensitive domains such as recruitment, healthcare, and law enforcement, where biased outcomes can negatively affect people's lives and amplify existing disparities. Data quality, representativeness, and fairness are crucial to avoiding these pitfalls and developing ethical, trustworthy AI solutions.

Moreover, an effective AI system requires more than quality data; it demands a comprehensive understanding of the context in which it will be deployed. AI models trained on data that lacks diversity or fails to reflect the real-world environment can face significant performance challenges when exposed to new, varied scenarios. For example, AI systems must consider demographic or situational data variations to provide accurate predictions across different groups and conditions. The failure to consider contextual relevance leads to unreliable outcomes, erodes trust in AI technologies, and can result in unintended consequences. Addressing these challenges requires careful data selection, regular audits for biases, and continuous improvement of the AI models to ensure they align with ethical standards and meet the needs of the diverse populations they serve.

Complexity and integration

AI systems are inherently complex, requiring seamless integration with existing technologies. This can be a daunting task. For instance, a large healthcare provider invested heavily in an AI system to streamline patient care. Despite significant resources, the integration process needed to be improved. The AI struggled to communicate with legacy systems, leading to service disruptions and staff frustration. The problem was not the AI itself but the need for a cohesive strategy for integration. This example illustrates how crucial it is to have a clear roadmap for merging new AI systems with existing infrastructure.

Ethical and legal concerns

Ethical and legal concerns present another layer of complexity. As AI systems become more pervasive, ensuring they operate within ethical and legal boundaries is paramount. Consider the example of facial recognition technology. Despite its potential benefits, its deployment has raised severe moral issues, particularly privacy and discrimination. Facial recognition systems have misidentified individuals in several instances, leading to wrongful arrests and public outcry. This highlights the need for robust ethical guidelines and compliance measures in AI system design.

Scalability and maintenance

Scalability and maintenance are also significant challenges. An AI system might perform well in a controlled environment but struggle under real-world conditions. A retail company, for example, implemented an AI-driven inventory management system. Initially, the system showed promise, accurately predicting stock levels and reducing waste. However, as the company expanded, the AI needed to catch up with the increased data volume and diversity, leading to errors and inefficiencies. This example underscores the importance of designing AI systems that scale and adapt to changing conditions.

Human-AI collaboration

Another pain point is fostering effective human-AI collaboration. AI systems are tools meant to augment human capabilities, not replace them. However, achieving this balance is often tricky. A global customer service company introduced AI chatbots to handle basic inquiries, aiming to free up human agents for more complex issues. Instead of easing the workload, the chatbots' limited understanding and inability to handle nuanced queries led to frustrated customers and overburdened human agents. This scenario exemplifies the challenge of designing AI systems that complement human efforts without causing additional strain.

Security risks

AI systems are also vulnerable to security risks. Cyber-attacks targeting AI models can lead to data breaches and manipulation of outputs, with potentially disastrous consequences. An autonomous vehicle company, for instance, faced a security breach where hackers manipulated the AI's image recognition system, causing it to misinterpret traffic signals. This incident raised alarms about the robustness of AI systems against cyber threats, emphasizing the need for rigorous security protocols.

Personal anecdote – learning the hard way

In my early days of working with AI, I was involved in a project for a financial institution aiming to predict market trends. We had access to vast amounts of historical data and cutting-edge algorithms. However, despite our best efforts, the model's predictions could have been better. We soon realized that the data we relied on needed to be updated and reflect current market dynamics. This experience taught me the importance of having good data and ensuring it is relevant and up to date. It was a humbling reminder that even the most sophisticated AI project can fail if built on a shaky foundation.

The stakes are high

The challenges of AI system design are significant, but so are the stakes. Businesses investing in AI are often under immense pressure to deliver results, with substantial financial and reputational risks on the line. AI can transform industries, but only if these systems are designed thoughtfully and strategically [1]. Poorly designed AI can lead to lost revenue, damaged reputations, and ethical violations, while well-designed AI can drive innovation, efficiency, and competitive advantage.

In summary, designing AI systems is fraught with challenges, from data quality and integration to ethical considerations and scalability. However, by understanding these pain points and addressing them head-on, businesses can navigate the complexities of AI and unlock its full potential. As we proceed in this chapter, we'll delve into practical strategies and best practices to overcome these challenges, ensuring your AI systems are robust, ethical, and effective. Let's move forward equipped with the knowledge to tackle these hurdles and pave the way for successful AI implementation.

The solution – step-by-step implementation

Now that we've identified the pain points and challenges in AI system design, let's delve into the solutions. I'll guide you through a step-by-step approach to designing compelling, ethical, and scalable AI systems. This methodology is built on years of experience and best practices, ensuring you can confidently navigate the complexities of AI design.

Step 1 – defining clear objectives

Before diving into the technical details, it's crucial to establish clear, measurable objectives. What problem are you trying to solve? What outcomes do you expect? Involve all stakeholders, from data scientists to end users, to ensure a shared understanding of goals. Clear objectives provide a roadmap for the entire project.

Example: A retail company aiming to reduce stock wastage set clear objectives: a 20% reduction in unsold inventory within 6 months. This goal guided every design decision, from data collection to model training.

Defining clear objectives helps ensure everyone is on the same page and working toward the same end goals. This alignment is crucial for the project's success. When everyone understands the objectives, they can make better decisions and align their efforts toward achieving them.

Step 2 – gathering and preparing quality data

High-quality data is the cornerstone of any successful AI system. Start by gathering relevant data and ensuring it is clean, accurate, and representative of the problem domain. Address any biases and gaps in the data to prevent skewed outcomes.

Actionable tip: Prepare your dataset using data preprocessing techniques such as normalization, outlier detection, and missing value imputation. Then, regularly update your data to reflect changing conditions.

Story: We struggled with inaccurate predictions during an early project due to outdated data. We significantly improved model accuracy by implementing a robust data pipeline that continuously updated our dataset.

Quality data is crucial for the accuracy and reliability of AI systems. It can lead to better model performance and accurate predictions. A robust data pipeline is essential to ensure the data is always up to date and correct.

Step 3 – selecting the right algorithms and tools

Choosing suitable algorithms and tools is critical. Consider the problem type, data characteristics, and computational resources. Experiment with different models and use interpretability and performance metrics to select the best one.

Best practices include the following:

- Try algorithms such as decision trees, random forests, or **neural networks** (**NNs**) for classification tasks
- Consider linear regression, **support vector machines** (**SVMs**), or ensemble methods for regression tasks

Tool recommendation: Utilize frameworks such as TensorFlow, PyTorch, or scikit-learn, which offer a wide range of pre-built models and tools.

Selecting suitable algorithms and tools can significantly impact the performance of the AI system. It's essential to understand the problem and choose the appropriate algorithms and tools to best address it.

Step 4 – developing and training your model

Developing and training your model involves iteratively refining it to improve performance. Split your data into training, validation, and test sets to evaluate model performance and avoid overfitting.

Actionable tip: Implement cross-validation to ensure your model generalizes well to unseen data. Use techniques such as hyperparameter tuning to optimize model performance.

Story: In a financial forecasting project, hyperparameter tuning and cross-validation helped us improve the model's accuracy by 15%, making it a reliable tool for predicting market trends.

Developing and training the model is an iterative process that requires continuous refinement. Techniques such as cross-validation and hyperparameter tuning are essential to improving the model's performance and ensuring it generalizes well to unseen data.

Step 5 – ensuring ethical and fair AI

Ethical considerations should be embedded in every stage of AI design [2]. Implement fairness checks to detect and mitigate biases. Ensure transparency in how your AI makes decisions.

Human-centered AI design focuses on creating solutions that prioritize diverse perspectives, assess the impact on various user groups, and uphold ethical and legal standards throughout the process:

- Engage diverse teams in the design process to bring multiple perspectives
- Conduct impact assessments to understand how your AI affects different user groups
- Establish clear guidelines for ethical AI use and ensure compliance with legal standards

Example: A healthcare provider used fairness metrics to adjust their diagnostic AI, ensuring accurate results across all patient demographics.

Ensuring ethical and fair AI is crucial for building trust and credibility. Fairness checks and impact assessments are essential to detect and mitigate biases and ensure the AI system operates within ethical and legal boundaries.

Step 6 – integrating and deploying your AI system

Integration and deployment involve embedding your AI system into the existing infrastructure. Ensure it works seamlessly with other technologies and processes.

Best practices for AI system design include the following:

- Use APIs to facilitate communication between the AI system and other software
- Implement robust monitoring to track performance and detect issues in real time
- Develop a rollback plan to address potential deployment failures quickly

Story: A logistics company successfully integrated an AI-driven route optimization system, reducing delivery times by 25%. They used APIs for seamless integration and continuous monitoring to maintain performance.

Integrating and deploying the AI system is a critical phase that requires careful planning and execution. Robust monitoring and a rollback plan ensure the system operates smoothly and issues are addressed quickly.

Step 7 – monitoring and maintaining your AI system

AI systems require ongoing monitoring and maintenance to remain effective. Update your model regularly with new data and refine it based on performance feedback.

Actionable tip: Set up automated alerts to notify your team of any anomalies in system performance. Periodically retrain your model to incorporate the latest data trends.

Example: An e-commerce platform used automated monitoring to detect a sudden drop in recommendation accuracy. They quickly retrained their model with updated data, restoring performance.

Monitoring and maintaining the AI system is an ongoing process that requires continuous attention. Automated alerts and periodic retraining are essential to ensure the system remains effective and up to date with the latest data trends.

Best practices for AI system design

To design effective and responsible AI systems, it's essential to follow best practices that address the unique challenges of AI development while ensuring ethical and reliable outcomes:

- **Collaborate across teams**: Involve diverse teams, from data scientists to end users, to ensure comprehensive design and implementation
- **Prioritize data quality**: Regularly update and clean your data to maintain model accuracy and relevance
- **Focus on ethical AI**: Embed fairness and transparency into every stage of the design process
- **Implement robust monitoring**: Continuously track system performance and have a plan for addressing issues swiftly
- **Iterate and improve**: View AI system design as an ongoing process, constantly changing, refining, and updating your models

Human-centered AI design

Human-centered AI design focuses on creating systems that augment human capabilities and foster trust. Here are the fundamental principles:

- **Empathy and inclusion**: Understand the needs and perspectives of all user groups, especially marginalized ones
- **Transparency and explainability**: Ensure users understand how AI decisions are made
- **Responsibility and accountability**: Establish clear guidelines for AI use and ensure accountability for its outcomes
- **Continuous feedback**: Encourage user feedback to refine and improve the AI system continuously

This step-by-step approach allows you to design effective, ethical, and scalable AI systems. These solutions address the pain points we identified, ensuring your AI projects succeed in driving innovation and business value. As we move forward, keep these principles in mind, and let's continue to explore the exciting possibilities AI offers.

Hypothetical case study – APEX Manufacturing and Distribution

To bring our framework to life, let's dive into a hypothetical case study involving APEX Manufacturing and Distribution. APEX is a mid-sized company specializing in producing and distributing industrial machinery. They approached us with a clear objective: to optimize their supply chain using AI to reduce costs and improve efficiency.

Initial situation

When APEX first approached us, they were facing several challenges:

- **Inefficiencies in inventory management**: APEX needed help maintaining optimal inventory levels, leading to either overstocking or stockouts
- **Supply chain disruptions**: Frequent disruptions in the supply chain caused delays and increased operational costs
- **Data silos**: Their data was scattered across different departments and systems, making it challenging to gain comprehensive insights

APEX had a wealth of data but needed more means to leverage it effectively. They needed a robust AI system to analyze their data and provide actionable insights to streamline their operations.

Step-by-step implementation

To successfully implement AI solutions, it's essential to follow a structured, step-by-step process to ensure that all aspects of the project are effectively addressed and optimized for the client's specific needs.

Step 1 – defining clear objectives

We began by collaborating with APEX's leadership team to define clear objectives. Our primary goals were the following:

- Reduce inventory holding costs by 15% within the first year
- Decrease supply chain disruptions by predicting potential issues and providing proactive solutions
- Improve data integration across departments to facilitate better decision-making

We conducted workshops with APEX's stakeholders, including supply chain managers, IT staff, and executives, to ensure everyone was aligned on the project goals. By involving diverse perspectives, we refined our objectives and gained a deep understanding of each department's specific challenges.

Step 2 – gathering and preparing quality data

Next, we conducted a thorough audit of APEX's data sources. We identified relevant data from their ERP system, supply chain management software, and sales databases. We then cleaned and integrated this data into a unified data warehouse.

Actionable tip: We implemented automated data cleaning pipelines to ensure data consistency and accuracy, reducing manual errors and freeing up valuable time for their team. This involved setting up scripts to handle missing values, outliers, and inconsistencies in the data, ensuring a clean and robust dataset for model training.

To address data silos, we worked with APEX's IT department to establish secure data pipelines that facilitated seamless data flow between departments. This not only improved data accessibility but also ensured real-time data updates, which were crucial for the AI system's performance.

Step 3 – selecting the right algorithms and tools

Given the nature of APEX's challenges, we chose a combination of **machine learning (ML)** algorithms for different tasks:

- **Inventory optimization**: We used a combination of time-series forecasting and **reinforcement learning (RL)** algorithms to predict demand and optimize inventory levels
- **Supply chain prediction**: We employed anomaly detection and predictive analytics algorithms to predict supply chain disruptions

Tool recommendation: We utilized TensorFlow for model development and Apache Spark for large-scale data processing, ensuring scalability and efficiency. These tools were chosen for their robustness and ability to handle complex computations at scale.

To determine the best algorithms, we conducted several **proof-of-concept (PoC)** tests. We experimented with **AutoRegressive Integrated Moving Average (ARIMA)** models, **Long Short-Term Memory (LSTM)** networks, and RL algorithms for inventory optimization. We tested various anomaly detection methods for supply chain prediction, including Isolation Forests and **Autoencoders (AEs)**, to identify the most effective approach.

Step 4 – developing and training the model

With the data prepared and algorithms selected, we developed and trained our models. We split the data into training, validation, and test sets to evaluate performance. We also conducted extensive hyperparameter tuning to optimize the models.

Story: During this phase, we encountered a challenge with the anomaly detection model, which initially had a high false-positive rate. We significantly improved its accuracy by iteratively refining the model and incorporating additional features, such as weather patterns and supplier performance data.

We leveraged feature engineering techniques to enhance the models, creating new features from existing data to improve model performance. For instance, we derived features such as seasonal demand trends and supplier reliability scores, which added valuable context to the predictions.

We also set up a continuous integration and continuous deployment (CI/CD) pipeline to automate model training and deployment. This ensured that the models were always up to date with the latest data and could be quickly retrained and redeployed if necessary.

Step 5 – ensuring ethical and fair AI

We implemented fairness checks to ensure our models were unbiased and provided equal benefits across all APEX operations segments. We also established transparency in our AI decision-making processes, providing clear explanations for the model's predictions and recommendations.

Human-centered AI design: We conducted workshops with APEX's employees to gather feedback and ensure the AI system met their needs and expectations. This human-centered approach fostered trust and collaboration.

We conducted a series of fairness audits to ensure ethical AI, analyzing the model's predictions across different demographic groups to identify and mitigate any biases. We also established clear documentation and transparency practices, ensuring that APEX's employees could understand and trust the AI system's decisions.

We also developed an ethics review board, composed of representatives from different departments, to oversee the AI system's deployment and ensure it adhered to ethical guidelines. This board addressed ethical concerns during the implementation and deployment phases.

Step 6 – integrating and deploying the AI system

We developed APIs to integrate the AI system with APEX's ERP and supply chain management software. We also set up a robust monitoring system to track performance and detect issues in real time.

Best practices for AI system design: We ensured seamless integration by conducting extensive testing in a controlled environment before full-scale deployment. We also developed a rollback plan to address any deployment failures quickly.

To ensure a smooth integration, we worked closely with APEX's IT department to test the AI system in a staging environment that mirrored their production setup. This allowed us to identify and address compatibility issues before the system went live.

We also implemented a detailed deployment plan, including training sessions for APEX's staff to ensure they were comfortable using the new AI system. This training covered everything from interpreting the AI's recommendations to troubleshooting common issues.

Step 7 – monitoring and maintaining the AI system

We established an ongoing monitoring process post-deployment to track the AI system's performance. We set up automated alerts to notify APEX's team of any anomalies. We also scheduled regular retraining sessions to incorporate new data and maintain model accuracy.

Actionable tip: We provided APEX with detailed documentation and training sessions to ensure their team could effectively manage and maintain the AI system.

We set up a maintenance schedule to ensure the system's longevity, including regular audits, performance reviews, and updates. This proactive approach helped prevent issues before they became critical, ensuring the system remained effective and reliable.

We also established a feedback loop with APEX's staff, encouraging them to report any issues or suggestions for improvement. This ongoing dialogue helped us continuously refine and enhance the AI system.

Results achieved

Within the first year of implementation, APEX achieved remarkable results:

- **Reduced inventory holding costs**: APEX saw a 20% reduction in inventory holding costs, surpassing their initial goal
- **Decreased supply chain disruptions**: The AI system accurately predicted potential supply chain disruptions, reducing delays by 30%
- **Improved data integration**: APEX gained comprehensive insights with a unified data warehouse, enabling better decision-making across departments

The success of the AI system at APEX had a profound impact on their operations. By reducing inventory holding costs and minimizing supply chain disruptions, APEX saved money and improved overall efficiency and customer satisfaction.

The integration of the AI system also fostered a culture of innovation within APEX. Employees across different departments began to see the value of AI and became more open to leveraging technology to solve problems and improve processes.

The successful implementation of the AI system at APEX Manufacturing and Distribution illustrates the power of a well-designed, ethical, and scalable AI framework. Following a structured approach, we addressed APEX's challenges and significantly improved its operations. This case study demonstrates that with clear objectives, quality data, suitable algorithms, and a human-centered approach, businesses can harness the full potential of AI to drive efficiency and innovation.

Reflection and practical next steps

As we wrap up our journey through the intricacies of AI system design, it's time to pause and reflect on the insights we've gathered. Think back to the road trip analogy we started with. Just as every journey shapes the traveler, each AI project you undertake will undoubtedly shape your understanding and approach to technology.

Consider for a moment: How does the structured approach we've discussed compare to your current practices? Perhaps you've experienced the frustration of an AI project that didn't quite hit the mark, much like our example of the biased recruitment tool. Or maybe you've witnessed the transformative power of well-designed AI, similar to APEX's supply chain optimization success story.

These reflections aren't just academic exercises. They're the foundation for real, impactful change in how we approach AI design [3]. Let's challenge ourselves to think critically about our current situations:

- **Data quality and bias**: How confident are you in the quality and representativeness of your data? Are there hidden biases lurking in your datasets that could skew your AI's decision-making?
- **Ethical considerations**: Have you established clear ethical guidelines for AI development in your organization? How can you ensure these principles are not just written down but actively practiced?
- **Human-AI collaboration**: How could AI augment and enhance your team's capabilities rather than replace them? Are there tasks currently overwhelming your staff that could benefit from AI assistance?
- **Scalability and maintenance**: How prepared are you to scale your AI systems as your organization grows? Do you have processes in place for ongoing monitoring and refinement?

These questions might seem daunting, but every journey begins with a single step. Here are some tangible, realistic steps you can take to start implementing these strategies:

1. **Conduct a data audit**: Thoroughly examine your data sources. Identify any gaps or potential biases. This could be as simple as creating a spreadsheet that lists all your data sources, their update frequency, and any known issues.
2. **Establish an ethics committee**: Form a diverse group of stakeholders to oversee AI development and deployment. This doesn't have to be a formal board – even regular meetings with representatives from different departments can make a significant difference.
3. **Pilot a small-scale AI project**: Choose a contained, low-risk area of your operations to test an AI solution. For example, you could use AI to optimize meeting scheduling or analyze customer feedback. Use this as a learning opportunity to refine your approach before tackling larger projects.

4. **Invest in training**: Organize workshops or training sessions to educate your team about AI basics and ethical considerations. This could involve bringing in external experts or leveraging online courses.

5. **Develop a monitoring dashboard**: Create a simple dashboard to track the performance of your AI systems. Start with basic metrics such as accuracy and user satisfaction, and refine them as you learn what's most important for your specific use case.

The goal isn't to transform your organization overnight. It's about taking steady, thoughtful steps toward more effective and ethical AI implementation [4]. Each small improvement compounds over time, leading to significant long-term benefits.

Remember the APEX Manufacturing and Distribution story as you embark on this journey. They didn't just implement an AI system; they changed their entire approach to data and decision-making. The result wasn't just cost savings but a cultural shift toward innovation and efficiency.

You have the power to drive similar transformations in your context. Whether you're part of a large corporation or working on personal projects, these principles of careful planning, ethical consideration, and continuous improvement apply universally.

So, what will your first step be? Perhaps it's scheduling a meeting to discuss data quality or sketching an idea for a small AI pilot project. Whatever it is, take that step with confidence. Remember – every AI success story starts with someone approaching the challenge thoughtfully and systematically.

As you move forward, stay curious, remain ethical, and don't be afraid to iterate. The field of AI is constantly evolving, and so should our approaches to designing and implementing these systems. Your journey in AI system design is just beginning, and the potential for positive impact is immense. Embrace the challenge, learn from each experience, and watch your AI initiatives transform from mere ideas into powerful tools for innovation and growth.

Summary

In this chapter, we navigated the complex terrain of AI system design, equipping you with a roadmap for creating intelligent, ethical, and scalable solutions. We explored the critical stages of AI development, from defining clear objectives and ensuring data quality to selecting appropriate algorithms and implementing robust monitoring systems. Along the way, we emphasized the importance of ethical considerations and human-centered design, illustrating how these principles can lead to more effective and trustworthy AI systems. Remember – designing AI isn't just about cutting-edge technology; it's about creating tools that enhance human capabilities and drive meaningful progress in your organization.

As we close this chapter, take a moment to reflect on how you might apply these insights to your projects or challenges. What aspects of your approach could benefit from a more structured, ethical framework? In our next chapter, we'll build on this foundation as we delve into the intricacies of training AI models, exploring techniques to transform your carefully designed systems into powerful learning machines.

Questions

1. What analogy does the chapter use to describe designing AI systems?
2. Name three main challenges in AI system design discussed in the chapter.
3. What was the primary goal of APEX Manufacturing and Distribution in implementing an AI system?
4. In the step-by-step implementation process, why is defining clear objectives the first crucial step?
5. How does the chapter suggest addressing potential biases in AI systems?
6. What role does human-centered AI design play in the development process?
7. In the APEX case study, what were two significant areas of improvement achieved after implementing the AI system?

References

1. theinsaneapp.com. *Hugging Face VS OpenAI.* https://www.theinsaneapp.com/2023/03/hugging-face-vs-openai.html
2. ValueCoders™. *AI Use Cases: Healthcare, E-commerce, Finance, Logistics & More.* https://www.valuecoders.com/ai/use-cases
3. techpoint.org. *Artificial Intelligence TechPoint.* https://techpoint.org/artificial-intelligence/
4. Digital Care. *How to Determine the Perfect Digital Marketing Budget for Your Business.* https://www.digitalcare.org/perfect-digital-marketing-budget/

10
Training AI Models

Once you trust a self-driving car with your life, you pretty much will trust artificial intelligence with anything.

– Dave Waters

Have you ever wondered what it takes to teach a machine to recognize a cat from a dog, understand human language, or even predict market trends? Imagine if you could train a team of tireless assistants who never sleep, never get bored, and can process more information in a day than you could in a lifetime. Welcome to the world of training AI models, where algorithms evolve from mere lines of code into intelligent systems capable of extraordinary feats.

Picture this: you're sitting at your desk, sipping your morning coffee, when your AI assistant alerts you to an opportunity that could save your company millions. Sounds like science fiction? It's not. Training AI models are the cornerstone of turning this vision into reality. But it's more complex than pressing a button and letting the magic happen. It's more like training a very eager, brilliant puppy that needs to be guided with precision, patience, and much practice.

Let's dive into the fascinating journey of training AI models. This chapter will help you understand how AI models are trained and appreciate the delicate balance between art and science that goes into creating these technological marvels.

In this chapter, we will cover the following key topics:

- Selecting the right algorithms
- Model training and optimization
- Handling bias and fairness in AI

By the end of this chapter, you will be able to understand the crucial steps in training AI models, from choosing appropriate algorithms to optimizing model performance. You'll gain insights into mitigating bias and ensuring fairness in AI systems, equipping you with the knowledge to develop more effective and ethical AI solutions for real-world business challenges.

AI model training – from data to insights

In AI, training models is a complex and nuanced process that combines technical expertise and creative problem-solving. This journey begins with carefully selecting and curating high-quality data and extends through feature engineering, model training, evaluation, and continuous improvement. Each step is crucial in developing AI systems that perform well, provide valuable insights, and adapt to changing environments.

As we explore the intricacies of AI model training, we'll use familiar analogies to demystify complex concepts. From comparing data selection to choosing ingredients for a gourmet meal to likening the training process to kneading dough, these comparisons will help illustrate the delicate balance of art and science in AI development. Whether you're predicting patient outcomes in healthcare, detecting fraud in banking, or uncovering unexpected retail trends, the principles we'll discuss are fundamental to creating robust, effective, and insightful AI models.

The importance of data selection

Imagine you're preparing a gourmet meal. You wouldn't just grab any random ingredients from your pantry. You'd select the freshest, highest-quality produce, spices, and proteins to ensure your dish is perfect. Training an AI model starts similarly, with data selection being paramount. High-quality, diverse data is the backbone of a successful AI model. As the saying goes, "Garbage in, garbage out." Your data's relevance and quality directly influence your AI model's effectiveness.

Consider a healthcare AI system designed to predict patient outcomes. If the dataset includes only young, healthy individuals, the model will likely fail to accurately predict outcomes for older or chronically ill patients. This highlights the necessity of a representative dataset that encompasses the full spectrum of the target population.

The art of feature engineering

Feature engineering is akin to marinating your ingredients to enhance their flavors. It involves selecting the correct variables, creating new features, and transforming existing ones to make them more beneficial for learning. For instance, if you're building a model to predict customer churn, relevant features include customer tenure, purchase history, and engagement metrics. Creating meaningful features can significantly improve your model's performance.

Take the example of a financial model predicting loan defaults. Instead of merely using raw income data, you might create features such as income stability (variability in income over time) and debt-to-income ratio. These engineered features provide more context and can help the model learn more effectively.

The training process

Training an AI model is much like kneading dough. It's an iterative process that involves starting with an initial model, evaluating its performance, making adjustments, and repeating the cycle until you achieve the desired results. This process requires fine-tuning parameters, adjusting the learning rate, and sometimes rethinking your entire approach if the model isn't performing as expected.

Consider a speech recognition system. Initial models might need help with accents or background noise. The system can improve its accuracy and robustness by iteratively refining the model, incorporating more diverse speech data, and tweaking parameters.

Model evaluation

How do you know if your AI model is any good? Evaluation metrics come into play here. Depending on your task, you might use accuracy, precision, recall, F1 score, or a combination of these to measure your model's performance [1]. But remember – a high accuracy sometimes means a good model. It's essential to consider your application's context and specific needs.

For instance, a false negative (missing a disease) might be far more critical in medical diagnosis than a false positive (wrongly diagnosing a disease). Therefore, metrics such as recall (sensitivity) and precision become crucial in such applications.

Continuous learning and improvement

Training an AI model is not a set-it-and-forget-it task. Models must be regularly updated with new data and retrained to remain accurate and relevant. This is particularly important in dynamic fields such as finance or social media, where patterns and trends can change rapidly. It's like tending to a garden; you must constantly nurture and care for your models to keep them flourishing.

Consider a fraud detection system in banking. As fraudsters develop new tactics, the model must be continuously updated with the latest data to recognize new patterns of fraudulent activity.

Unexpected insights

One of the most exciting aspects of training AI models is the unexpected insights they can provide. Sometimes, models reveal patterns and correlations that we humans might miss. For instance, a retail company might discover that umbrella sales spike not only during rainy days but also on days with high pollen counts. These kinds of insights can lead to innovative business strategies and competitive advantages.

So, as we delve deeper into training AI models, remember that it's both an art and a science. It requires technical expertise, creativity, and a willingness to experiment and learn from failures. But the rewards are immense. Successfully trained AI models can transform businesses, drive innovation, and solve some of today's most complex challenges.

The problem – pain points and challenges

Training AI models, while incredibly powerful, presents a host of challenges that can be daunting for businesses. From securing high-quality data to navigating complex algorithms, the journey to a well-trained AI model is fraught with obstacles. Let's dive into some of the most pressing pain points for organizations.

Data quality and availability

The foundation of any AI model is data. However, securing high-quality, diverse data is easier said than done. Businesses often need help with complete, consistent, or biased data, which can lead to inaccurate or unfair models.

Consider a company attempting to build a predictive maintenance model for its manufacturing equipment. If the historical data is sparse or poorly labeled, the model may fail to accurately predict equipment failures. A logistics firm I worked with had years of operational data, but much of it was riddled with inaccuracies and missing entries. We spent months cleaning and validating the data before we could even begin training the model. This delay not only increased costs but also pushed back critical project milestones.

Feature engineering complexity

Transforming raw data into meaningful features is both an art and a science. Identifying the right features that will allow the model to learn effectively can be incredibly challenging. It requires domain expertise and a deep understanding of the data [2].

For instance, features such as transaction frequency, average transaction amount, and geographic location are critical in a bank's fraud detection system. Creating these features from raw transactional data involves complex data wrangling and a thorough understanding of fraudsters' operations. During a project with a financial services company, our team had to work closely with fraud analysts to develop features that captured the nuances of fraudulent behavior, which was a painstaking process.

Additionally, feature engineering can sometimes reveal unexpected correlations. For example, in an e-commerce setting, we discovered that the time of day a purchase was made significantly impacted the likelihood of a return. Incorporating this feature improved our model's accuracy significantly.

Model selection and tuning

Another major hurdle is choosing and tuning the correct algorithm for optimal performance. With so many algorithms available, each with its strengths and weaknesses, selecting the best one for a particular task can be overwhelming.

The problem – pain points and challenges

I once consulted for a retail company that wanted to predict customer churn. We started with a basic logistic regression model, but it quickly became apparent that it needed to capture the complexity of customer behavior. After experimenting with decision trees, random forests, and, finally, **gradient-boosting machines** (**GBMs**), we found a model that significantly improved our predictive accuracy. However, this trial-and-error approach took time and effort.

Moreover, hyperparameter tuning, which involves tweaking the algorithm's settings to improve performance, can be particularly challenging. Grid and random search techniques are commonly used but can be computationally expensive and time-consuming. **Automated machine learning** (**AutoML**) tools are emerging to help address this challenge, but they are not a panacea and still require human oversight and expertise.

Computational resources

Training sophisticated AI models often requires substantial computational power, which can be a significant barrier for many businesses. High-performance GPUs, vast amounts of memory, and scalable cloud infrastructure are essential, but they come at a cost.

A medium-sized e-commerce company I worked with wanted to implement a recommendation system similar to Amazon's. They quickly realized that their existing infrastructure couldn't handle the computational demands of training such a model. They had to invest in cloud-based solutions, which strained their budget and required significant time to integrate and optimize.

Additionally, the cost of computational resources is not just a one-time expense. The operational costs can add up quickly for models that require continuous retraining or real-time processing. Organizations must carefully balance the benefits of advanced models with their infrastructure's financial and logistical constraints.

Interpretability and trust

Once a model is trained, it is crucial to interpret its decisions and build trust in its predictions, especially in high-stakes industries such as healthcare and finance. Many advanced models, such as **deep neural networks** (**DNNs**), are often criticized for being "black boxes."

For instance, a healthcare provider I collaborated with developed an AI model to diagnose diseases. While the model showed high accuracy, the medical professionals hesitated to rely on it because they couldn't understand how it was making its decisions. We had to implement additional techniques, such as **SHapley Additive exPlanations** (**SHAP**) values, to explain the model's predictions. This added another layer of complexity to the project but was essential for gaining the trust of the end users.

In finance, regulators are increasingly scrutinizing AI models to ensure they are fair and transparent. Financial institutions must, therefore, invest in interpretability tools and techniques to explain their models to regulators, auditors, and other stakeholders. This helps build trust and ensures compliance with legal and ethical standards.

Ethical and legal considerations

Ensuring that AI models adhere to ethical standards and comply with legal regulations is an increasingly significant challenge. Issues such as data privacy, bias, and accountability must be carefully managed.

During a project with a multinational corporation, we developed a hiring algorithm designed to streamline their recruitment process. However, we soon discovered that the model was inadvertently biased against specific demographics. Addressing this bias required technical adjustments and a broader conversation about ethical AI practices within the organization [3]. We implemented fairness constraints and regularly monitored the model to ensure it met ethical standards.

Moreover, data privacy regulations such as the **General Data Protection Regulation** (**GDPR**) and the **California Consumer Privacy Act** (**CCPA**) impose strict requirements for collecting, storing, and using data. Businesses must navigate these regulations carefully to avoid hefty fines and reputational damage. This often involves anonymizing data, obtaining explicit user consent, and implementing robust security measures to protect sensitive information.

Continuous learning and maintenance

AI models are not static. They must be continuously updated with new data and retrained to maintain accuracy and relevance. This ongoing maintenance can be resource-intensive and requires a robust strategy for monitoring and updating models.

A real estate company I advised had developed a pricing model for property valuations. Initially, the model performed well, but its accuracy declined as market conditions changed. They realized the importance of creating a continuous learning pipeline to regularly update the model with the latest market data, ensuring it remained accurate and valuable.

In addition to retraining, businesses must monitor their models for performance degradation, drift, and other issues. This requires setting up automated alerts and dashboards to track key metrics and intervene when necessary. Implementing a robust **Machine Learning Operations** (**MLOps**) framework can help streamline these processes and ensure that models remain reliable and effective over time.

Integration with business processes

Integrating AI models into existing business processes is another significant challenge. Even the most accurate model can fail to deliver value if it is not seamlessly integrated into the workflow and adopted by end users.

For example, a sales team might only accept using an AI-driven lead scoring model if it disrupts their established workflow or they trust its recommendations. Successful integration requires technical solutions and change management strategies to ensure employees understand and embrace the new tools.

During a project with a telecommunications company, we developed a customer support chatbot to handle routine inquiries. However, integrating the chatbot with the existing **customer relationship management** (**CRM**) system proved more complex than anticipated. It required extensive collaboration between the AI and IT departments to ensure that data flowed smoothly between the systems and that the chatbot could access and update customer records in real time.

Scaling AI solutions

Once a model is successfully trained and integrated, scaling the solution to handle larger volumes of data or more complex tasks can be challenging. This often involves optimizing the performance model, deploying it on scalable infrastructure, and ensuring it can handle real-world usage demands.

A retail company I worked with wanted to scale its personalized recommendation system to serve millions of customers. This required optimizing the model to run efficiently on large datasets and setting up a scalable deployment architecture using containerization and microservices. Ensuring the system could handle peak loads during holiday shopping seasons added another layer of complexity.

User adoption and feedback

Finally, user adoption and feedback are critical to the success of any AI initiative. Even the most advanced models can fail to deliver value if they are not used effectively by the intended audience. Gathering user feedback, iterating on the model based on their input, and providing training and support are essential to ensure that AI solutions deliver tangible business benefits.

In conclusion, the challenges of training AI models are multifaceted and can be daunting. However, these obstacles can be overcome with a strategic approach and the right resources. In the following sections, we'll explore solutions and best practices to navigate these challenges, turning potential pitfalls into stepping stones for success. As we delve deeper, you'll gain insights and tools to train AI models effectively, transforming complex data into powerful, actionable intelligence.

The solution and process – step-by-step implementation

Effectively training AI models requires a strategic and structured approach. Let's explore a comprehensive, step-by-step guide to implementing solutions that address businesses' common challenges. We'll break this down into three key sections: selecting the right algorithms, model training and optimization, and handling bias and fairness in AI.

Step 1 – selecting the right algorithms

Solution: Choosing the most suitable algorithms for different AI applications is crucial for achieving desired outcomes. The effectiveness of specific algorithms depends on the nature of the problem, the quality and quantity of data, and the computational resources available. For instance, **deep learning** (**DL**) algorithms excel in image and speech recognition tasks because they can handle large, complex datasets. In contrast, simpler algorithms such as logistic regression might be sufficient for binary classification problems with structured data.

Implementation: Here's a step-by-step guide to selecting suitable algorithms:

1. **Understand the problem**:

    - **Define the problem**: Clearly define the problem you are trying to solve. Is it a classification, regression, clustering, or **reinforcement learning** (**RL**) problem? Understanding the problem type helps narrow down the algorithm choices.

    - **Output requirements**: Determine the output requirements and the data type you have (structured, unstructured, text, images, and so on). For example, image data might require **convolutional neural networks** (**CNNs**), while time-series data could benefit from **recurrent neural networks** (**RNNs**).

2. **Assess data characteristics**:

    - **Data volume**: Evaluate the volume of data you have. Large datasets might be well suited for complex models such as DL models, while smaller datasets may perform better with simpler algorithms.

    - **Data variety**: Identify the data types available (numerical, categorical, text, image) and any specific data characteristics, such as missing values, outliers, or imbalances.

    - **Data velocity**: Consider the rate at which data is generated and requires processing. Real-time data may require algorithms optimized for speed and low latency.

3. **Match algorithms to problem type**:

    - **Classification problems**: For tasks such as spam detection, image classification, or sentiment analysis, consider algorithms such as logistic regression, decision trees, random forests, **support vector machines** (**SVMs**), and DL models such as CNNs.

    - **Regression problems**: To predict continuous outcomes such as house prices or stock values, use algorithms such as linear regression, polynomial regression, ridge regression, **Least Absolute Shrinkage and Selection Operator** (**LASSO**), and **neural networks** (**NNs**).

    - **Clustering problems**: To group similar items or identify patterns, consider algorithms such as *k*-means clustering, hierarchical clustering, **Density-Based Spatial Clustering of Applications with Noise** (**DBSCAN**), and **Gaussian mixture models** (**GMMs**).

    - **RL**: For tasks that involve decision-making and reward optimization, such as game playing or robotic control, use algorithms such as Q-learning, **deep Q-networks** (**DQNs**), policy gradient methods, and actor-critic algorithms.

4. **Evaluate computational resources**:

   - **Assess infrastructure**: Evaluate the computational power and memory available. DL models may require high-performance GPUs, while simpler models can run on standard CPUs.

   - **Cloud versus on-premises**: Decide whether to use cloud-based solutions or on-premises infrastructure based on your scalability and cost requirements. Cloud platforms such as **Amazon Web Services** (**AWS**), Azure, and Google Cloud offer powerful tools for training large models.

5. **Experiment and iterate**:

   - **Cross-validation**: Use cross-validation techniques to experiment with different algorithms and evaluate their performance. This helps ensure that the chosen model generalizes well to new data.

   - **Ensemble methods**: Consider hybrid approaches, such as ensemble methods (for example, bagging and boosting), to combine the strengths of multiple algorithms and improve overall performance.

Tools and best practices include the following:

- **AutoML**: Platforms such as AutoML automate algorithm selection and tuning. AutoML tools can save time and help identify the best-performing models with minimal manual intervention.

- **Machine learning (ML) libraries**: Leverage libraries such as `scikit-learn`, `TensorFlow`, and `PyTorch` to implement and experiment with various algorithms. These libraries offer many pre-built models and tools for data preprocessing, model training, and evaluation.

Step 2 – model training and optimization

Solution: Training and optimizing AI models involves a series of best practices and techniques to ensure they learn effectively and perform well. These include data preprocessing, feature engineering, hyperparameter tuning, and regular evaluation.

Implementation: Here's a clear, direct guide to training and optimizing AI models:

1. **Data preprocessing**:

   - **Cleaning**: Handle missing values, remove duplicates, and correct errors in the data. Use imputation for missing values and outlier detection to ensure data quality.

   - **Normalization**: Scale numerical features to ensure a similar range, improving model performance. Techniques such as Min-Max scaling or Z-score normalization can be applied.

   - **Encoding**: Convert categorical variables into numerical values using one-hot or label encoding techniques. For instance, convert categorical features such as `'color'` (red, blue, green) into binary vectors.

2. **Feature engineering**:

    - **Selection**: Identify and select the most relevant features using techniques such as correlation analysis, mutual information, and feature importance scores from models such as random forests.
    - **Creation**: Generate new features from existing ones, such as aggregations (for example, average purchase amount), interactions (for example, the product of age and income), or domain-specific transformations (for example, text embeddings for **natural language processing** (**NLP**) tasks).

3. **Split data**:

    - **Training, validation, test sets**: To evaluate model performance accurately, split the dataset into training, validation, and test sets. A common split is 70% training, 15% validation, and 15% test.

4. **Model training**:

    - **Algorithm selection**: Choose the appropriate algorithm based on the problem type and data characteristics. Refer to the guidelines from the previous section, *Step 1 – selecting the right algorithms*.
    - **Training process**: Train the model using the training dataset, adjusting hyperparameters to optimize performance. Use libraries such as `TensorFlow`, `PyTorch`, and `scikit-learn` to facilitate training.

5. **Hyperparameter tuning**:

    - **Grid search**: Use grid search to systematically explore combinations of hyperparameters. This method tests all possible combinations within a specified range.
    - **Random search**: When the hyperparameter space is large, a random selection of combinations of hyperparameters to test can be more efficient than grid search.
    - **Bayesian optimization**: Use Bayesian optimization techniques to find the optimal set of hyperparameters based on past evaluations.
    - **Cross-validation**: Perform cross-validation to ensure the model generalizes well to unseen data and reduce the overfitting risk.

6. **Model evaluation**:

    - **Evaluation metrics**: Evaluate the model on the validation set using appropriate metrics (accuracy, precision, recall, F1 score, **Root Mean Squared Error** (**RMSE**), and so on). Choose metrics that align with the business goals and the specific problem.

- **Diagnostic tools**: To understand model performance and analyze confusion matrices, use **receiver operating characteristic** (**ROC**) curves and other diagnostic tools. These tools help identify areas where the model may be misclassifying or underperforming.

7. **Regularization and optimization**:

    - **Regularization techniques**: Apply regularization techniques (L1, L2 regularization) to prevent overfitting. Regularization adds a penalty for significant coefficients, encouraging simpler models.

    - **Optimization algorithms**: Use algorithms such as **stochastic gradient descent** (**SGD**), Adam, and RMSprop to improve training efficiency and convergence. These algorithms help adjust the model parameters to minimize the loss function effectively.

8. **Continuous monitoring and retraining**:

    - **Monitor performance**: Set up automated monitoring to track model performance over time. Use dashboards and alert systems to detect any degradation in accuracy or other metrics.

    - **Retrain models**: Regularly retrain models with new data to maintain accuracy and relevance. This is particularly important in dynamic environments where data patterns change frequently.

    - **MLOps framework**: Implement an MLOps framework to automate the monitoring, deployment, and retraining processes. MLOps integrates DevOps practices with ML, ensuring smooth and reliable model operations.

Here is some practical advice:

- **Start simple**: Begin with simpler models and gradually increase complexity as needed. Simpler models are more accessible to interpret and debug.

- **Documentation**: Document your experiments and results to track what works best. Maintain a detailed log of model versions, hyperparameters, and performance metrics.

- **Cloud platforms**: Leverage cloud platforms for scalable training and optimization. Cloud services offer powerful computing resources and tools for efficient model development.

Step 3 – handling bias and fairness in AI

Solution: Ensuring fairness and mitigating bias in AI models is critical for ethical AI development. This involves identifying potential sources of bias, implementing strategies to reduce bias, and continuously monitoring models for fairness.

Implementation: Here's an outline of steps to ensure AI models are free from bias and adhere to fairness standards:

1. **Identify bias**:

   - **Data bias**: Examine your data for imbalances or underrepresented groups. For example, if training a facial recognition model, ensure the dataset includes diverse ethnicities. Use statistical measures to assess representation across different demographic groups.

   - **Label bias**: Check for biased labeling practices that may skew model predictions. Ensure labels are accurate and representative. Conduct manual reviews and use label verification tools to minimize label bias.

   - **Algorithmic bias**: Analyze how different algorithms may introduce or amplify biases. Specific algorithms might favor majority classes or particular feature values. Use fairness-aware algorithms that incorporate fairness constraints during training.

2. **Mitigate bias**:

   - **Balanced datasets**: Ensure your dataset is balanced and representative of the population. Use techniques such as oversampling, undersampling, or synthetic data generation to address imbalances. For instance, in a gender-biased dataset, oversample the minority gender to achieve balance.

   - **Fairness constraints**: Implement fairness constraints during model training to ensure equitable treatment of all groups. These constraints can be incorporated into the loss function or used as postprocessing adjustments.

   - **Bias detection tools**: Utilize tools such as IBM's AI Fairness 360 or Google's What-If Tool to detect and mitigate bias in your models. These tools provide metrics and visualizations to assess fairness and identify sources of bias.

3. **Monitor fairness**:

   - **Regular audits**: Regularly audit your models to identify and address emerging biases. This includes reviewing model performance across different demographic groups. Set up periodic reviews and incorporate fairness checks into your MLOps pipeline.

   - **Stakeholder engagement**: Engage with diverse stakeholders to understand the impact of your models and gather feedback. This helps identify biases that may not be immediately apparent. Conduct focus groups and surveys to collect insights from affected communities.

   - **Transparent reporting**: Maintain transparency in your AI processes by documenting your efforts to address bias and ensure fairness. This builds trust with users and regulators. Publish fairness reports and model cards detailing the measures taken to ensure fairness.

By following these structured steps, businesses can effectively tackle the challenges of training AI models, ensuring they are accurate, fair, and optimized for performance. The journey may be complex, but the rewards are immense with the right approach and tools. Data is transformed into powerful, actionable intelligence that drives innovation and success.

Hypothetical case study – APEX Manufacturing and Distribution

To illustrate the successful application of our framework in training AI models, let's explore the story of APEX Manufacturing and Distribution, a mid-sized company specializing in producing and distributing industrial components. APEX faced several challenges that hindered growth and efficiency, prompting it to explore AI solutions to streamline its citations.

Initial situation

APEX Manufacturing and Distribution was dealing with the following:

- **Inventory management issues**: Overstocking and stockouts were common, leading to high carrying costs and missed sales opportunities
- **Predictive maintenance needs**: Unexpected equipment failures caused significant downtime and production losses
- **Demand forecasting challenges**: Inaccurate demand forecasts led to inefficiencies in production planning and supply chain management

Recognizing AI's potential to address these issues, APEX sought our assistance in developing and implementing AI models tailored to their needs.

Step-by-step implementation

Let's go through the steps that were executed at APEX Manufacturing and Distribution:

Step 1 – understanding the problem and data collection

We began by conducting a thorough analysis of APEX's operations. This involved the following:

- **Inventory management**: We understood their current inventory practices and available data, including historical sales, lead times, and stock levels. We discovered they had an extensive 5-year dataset, but inconsistencies and missing entries plagued it.
- **Equipment maintenance**: Data was collected from sensors on machinery, including usage patterns, maintenance logs, and failure incidents. This data was crucial for developing a predictive maintenance model that could anticipate failures before they occurred.

- **Demand forecasting**: We gathered sales data, market trends, and external factors such as seasonal effects and economic indicators. We also integrated social media and web analytics data to capture real-time trends and customer sentiments.

Step 2 – selecting the right algorithms

Based on the analysis, we identified the following AI applications and corresponding algorithms:

- **Inventory management**: We chose a combination of demand forecasting and optimization algorithms. We used **AutoRegressive Integrated Moving Average (ARIMA)** and **Long Short-Term Memory (LSTM)** networks for forecasting. For optimization, we applied linear programming techniques. The combination allowed us to predict future inventory needs accurately and optimize stock levels.
- **Predictive maintenance**: We selected random forest and GBMs for their robustness in handling time-series sensor data and identifying patterns leading to equipment failures. These algorithms were particularly effective in capturing complex interactions between different sensor readings.
- **Demand forecasting**: To improve forecast accuracy, we combined traditional statistical methods such as ARIMA with advanced ML techniques, including XGBoost and LSTM networks. This hybrid approach leveraged the strengths of both methods to provide more reliable predictions.

Step 3 – data preprocessing and feature engineering

Next, we focused on data preprocessing and feature engineering:

- **Data cleaning**: We handled missing values, removed duplicates, and corrected any inaccuracies in the data. For example, we addressed gaps in sensor data by interpolating missing values and removing outliers from sales data using Z-score analysis.
- **Normalization and encoding**: Using one-hot encoding, we normalized numerical features to ensure consistent scales and encoded categorical variables, such as product categories and machine types. This step was crucial for ensuring the algorithms could process the data effectively.
- **Feature creation**: We generated new features such as moving sales averages, lagged variables to capture trends, and interaction terms between different product categories and seasons. For predictive maintenance, we created features that captured the duration since the last maintenance and the average usage intensity.

Step 4 – model training and hyperparameter tuning

We then proceeded with training and optimizing the models:

- **Training models**: We used the preprocessed data to train our selected algorithms. For instance, we trained the LSTM network on historical sales data to capture long-term dependencies and patterns. The training process involved multiple iterations to refine the model and improve its accuracy.

- **Hyperparameter tuning**: We applied grid and random search techniques to fine-tune hyperparameters. For the random forest model used in predictive maintenance, we tuned the number of trees and the depth of each tree to balance performance and computational efficiency. Bayesian optimization was also employed to optimize the hyperparameters of the LSTM networks.
- **Cross-validation**: We employed cross-validation to ensure our models were generalizing well to unseen data. This involved splitting the data into training, validation, and test sets and iteratively testing the models. We used *k*-fold cross-validation to assess the models' robustness and prevent overfitting.

Step 5 – model evaluation and deployment

After training, we evaluated and deployed the models:

- **Evaluation metrics**: We used metrics such as **Mean Absolute Error (MAE)** for demand forecasting, precision and recall for predictive maintenance, and service level and carrying costs for inventory optimization. These metrics provided a comprehensive view of the models' performance.
- **Performance analysis**: Our models demonstrated significant improvements. For example, the LSTM model reduced the MAE in demand forecasts by 20%, and the random forest model increased the precision of failure predictions by 15%. The linear programming optimization model improved the inventory turnover ratio by 25%.
- **Deployment**: We integrated the models into APEX's existing systems. The demand forecasting model was linked to their ERP system for real-time updates, while the predictive maintenance model was connected to the IoT platform monitoring equipment health. We also developed a custom dashboard for inventory management that provided actionable insights and alerts.

Step 6 – continuous monitoring and maintenance

To ensure the longevity and relevance of the models, we implemented a continuous monitoring and maintenance plan:

- **Automated monitoring**: We set up automated monitoring to track the models' performance over time. This included real-time alerts for any significant deviations in predictions or model accuracy.
- **Regular updates**: To maintain their accuracy, the models were regularly updated with new data. For instance, the demand forecasting model was retrained monthly with the latest sales data, and the predictive maintenance model was updated with new sensor readings.
- **User feedback**: We collected feedback from APEX's staff to improve the models continuously. This feedback loop helped identify any practical issues and provided insights into further enhancements.

Results achieved

The implementation of AI models brought transformative results for APEX Manufacturing and Distribution:

- **Improved inventory management**: The optimization model reduced excess inventory by 30% and minimized stockouts, resulting in a 15% reduction in carrying costs. The improved inventory turnover ratio also freed up capital previously tied up in overstocked items.

- **Enhanced predictive maintenance**: The predictive maintenance model decreased unexpected equipment failures by 25%, significantly reducing downtime and maintenance costs. This improvement translated into an increase in **overall equipment effectiveness** (**OEE**) by 10%.

- **Accurate demand forecasting**: The enhanced demand forecasting accuracy led to better production planning, reduced waste, and timely order fulfillment. This improved customer satisfaction and increased sales by 10%. The accurate forecasts also allowed APEX to negotiate better terms with suppliers based on predicted demand.

The journey with APEX Manufacturing and Distribution exemplifies the power of AI in transforming business operations. Following a structured approach, from problem identification to model deployment, we achieved tangible results that drove efficiency, reduced costs, and enhanced competitiveness. This case study serves as a testament to the potential of AI when applied thoughtfully and strategically, providing valuable lessons and inspiration for other businesses embarking on their AI journey. The success of this project not only improved APEX's operational performance but also highlighted the importance of continuous learning and adaptation in the ever-evolving landscape of AI.

Reflection and practical next steps

As we wrap up this journey through the intricacies of AI model training, take a moment to reflect on the key insights we've explored. Think about how the process of selecting high-quality data resonates with your own experiences. Have you ever encountered a situation where poor data quality led to unreliable results? Consider how the art of feature engineering might apply to your current problems. Are there creative ways you could transform your existing data to uncover new insights?

Let's challenge ourselves to apply these concepts in our daily work or personal projects. Ask yourself the following questions:

- How can I improve the quality and diversity of the data I'm working with?
- What unexpected features or combinations might provide valuable insights into my current projects?
- Am I evaluating my models effectively, considering my applications' specific context and needs?
- How can I implement a continuous learning and improvement system in my AI initiatives?

These questions aren't just theoretical – they're stepping stones to practical improvements. Maybe you've realized that your customer churn prediction model could benefit from more diverse data sources.

Or perhaps you've identified an opportunity to create more meaningful features in your financial risk assessment tool. These realizations are the first step toward tangible progress.

Let's turn these reflections into action. Here are some practical next steps you can take:

1. **Data audit**: Conduct a thorough review of your current data sources. Identify any gaps or biases in your datasets. Can you integrate new data sources to provide a more comprehensive view?
2. **Feature engineering workshop**: Organize a brainstorming session with your team. Challenge each other to think creatively about new features that enhance your models. Remember – sometimes, the most insightful features come from unexpected combinations or transformations of existing data.
3. **Evaluation metric review**: Reassess the metrics you use to evaluate your models. Are they truly aligned with your business objectives? Consider implementing a more holistic evaluation framework that captures the nuanced performance requirements of your specific application.
4. **Continuous learning plan**: Develop a structured plan for regularly updating and retraining your models. This could involve setting up automated data pipelines, scheduling periodic model reviews, or establishing a feedback loop with end users to capture evolving needs and patterns.
5. **Ethical AI checklist**: Create a checklist for ensuring fairness and mitigating bias in your AI models. Make this a standard part of your development process, fostering a culture of responsible AI within your organization.

Remember – the journey of AI model training is ongoing. Each step you take to improve your approach brings you closer to more accurate, insightful, and impactful AI solutions. Whether working on a small personal project or leading a large-scale AI initiative, these principles can guide you toward success.

So, what's your next move? Perhaps it's as simple as scheduling that data audit or as ambitious as revamping your entire model evaluation process. Whatever it is, take that first step today. The world of AI is constantly evolving, and by actively applying these strategies, you're not just keeping pace – you're positioning yourself at the forefront of innovation.

Embrace the challenges, celebrate the unexpected insights, and, most importantly, keep learning and experimenting. Your journey in mastering AI model training is just beginning, and the possibilities are endless. What exciting discoveries will your next AI project unveil?

Summary

In this chapter, we navigated the intricate landscape of training AI models, from selecting high-quality data to the art of feature engineering and the iterative model refinement process. You learned that training an AI model is both a science and an art, requiring technical expertise and creative problem-solving. We explored how to evaluate model performance, the importance of continuous learning, and the potential for AI to uncover unexpected insights. Remember – the journey doesn't end with a trained model; it's an ongoing process of improvement and adaptation.

As you reflect on these concepts, consider how you might apply them to your projects or challenges. Whether you're fine-tuning a recommendation system or developing a predictive maintenance model, the principles we've discussed form the foundation of effective AI development. Our next chapter will build on this knowledge as we explore the crucial step of deploying AI solutions. We'll examine how to take your carefully trained models from the development environment to real-world applications, ensuring they deliver value and perform reliably in production settings.

Questions

1. What analogy describes the importance of data selection in AI model training?
2. How does feature engineering improve an AI model's performance?
3. Why is the training process for AI models described as iterative?
4. Name the evaluation metrics mentioned in the chapter for assessing AI model performance.
5. In medical diagnosis, why might recall be a more critical metric than precision?
6. How is continuous learning and improvement in AI models compared to gardening?
7. What unexpected insight about umbrella sales was discovered by an AI model, as mentioned in the chapter?
8. Why is it said that training AI models requires technical expertise and creativity?
9. How might poor data quality affect the performance of an AI model predicting patient outcomes in healthcare?
10. What steps were suggested in the *Reflection and practical next steps* section for implementing continuous learning in AI initiatives?

References

1. *Python for Geeks*. packtpub.com. `https://www.packtpub.com/product/python-for-geeks/9781801070119`
2. DPG Webinar. *Art of Feature Engineering for Machine Learning – DataPlatformGeeks*. `https://www.dataplatformgeeks.com/events/dpg-webinar-17th-october-2019-0300-pm-0400-pm-ist-sandip-pani-art-of-feature-engineering-for-machine-learning/`
3. machinelearninghowto.com. *The Role of Machine Learning in Cybersecurity: Detecting and Preventing Threats - Machine Learning how to*. `https://machinelearninghowto.com/the-role-of-machine-learning-in-cybersecurity/`

11
Deploying AI Solutions

When deploying AI, whether you focus on top-line growth or bottom-line profitability, start with the customer and work backward.

– Rob Garf

Have you ever wondered how your favorite streaming service always seems to know precisely what you want to watch next? Or how your online shopping cart gets eerily populated with items you didn't even realize you needed? The magic behind these personalized experiences results from meticulously deployed AI solutions. But what if I told you that behind every seamless AI interaction lies a labyrinth of complexities and challenges that can make or break its success?

Imagine that deploying AI solutions is like orchestrating a grand symphony. Each component – data, algorithms, infrastructure, and user interaction – plays a crucial role, and even the slightest discord can disrupt the entire performance. But when done right, it creates a harmony that feels almost magical to the end user.

Deploying AI is more than just flipping a switch; it's akin to launching a space mission where precision, timing, and meticulous planning are paramount. One miscalculation could cause the whole operation to fail. But unlike rocket science, AI deployment is a journey you can learn and master with the proper guidance and patience.

Consider this: many AI projects never make it past the experimental stage. They languish in what some call the "AI Graveyard," where great ideas die due to poor planning, lack of scalability, or insufficient integration with existing systems. Yet, those who succeed in deploying AI solutions reap transformative benefits, from increased efficiency and cost savings to new revenue streams and competitive advantages.

Let's take a real-world example to illustrate the stakes. Imagine a global retailer aiming to implement an AI-driven supply chain optimization tool. The goal is to reduce stockouts and overstock situations, thus saving millions annually. However, with proper deployment, this ambitious project could continue. Inaccurate data integration, underestimating computational power needs, or failing to align the tool with actual business processes could all lead to a costly failure.

Now, let's flip the script. Picture a healthcare provider deploying an AI system to predict patient readmissions. By meticulously planning every step – from data collection and model training to integration with electronic health records and staff training – the provider can significantly reduce readmission rates, improve patient outcomes, and save millions in penalties. This is not science fiction; it's happening today, transforming industries and improving lives.

Deploying AI solutions is a journey filled with insights, challenges, and opportunities. Along the way, we'll uncover surprising facts, share real-world stories, and provide actionable advice to empower you to transform your AI initiatives from concept to reality.

In this chapter, we will cover the following topics:

- Scaling from prototype to production
- **Continuous integration and continuous deployment (CI/CD) for AI**
- Monitoring and maintaining AI systems

By the end of this chapter, you will be able to understand the key challenges in deploying AI solutions at scale, implementing effective CI/CD pipelines tailored for AI projects, and establishing robust strategies for monitoring and maintaining AI systems in production environments. You'll gain practical insights into transitioning AI prototypes to full-scale production systems, ensuring their ongoing reliability and performance, and addressing common pitfalls in AI deployment.

The problem – pain points and challenges

Deploying AI solutions in a business environment can feel like navigating a minefield. Despite AI's immense potential, the journey from prototype to production is fraught with challenges that can derail even the most promising projects. Let's explore some key pain points for organizations, illustrating them with compelling examples and insightful analysis.

Scaling from prototype to production

One of the most significant hurdles in deploying AI solutions is scaling from a successful prototype to a full-fledged production system. During the prototype phase, everything works smoothly. The model performs well on test data, and the team is optimistic about its potential. However, transitioning to production often reveals hidden complexities.

Consider a mid-sized retail company that developed a recommendation engine to personalize customer shopping experiences. The prototype was a hit, showing impressive accuracy in recommending products. However, when scaling up, they encountered data volume and variability issues. The model needed help to handle the real-time data influx, leading to slow response times and inaccurate recommendations. The company had to invest heavily in infrastructure upgrades and data engineering efforts to make the solution viable at scale.

In another instance, a logistics firm created an AI model to optimize delivery routes. The prototype, tested in a controlled environment with a limited dataset, significantly reduced delivery times. However, the model's performance dropped when deployed across multiple cities with varying traffic conditions and delivery schedules. The increased complexity of real-world variables overwhelmed the system, necessitating a redesign of the model to handle broader and more dynamic data.

Managing CI/CD for AI

Continuous Integration and **Continuous Deployment (CI/CD)** are critical for maintaining and updating AI models. However, implementing CI/CD for AI poses unique challenges compared to traditional software development. AI models require frequent retraining with new data, and changes in data distribution can unpredictably impact model performance.

A financial services firm faced this issue when deploying an AI system for fraud detection. They set up a CI/CD pipeline to continuously update the model with new transaction data. However, they found that model retraining caused fluctuations in performance. Some updates improved detection rates, while others inadvertently increased false positives, frustrating customers. The firm had to implement rigorous validation processes and rollback mechanisms to ensure stability and reliability in its CI/CD pipeline.

Furthermore, integrating CI/CD with AI requires specialized tools and practices. AI models often depend on large datasets and complex processing, unlike traditional software. Ensuring these elements are correctly versioned, tested, and deployed requires a sophisticated setup. For example, a CI/CD pipeline for an AI-driven marketing recommendation engine must manage not just the code but also the datasets, feature engineering processes, and hyperparameters. Any change in these components can have significant downstream effects on model performance.

Ongoing monitoring and maintenance

Deploying an AI solution is not a one-time event; it requires ongoing monitoring and maintenance to ensure sustained performance. Models can degrade over time due to changes in data patterns, a phenomenon known as model drift [1]. External factors such as regulatory changes or market dynamics can also necessitate model adjustments.

Take the case of a healthcare provider using AI to predict patient readmissions. Initially, the system performed admirably, reducing readmission rates and improving patient care. However, changes in patient demographics and treatment protocols led to a decline in model accuracy. The healthcare provider had to establish a robust monitoring framework, including regular performance audits and retraining schedules, to maintain the model's effectiveness.

Another example is an e-commerce platform that uses AI to detect fraudulent transactions. When initially deployed, the model effectively identified fraudulent activities. However, as fraud tactics evolved, the model's effectiveness waned. The company had to continuously update the model with new fraud patterns and incorporate feedback from human analysts to keep the system robust. This ongoing maintenance required dedicated resources and a proactive approach to model management.

Integrating AI with business processes

Integration with existing business processes is often underestimated but is crucial for the success of AI solutions. AI systems must work seamlessly with other software and operational workflows to provide value. Misalignment can lead to inefficiencies and user resistance.

For instance, an insurance company implemented an AI tool to automate claims processing. While the AI performed well in isolation, integrating it with the company's legacy systems was a nightmare. Data transfer between systems could have been faster and it was more error-prone, causing employee delays and frustration. The project required a complete overhaul of the integration approach, including updating legacy systems and implementing new data pipelines to facilitate smooth interactions.

Addressing ethical and compliance issues

Deploying AI solutions also brings ethical and compliance challenges. Ensuring that AI models adhere to ethical standards and regulatory requirements is vital to avoid legal pitfalls and maintain public trust.

Consider a social media platform that deployed an AI model to moderate content. While the model efficiently flagged inappropriate content, it also disproportionately targeted posts from specific user groups, leading to accusations of bias. The company faced a public relations crisis and regulatory scrutiny. To address this, they had to thoroughly audit their AI system, implement fairness checks, and establish transparency measures to rebuild trust.

The solution and implementation process

Deploying AI solutions effectively requires a structured and well-planned approach. Here, we present a comprehensive solution to the earlier challenges, focusing on transitioning from prototype to production, implementing CI/CD for AI, and ensuring ongoing monitoring and maintenance. Our step-by-step guide will provide practical advice and actionable insights, making the implementation process transparent and accessible.

From prototype to production

Successfully transitioning AI prototypes to full-scale production systems is no small feat. It involves careful planning, rigorous testing, and a strategic approach to scalability.

The methodology for transitioning AI prototypes includes the following:

- **Evaluate prototype performance**: Start by thoroughly evaluating your prototype's performance. Ensure that it meets the desired accuracy, precision, and recall metrics. Cross-validation and A/B testing will validate the results across different datasets.
- **Assess scalability requirements**: Determine the scalability requirements for your AI solution. This involves understanding the expected data volume, processing power, and infrastructure needed to support the system at full scale.

- **Design for scalability**: Architect your system to handle increased load. This may involve optimizing your data pipelines, using distributed computing frameworks such as Apache Spark, and ensuring your models can process data in parallel.
- **Develop robust data pipelines**: Ensure your pipelines handle real-time data ingestion, processing, and storage. Use technologies such as Apache Kafka for real-time data streaming and ETL tools to manage data transformations.
- **Implement load testing**: Conduct load testing to simulate the production environment. This will help identify potential bottlenecks and performance issues before the system goes live.
- **Deploy in phases**: Roll out the AI solution in phases. Start with a small user group or region and gradually expand as you gain confidence in the system's performance and stability [2].
- **Monitor and iterate**: Continuously monitor the system's performance and gather feedback. Use this data to make iterative improvements and ensure the solution scales effectively.

However, there are some critical steps and considerations to be accounted for as well:

- **Data management**: Ensure data quality, consistency, and availability. Implement data governance policies to manage the data lifecycle and compliance.
- **Model optimization**: Regularly retrain and fine-tune models to adapt to changing data patterns and maintain accuracy.
- **Infrastructure**: Leverage cloud services for scalable infrastructure. Use auto-scaling features to handle variable workloads efficiently.

CI/CD for AI

Implementing CI/CD practices tailored for AI projects is essential for effectively maintaining and updating models. Here's a comprehensive guide to setting up CI/CD pipelines for AI projects.

Frameworks for CI/CD in AI are as follows:

- **Version control for code and data**: Use version control systems such as Git for code and tools such as **Data Version Control** (**DVC**) for managing datasets and model files. This ensures reproducibility and traceability.
- **Automated testing**: Implement automated testing for your AI models. This includes unit tests for data preprocessing code, integration tests for data pipelines, and model performance tests.
- **Continuous integration**: Set up a CI pipeline using tools such as Jenkins or GitLab CI. This pipeline should automatically trigger tests and validations whenever new code or data is committed.
- **Model validation**: Include model validation steps in your CI pipeline. This involves evaluating model performance on validation datasets and comparing it to predefined benchmarks.

- **Artifact management**: Store trained models in artifact repositories, ensuring each version is appropriately documented and accessible for deployment.
- **Continuous deployment**: Set up a CD pipeline that automates the deployment of models to production. Use containerization technologies such as Docker and orchestration tools such as Kubernetes for seamless deployment.
- **Monitoring and rollback mechanisms**: Implement monitoring tools to track model performance in production. Set up automated rollback mechanisms to revert to previous versions if performance degrades.

Items to keep in mind for CI/CD pipelines are as follows:

- **Define pipeline stages**: Identify and define each stage of your CI/CD pipeline, including code testing, model training, validation, and deployment.
- **Use Infrastructure as Code (IaC)**: Implement IaC practices to manage your deployment infrastructure. Tools such as Terraform and AWS CloudFormation can help automate infrastructure provisioning.
- **Security and compliance**: Ensure your CI/CD pipeline adheres to security best practices and requirements. This includes securing data access, encrypting sensitive information, and performing regular security audits.

Monitoring and maintaining AI systems

Effective monitoring and maintenance are crucial for ensuring the reliability and performance of AI systems in production [3]. Here are strategies and best practices to achieve this.

Strategies for monitoring AI systems:

- **Performance monitoring**: Continuously track key performance metrics such as accuracy, precision, recall, and latency. Monitoring tools such as Prometheus and Grafana can visualize and alert performance anomalies.
- **Model drift detection**: Implement techniques to detect model drift, where the model's performance degrades due to changes in data patterns. Use statistical methods and continuous validation to monitor drift.
- **Logging and auditing**: Maintain detailed logs of model predictions, data inputs, and system activities. This helps debug issues and conduct audits to ensure compliance.
- **User feedback integration**: Incorporate feedback mechanisms to collect user input on model performance. Use this feedback to refine and improve the models.

Best practices for ongoing maintenance are as follows:

- **Regular retraining**: Schedule regular retraining of models using updated data to maintain performance and adapt to new trends
- **System health checks**: Perform regular health checks on the entire AI system, including data pipelines, model servers, and deployment infrastructure
- **Proactive incident management**: Establish a proactive incident management process to address and resolve any issues that arise in production quickly

Aligning AI with business processes

Seamless alignment of AI solutions with existing business processes is crucial for realizing their full potential. The process begins with thoroughly mapping existing workflows that will interact with the AI system, helping you identify potential friction points and integration opportunities. Engaging key stakeholders from different departments early in the integration process ensures that the AI solution aligns with business needs and workflows. Developing robust APIs facilitates smooth communication between the AI system and existing software, allowing for more flexible and scalable integration.

Optimizing data pipelines is essential to ensure efficient and accurate data transfer between systems, which may involve implementing ETL processes or real-time data streaming solutions. Designing intuitive user interfaces seamlessly incorporating AI functionalities into existing workflows reduces the learning curve and improves user adoption. Implementing the AI solution in phases, starting with non-critical processes and allowing for testing and refinement before full-scale deployment, is often beneficial. Where necessary, legacy systems may need to be updated to better interface with modern AI solutions, which might involve system upgrades or implementing middleware solutions. Throughout this process, providing ongoing training to employees on effectively using and interacting with the new AI-enhanced processes is crucial for successful adoption.

Navigating ethical and compliance issues

Ensuring ethical deployment and regulatory compliance of AI solutions is paramount for maintaining trust and avoiding legal issues. This begins with establishing a clear ethical framework for AI development and deployment within your organization, aligning with company values and industry best practices. Implementing rigorous testing processes to detect and mitigate biases in AI models, including using diverse datasets and employing fairness metrics in model evaluation, is crucial. Developing methods to make AI decision-making processes more transparent and explainable builds user trust and satisfies regulatory requirements.

Ensuring that AI systems adhere to data protection regulations such as GDPR and CCPA and implementing robust data anonymization and security measures is non-negotiable. Regular ethical and compliance audits of AI systems help identify potential issues before they escalate into larger problems. Establishing an ethical review board to oversee AI projects and provide guidance on ethical considerations can provide valuable oversight. Maintaining detailed documentation of AI development processes, decision-making criteria, and model behaviors supports accountability and helps address future concerns.

Engaging with external stakeholders, including users, regulators, and ethics experts, gathers diverse perspectives on the ethical implications of your AI solutions. Implementing ongoing monitoring systems to track the ethical performance of AI models in production allows for quick identification and resolution of emerging ethical issues. Finally, providing ethics training to AI development teams ensures they understand and can apply ethical principles in their work. By addressing these aspects of integration and ethical deployment, organizations can significantly improve the success rate of their AI implementations while maintaining public trust and regulatory compliance.

Hypothetical case study – APEX Manufacturing and Distribution

APEX Manufacturing and Distribution, a mid-sized company specializing in industrial machinery, faced several challenges in its operations. Despite having a solid reputation in the industry, APEX struggled with inefficiencies in its supply chain, leading to frequent stockouts and overstock situations. These issues caused delays in production schedules, increased operational costs, and frustrated customers. Additionally, their manual inventory management system is needed to help keep up with their product lines' growing demand and complexity.

Step 1 – assessment and prototype development

Our journey with APEX began with a thorough assessment of their current operations. We identified key pain points, including the following:

- **Inefficient inventory management**: The manual system was prone to errors and unable to provide real-time inventory updates
- **Production delays**: Frequent stockouts caused production halts, while overstocking led to unnecessary storage costs
- **Customer dissatisfaction**: Delayed deliveries affected customer satisfaction and loyalty

We proposed developing an AI-driven supply chain optimization tool to address these issues. We started with a prototype that used historical sales data to predict demand and optimize inventory levels [4]. The prototype showed promising results, with a 20% improvement in demand forecasting accuracy during initial testing.

Step 2 – scaling from prototype to production

Transitioning the successful prototype to a full-scale production system required careful planning and execution. Here's how we did it:

- **Infrastructure upgrade**: We upgraded APEX's infrastructure to support the increased data volume and computational requirements. This included migrating to a cloud-based platform with scalable storage and processing capabilities.
- **Data pipeline development**: We developed robust data pipelines using Apache Kafka for real-time data streaming and ETL tools to manage data transformations. This ensured that the AI model received timely and accurate data.
- **Model optimization**: We fine-tuned the AI model to handle the variability in real-world data. This involved retraining the model with additional datasets and optimizing hyperparameters to improve performance.
- **Load testing**: We conducted extensive load testing to ensure the system could handle peak loads. This helped us identify and address potential bottlenecks before going live.
- **Phased deployment**: We rolled out the AI solution in phases, starting with a small subset of products. This allowed us to monitor performance, gather feedback, and make necessary adjustments before a full-scale launch [5].

Step 3 – implementing CI/CD for AI

We established a robust workflow to ensure a reliable, efficient, and scalable AI deployment. This process ensured consistent performance, adaptability to new data, and the ability to scale as the business grows:

- **Version control**: We used Git for code versioning and DVC for managing datasets and model files. This ensured the reproducibility and traceability of model versions.
- **Automated testing**: We set up automated tests for data preprocessing, model training, and performance validation. This helped catch issues early and ensure the integrity of the AI system.
- **Continuous integration**: Using Jenkins, we created a CI pipeline that automatically triggered tests and validations whenever new code or data was committed. This streamlined the development process and maintained code quality.
- **Model validation and deployment**: Our CI pipeline included model validation steps to evaluate performance on validation datasets. Successful models were deployed using Docker and Kubernetes, ensuring a consistent and scalable deployment process.
- **Monitoring and rollback mechanisms**: We implemented monitoring tools such as Prometheus and Grafana to track model performance in production. Automated rollback mechanisms were set up to revert to previous versions if performance degraded.

Step 4 – monitoring and maintenance

To ensure the ongoing reliability of the AI system, we established comprehensive monitoring and maintenance strategies:

- **Performance monitoring**: Performance metrics such as accuracy, recall, and latency were continuously tracked. Alerts were set up to notify the team of any anomalies.
- **Model drift detection**: Using updated data, we implemented statistical methods to detect model drift and scheduled regular model retraining sessions.
- **User feedback integration**: Feedback mechanisms were incorporated to collect input from APEX employees using the system. This feedback was crucial for iterative improvements and addressing any usability issues.
- **Regular health checks:** We conducted health checks on the entire AI system, including data pipelines, model servers, and deployment infrastructure. This proactive approach helped maintain system stability and performance.

Results achieved

The successful deployment of the AI-driven supply chain optimization tool brought transformative results for APEX Manufacturing and Distribution:

- **Improved inventory management**: The AI system provided real-time inventory updates and optimized stock levels, reducing stockouts by 30% and overstock situations by 25%
- **Enhanced production efficiency**: Better inventory management decreased production delays significantly, resulting in a 20% increase in production efficiency
- **Increased customer satisfaction**: Timely deliveries and improved product availability boosted customer satisfaction scores by 40%
- **Cost savings**: APEX saw a 15% reduction in operational costs due to optimized inventory levels and reduced storage expenses

Relatable anecdote – the turning point

During one of our feedback sessions, an APEX warehouse manager shared a story that perfectly encapsulated the impact of the AI solution. Previously, the manager would spend hours manually reconciling inventory records and placing weekly orders. These tasks were automated with the new AI system, freeing his time to focus on more strategic activities. He mentioned, "It's like having an extra pair of hands that never tire and always get it right. Our team can now focus on what truly matters – improving our processes and serving our customers better."

Reflection and practical next steps

Before we conclude this chapter, it's time to pause and reflect on our journey through the complex landscape of AI deployment. Whether you're a data scientist, IT manager, or business leader, the challenges and strategies we've discussed will likely resonate with your experiences or future aspirations in AI.

Think back to when you faced the exhilarating – and perhaps daunting – task of moving an AI project from a promising prototype to a full-fledged production system. Did you experience the thrill of seeing your model perform well in controlled conditions, only to face unexpected hurdles when scaling up? Or maybe you're still in the planning stages, envisioning how an AI solution could revolutionize your organization's operations, much like it did for APEX Manufacturing and Distribution.

Let's dive deeper with some thought-provoking questions to challenge our understanding and readiness:

- **Infrastructure readiness**: How prepared is your organization's technical infrastructure to handle the demands of AI deployment? Consider aspects such as these:
  - Do you have scalable computing resources on-premise or in the cloud?
  - Are your data storage solutions capable of handling the volume and velocity of data required for AI operations?
  - Is your network infrastructure robust enough to support real-time data streaming and model serving?

- **Data pipeline maturity**: Reflect on your current data processes:
  - How efficient and reliable are your data collection and preprocessing pipelines?
  - Can your systems handle real-time data ingestion and transformation?
  - Do you have mechanisms in place to ensure data quality and consistency?

- **CI/CD implementation**: If you were to implement a CI/CD pipeline for your AI projects tomorrow, consider the following:
  - What would be your biggest technical hurdle? Is it automating model training, implementing robust testing, or ensuring smooth deployment?
  - How would you manage version control for both code and data?
  - Are your team members familiar with DevOps practices and tools such as Jenkins, Docker, or Kubernetes?

- **Monitoring and maintenance strategy**: Considering the ongoing care of AI systems, think about the following:

    - Do you have a proactive approach to detecting model drift and performance degradation?
    - How would you handle retraining and redeploying models without disrupting ongoing operations?
    - Are you equipped to explain model decisions, especially in regulated industries?

- **Organizational readiness**: Beyond technical aspects, consider the following:

    - How aligned are your AI initiatives with broader business objectives?
    - Is there buy-in from leadership and end users for AI adoption?
    - Do you have the right mix of skills in your team, spanning data science, engineering, and domain expertise?

These questions are designed to spark critical thinking about your AI deployment readiness and identify areas for growth. Now, let's translate this reflection into actionable steps:

1. **Conduct a comprehensive AI readiness assessment**:

    - **Technical infrastructure**: Evaluate your computing, storage, and networking capabilities. If you're not leveraging cloud services, consider a pilot project to test scalability and flexibility.
    - **Data management**: Audit your data pipelines. Look for bottlenecks, quality issues, and opportunities for automation. Tools such as Apache NiFi and Airflow can help streamline data workflows.
    - **Skills gap analysis**: Assess your team's capabilities across data science, engineering, and DevOps. Identify training needs or potential new hires to fill critical gaps.

2. **Start small, but think strategically**:

    - **Choose a pilot project**: Select a manageable AI project aligning with a business need. For instance, if you're in retail, you might start with a demand forecasting model for a specific product category.
    - **Define clear success metrics**: Establish KPIs that tie directly to business value, such as reduced stockouts or improved customer satisfaction scores.
    - **Plan for scalability**: Even as you start small, design your pilot with future scaling in mind. This might involve choosing cloud-native technologies or implementing modular architecture.

3. **Build a CI/CD sandbox for AI**:

    - **Set up a test environment**: Create a controlled environment to experiment with CI/CD pipelines tailored for AI. Use tools such as GitLab CI or Jenkins for automation.

    - **Implement version control for everything**: Use Git for code versioning and explore tools such as DVC for managing datasets and model artifacts.

    - **Automate testing**: Develop a suite of tests covering data validation, model performance, and integration checks. Tools such as pytest for Python can be invaluable here.

4. **Cultivate a culture of continuous monitoring**:

    - **Implement monitoring tools**: Set up dashboards using tools such as Prometheus and Grafana to track model performance, data drift, and system health.

    - **Establish alert mechanisms**: Define thresholds for key metrics and set up alerting systems to notify relevant team members when issues arise.

    - **Regular audits**: Schedule periodic reviews of your AI systems, examining technical performance, business impact, and ethical considerations.

5. **Invest in knowledge and best practices**:

    - **Continuous learning**: Allocate time and resources for your team to stay updated on AI deployment best practices. This could involve online courses, attending conferences, or bringing in external trainers.

    - **Create internal knowledge bases**: Document lessons learned, best practices, and common pitfalls specific to your organization's AI journey.

    - **Foster a community of practice**: Encourage knowledge sharing across teams and departments. This could be through regular tech talks, hackathons, or collaborative projects.

6. **Engage stakeholders across the organization**:

    - **Education sessions**: Conduct workshops for non-technical stakeholders to demystify AI and its potential impact on the business.

    - **Feedback loops**: Establish mechanisms for end users to provide feedback on AI systems. This could be through regular surveys or user testing sessions.

    - **Showcase success**: Regularly communicate the wins and learnings from your AI initiatives to build enthusiasm and support across the organization.

Remember, the journey of AI deployment is not a sprint but a marathon. Each step you take, no matter how small, moves you closer to harnessing AI's full potential in your organization. The key is to start, learn, and continuously improve.

As you progress, keep the lessons from APEX Manufacturing and Distribution in mind. Their story illustrates that, with careful planning, phased implementation, and a commitment to continuous improvement, AI can transform operations and drive significant business value. They didn't just focus on the technical aspects and ensured that their AI solution integrated seamlessly with existing business processes and addressed real pain points.

So, what will your first step be? Perhaps it's initiating a discussion with your leadership team about conducting an AI readiness assessment. Maybe it's revisiting an AI prototype sitting on the shelf and planning its path to production. Or it could be as simple as setting up a small data science sandbox environment where your team can experiment with CI/CD practices for machine learning models.

Whatever your starting point, approach it confidently, knowing you're now equipped with insights and strategies to guide your path. Remember, every tech giant started with a single line of code, and every successful AI deployment began with a single step.

The future of AI is not just about groundbreaking algorithms or massive computing power – it's about successfully deploying these innovations in the real world, creating tangible value, and driving meaningful change. You're now part of that future. Embrace the challenges, celebrate the successes, and keep pushing forward. Your AI deployment journey starts now, and the possibilities are limitless!

Summary

In this chapter, we navigated the complex terrain of deploying AI solutions, from scaling prototypes to production to implementing robust CI/CD pipelines and maintaining AI systems in the wild. You gained insights into the challenges that organizations such as APEX Manufacturing face and learned practical strategies to overcome them. Successful AI deployment isn't just about cutting-edge algorithms – it's also about thoughtful integration, continuous monitoring, and alignment with business objectives.

Consider how you might apply them in your context. Whether you're fine-tuning your first model or managing a fleet of AI systems, the principles we've explored – scalability, reliability, and continuous improvement – will serve as your compass. But our journey doesn't end here. As we venture into AI systems, we must consider their broader implications.

In the next chapter, we'll explore the critical realm of AI governance and ethics. As AI becomes more prevalent in our lives and businesses, understanding how to deploy these systems responsibly and ethically is paramount. We'll delve into the frameworks and considerations that ensure our AI solutions perform well and align with our values and societal norms.

Questions

1. What is one of the main challenges in scaling an AI prototype to a production system?
2. Name two key CI/CD pipeline components tailored to AI projects.
3. Why is ongoing monitoring crucial for deployed AI systems?

4. In the APEX Manufacturing case study, what was one of the main issues they faced before implementing the AI solution?
5. What strategy did APEX use to transition their AI system from prototype to production safely?
6. How can version control be implemented for code and data in AI projects?
7. What are two potential consequences of not properly maintaining an AI system after deployment?

References

1. hgpu.org. *Deep-Edge: An Efficient Framework for Deep Learning Model Update on Heterogeneous Edge.* https://hgpu.org/?p=20596
2. alpha-sense.com. *Generative AI in Financial Services: Use Cases, Benefits, and Risks.* https://www.alpha-sense.com/blog/trends/generative-ai-in-financial-services/
3. MatrixLabX. *AI Data Science Consulting: Transform Your Business with Data-Driven Insights.* https://matrixlabx.com/ai-data-science-consulting/
4. automarketinsights.com. *How AI is Disrupting Automotive Retail.* https://www.automarketinsights.com/post/how-ai-is-distrupting-automotive-retail
5. launchnotes.com. *Minimum Viable Product (MVP): Product Management & Operations Explained.* https://www.launchnotes.com/glossary/minimum-viable-product-mvp-in-product-management-and-operations

Part 3: Governance, Ethics, Security, and Compliance

Ensuring AI's responsible use is crucial as it becomes integral to business operations. This part explores the critical aspects of governing AI systems, maintaining ethical standards, and addressing security, privacy, and compliance challenges. From establishing robust AI governance frameworks to safeguarding sensitive data and navigating regulatory landscapes, these chapters provide essential guidance for mitigating risks and fostering trust. Focusing on responsible AI practices empowers leaders to balance innovation with accountability, ensuring their AI initiatives are secure, ethical, and compliant.

This part has the following chapters:

- *Chapter 12, AI Governance and Ethics*
- *Chapter 13, Security in AI Systems*
- *Chapter 14, Privacy in the Age of AI*
- *Chapter 15, AI Compliance*

12

AI Governance and Ethics

Responsible AI is not just about liability — it's about ensuring what you are building is enabling human flourishing.

– Rumman Chowdhury

Imagine waking up in a world where your morning coffee is brewed by an AI-powered machine that remembers your favorite blend and makes health-based decisions based on your latest medical records. Sounds like a futuristic convenience. But what if that same AI decides you shouldn't have that second cup of coffee because it deems it unhealthy, effectively locking you out of your kitchen appliance? This scenario highlights the critical importance of AI governance and ethics.

As we navigate the complexities of AI, it becomes evident that the rise of this technology isn't just about sophisticated algorithms and vast amounts of data. It is also about the profound ethical implications and governance frameworks necessary to ensure these technologies serve humanity's best interests. AI can easily drift into uncharted and potentially hazardous territory without a robust ethical compass.

Consider the 2020 incident involving a leading tech company that released an AI hiring tool, only to find that it inadvertently favored male candidates over female ones. The AI was trained on historical hiring data, where men were predominantly favored, perpetuating a biased cycle. This isn't merely a technical glitch; it's a stark reminder of our ethical responsibilities when deploying AI.

Another prominent example is facial recognition technology, which has been praised for its potential to enhance security and convenience. However, it has also raised significant concerns due to privacy violations and inaccuracy. In several instances, the technology has struggled to differentiate between individuals with similar features, such as identical twins, leading to misidentifications and false alerts. This raises critical questions about fairness, accountability, and the societal impact of these technologies [1].

In this chapter, we will cover the following key topics:

- Understanding AI ethics
- Building ethical AI frameworks
- Governance of AI solutions and capabilities

By the end of this chapter, you will be able to recognize the fundamental principles of AI ethics and their importance in responsible AI development. You'll know how to construct ethical AI frameworks tailored to your organization's needs and implement effective governance structures for AI solutions. Additionally, you'll be equipped to navigate the complex landscape of AI ethics, ensuring your AI initiatives are innovative and align with ethical standards and regulatory requirements.

The problem – pain points and challenges

As organizations increasingly integrate AI into their operations, they encounter myriad challenges related to governance and ethics. These challenges are not merely theoretical but have profound real-world implications that can significantly impact a company's reputation, legal standing, and overall success [2].

Bias and fairness

One of the most pressing issues is the potential for bias in AI systems. AI models are trained on historical data, often containing inherent bias reflective of societal inequality [3]. This can result in AI systems perpetuating and even amplifying this bias. For instance, a study by the MIT Media Lab found that facial recognition systems had an error rate of 34.7% for dark-skinned women compared to just 0.8% for light-skinned men. This disparity can lead to unfair treatment and discrimination, eroding public trust in AI systems. In hiring, biased algorithms can lead to homogeneous workforces, undermining diversity and inclusion efforts.

Lack of transparency

AI algorithms often function as "black boxes," making decisions without providing clear, understandable explanations. This opacity can be particularly problematic in high-stakes areas such as healthcare, finance, and criminal justice. For example, if an AI system denies a loan application, the applicant and the lender must understand the rationale behind the decision. With transparency, it becomes easier to identify and rectify potential bias or errors in the decision-making process, thereby reducing accountability and trust in AI systems [4].

Accountability

Determining responsibility when an AI system makes an error is a significant challenge. If an autonomous vehicle causes an accident, questions arise: is the manufacturer, the software developer, or the vehicle owner at fault? This lack of clear accountability creates legal and ethical dilemmas, complicating the deployment and acceptance of AI technologies. In addition, delegating decision-making to machines can blur the lines of human oversight, leading to potential negligence.

Data privacy and security

AI systems require vast data to function effectively. Ensuring the privacy and security of this data is crucial. The unauthorized collection and exploitation of personal data can result in significant financial losses and irreparable harm to a company's reputation. A prime example is the Cambridge Analytica scandal, where millions of Facebook users' data were harvested without their consent and used to influence political campaigns. Ensuring data privacy is not just about compliance but also about maintaining user trust and ethical responsibility.

Ethical decision-making

AI systems can face ethical dilemmas that are difficult to resolve. In healthcare, an AI system might need to decide between allocating limited resources to a few patients with severe conditions or many patients with less critical needs. These ethical decisions require careful consideration and a framework that aligns with societal values and norms. For example, an AI system prioritizing organ transplants must balance urgency, survival probability, and fairness. These complex ethical decisions necessitate a governance framework incorporating diverse perspectives and principles.

Regulatory compliance

Maintaining evolving regulations and ensuring compliance is daunting for businesses. Rules such as the EU's **General Data Protection Regulation (GDPR)** impose strict guidelines on data usage and require companies to implement robust data protection measures. Non-compliance can result in hefty fines and legal repercussions, adding to the complexity of AI governance. Additionally, different jurisdictions may have varying regulations, making it challenging for global companies to maintain consistent compliance standards.

Compelling examples

Consider the case of a major financial institution that implemented an AI-driven credit scoring system to improve efficiency and accuracy in evaluating loan applications. However, it quickly became apparent that the system disproportionately denied loans to applicants from certain demographic groups. The backlash was swift, leading to a public relations crisis and calls for regulatory scrutiny. The institution had to halt the use of the AI system, conduct a thorough audit, and implement corrective measures, which were both costly and time-consuming. This example illustrates how bias in AI systems can have far-reaching consequences, affecting individuals' lives and a company's reputation.

Another compelling example involves a healthcare provider that used AI to predict patient outcomes and optimize treatment plans. While the AI system showed promise, it inadvertently introduced bias against certain patient groups. For instance, it consistently under-prioritized elderly patients for specific treatments. This led to ethical concerns and prompted the provider to revisit and revise their AI model to ensure it aligned with ethical standards and provided equitable care. This example highlights the importance of ethical oversight and the potential harm biased AI systems can cause in critical sectors such as healthcare.

Personal anecdotes

Reflecting on my own experiences, I recall a project where we developed an AI tool for predictive maintenance in manufacturing. The goal was to reduce downtime by anticipating equipment failures. However, we soon discovered that the AI was biased towards certain types of machinery, leading to an imbalance in maintenance schedules. Addressing this issue required revisiting our data sources and incorporating a more diverse set of inputs to ensure fair and effective predictions. This experience underscored the importance of continuously monitoring and adjusting AI systems to prevent and mitigate bias.

In another instance, while working on an AI-driven customer service solution, we faced significant challenges related to data privacy. Customers were concerned about how their data was being used and stored. To address these concerns, we implemented rigorous data protection protocols and ensured our AI systems were transparent in their operations. This improved customer trust and helped us comply with regulatory requirements. This anecdote illustrates how addressing privacy concerns can enhance customer relationships and ensure regulatory compliance.

These examples and anecdotes underscore the multifaceted challenges of AI governance and ethics. Addressing these issues requires a comprehensive approach that blends technical expertise with a deep understanding of ethical principles and regulatory landscapes. As we proceed through this chapter, we will explore strategies and best practices to navigate these challenges effectively, ensuring that AI systems are developed and deployed responsibly.

The solution and process – implementation

Addressing AI governance and ethics challenges requires a multifaceted approach that combines foundational understanding, practical frameworks, and robust governance structures. This section will detail our unique solution to these challenges, providing a comprehensive, step-by-step guide to implementation. The aim is to offer a blend of strategic insight, practical tools, and actionable steps to ensure ethical AI development and deployment.

Understanding AI ethics

The first step in addressing AI ethics is establishing a foundational understanding of the core principles governing ethical AI. These principles include fairness, accountability, transparency, and privacy. A deep understanding of these principles is essential for anyone developing and deploying AI systems.

The implementation steps are as follows:

1. **Educate your team and stakeholders:**
    - **Training sessions**: Conduct comprehensive training sessions focused on the fundamental principles of AI ethics. These sessions should cover why these principles matter and how they can be integrated into AI projects. Utilize case studies and real-world examples to illustrate the practical implications of ethical AI.

- **Workshops and seminars**: Organize interactive workshops and seminars featuring industry experts who can provide insights into current ethical dilemmas in AI. These sessions should encourage active participation and discussion, helping to deepen the understanding of ethical considerations.

- **Ethics committees**: Establish ethics committees within your organization to oversee training programs and ensure ongoing education on AI ethics.

Consider implementing a series of workshops where employees analyze incidents such as bias in facial recognition technology. Through group discussions and expert-led seminars, participants can explore the ethical implications and develop strategies to address similar challenges in their work. This hands-on approach fosters a more profound commitment to ethical AI practices.

2. **Incorporate ethical discussions into regular meetings**:

   - **Weekly ethics roundtables**: Host weekly roundtable discussions where team members can share insights, discuss recent developments in AI ethics, and explore the ethical dimensions of ongoing projects. These sessions should be a staple of your organizational culture, ensuring continuous engagement with ethical issues.

   - **Case study analysis**: Review and discuss case studies of ethical challenges and successes in AI regularly to keep the conversation relevant and grounded in real-world applications.

Building ethical AI frameworks

Creating and implementing ethical AI frameworks involves developing structured policies and practices that guide ethical AI development and deployment. These frameworks should ensure that ethical considerations are embedded at every stage of the AI lifecycle.

The implementation steps are as follows:

1. **Drafting policies**:

   - **Ethical guidelines**: Develop comprehensive ethical guidelines that outline the principles and standards for AI development within your organization. These guidelines should be clear, actionable, and aligned with industry best practices and regulatory requirements.

   - **Policy documentation**: Thoroughly document these guidelines and policies. Make them accessible to all team members and regularly update them to reflect evolving ethical standards and regulatory changes.

2. **Creating cross-functional teams**:

   - **Diverse teams**: Form cross-functional teams that include members from various departments, such as AI developers, legal experts, ethicists, data scientists, and customer representatives. This diversity ensures a broad perspective on ethical issues and promotes holistic decision-making.

- **Regular meetings**: Schedule regular meetings for these teams to discuss ongoing projects, review ethical concerns, and make collaborative decisions. Encourage open communication and diverse viewpoints to ensure comprehensive ethical oversight.

3. **Integrating ethical checks**:

   - **Ethical checkpoints**: Establish ethical checkpoints at key stages of the AI development lifecycle. These checkpoints should include data collection, model training, validation, and deployment, ensuring that ethical considerations are assessed and documented at each stage.

   - **Review boards**: Set up ethical review boards to periodically audit AI systems. These boards should evaluate the systems against the established ethical guidelines and recommend necessary adjustments.

Governance of AI solutions and capabilities

Effective governance structures and policies are essential for ethically managing AI systems. These structures provide ongoing oversight, ensure accountability, and maintain compliance with ethical standards and regulatory requirements.

Let's look at the implementation steps:

1. **Establish governance committees**:

   - **AI ethics committee**: Create an AI ethics committee responsible for overseeing all AI-related activities within your organization. This committee should include senior leaders, AI experts, ethicists, and legal advisors to ensure comprehensive oversight.

   - **Roles and responsibilities**: Clearly define each committee member's roles and responsibilities. Ensure accountability for monitoring and addressing ethical concerns and that the committee can make impactful decisions.

2. **Define governance policies**:

   - **Governance framework**: Develop a comprehensive governance framework that outlines policies for data usage, transparency, accountability, and compliance. This framework should be aligned with industry best practices and regulatory requirements [5].

   - **Documentation and communication**: Thoroughly document and communicate these policies across the organization. Ensure that all team members understand their responsibilities under the governance framework and are committed to upholding these standards.

3. **Continuous monitoring and auditing**:

   - **Monitoring systems**: Implement advanced monitoring systems to continuously oversee AI systems' compliance with ethical standards. These systems should include automated tools to detect bias and irregularity, providing real-time alerts for potential issues.

- **Regular audits**: Conduct audits of AI systems to ensure ongoing compliance with ethical guidelines and regulatory requirements. These audits should assess the systems against the governance framework, identify areas for improvement, and recommend necessary adjustments.

Consider a financial institution deploying an AI-based credit scoring system. By establishing an AI ethics committee, they can ensure that the system adheres to ethical guidelines and prevents bias that could lead to discriminatory practices [6]. Regular audits and continuous monitoring systems help detect and address bias, ensuring fair treatment of all applicants and maintaining the institution's reputation for ethical practices.

Implementing these solutions requires a deep commitment to ethical principles and a proactive approach to governance. By educating your team, building robust ethical frameworks, and establishing effective governance structures, you can ensure that your AI systems are developed and deployed responsibly [7]. This mitigates risks and builds trust and credibility, positioning your organization as a leader in ethical AI.

Understanding and implementing these practices is about regulatory compliance and setting a standard for responsible AI development. This journey, while complex, is essential for harnessing AI's transformative potential while safeguarding against its risks.

Hypothetical case study – APEX Manufacturing and Distribution

To illustrate the successful application of our AI governance and ethics framework, let's delve into a hypothetical case study of APEX Manufacturing and Distribution. This case study demonstrates how APEX navigated its initial challenges, implemented our recommended steps, and achieved significant results through ethical AI practices.

Client's initial situation

APEX Manufacturing and Distribution was at the forefront of integrating AI into their operations to enhance efficiency and competitiveness. However, they faced several critical challenges:

- **Bias in predictive models**: Their AI-driven predictive maintenance tool exhibited significant bias, prioritizing certain machinery over others. This led to uneven maintenance schedules, causing frequent downtime for under-prioritized equipment and increased operational inefficiency.
- **Lack of transparency**: The AI systems used by APEX operated as black boxes, making decisions without providing clear explanations. This lack of transparency fostered distrust among employees and stakeholders, complicating the adoption of AI solutions.
- **Data privacy concerns**: Substantial concerns were raised about the privacy and security of the customer and operational data used in their AI systems. Ensuring compliance with data protection regulations across multiple jurisdictions was particularly challenging.

- **Regulatory compliance**: APEX struggled to keep pace with evolving regulations, particularly in regions with stringent data protection laws such as the GDPR. Ensuring compliance across their global operations was a significant burden.

Steps taken

The following steps were implemented to tackle the challenges faced at APEX Manufacturing and Distribution.

Step 1 – understanding AI ethics

The first step was comprehensively understanding AI ethics among all employees and stakeholders. This foundational knowledge is crucial for embedding ethical principles throughout the organization.

The implementation steps are as follows:

1. **Educational workshops**:
   - **Comprehensive training**: We organized extensive training sessions that covered the fundamental principles of AI ethics, including fairness, accountability, transparency, and privacy. These sessions were designed to be interactive and incorporate real-world examples and case studies to highlight the importance of ethical AI.
   - **Expert-led seminars**: Industry experts led seminars to delve deeper into ethical dilemmas specific to the manufacturing and logistics sectors. These sessions provided insights into the latest ethical standards and practices in AI.

2. **Interactive seminars and continuous learning**:
   - **Ethics committees**: We established ethics committees within APEX to oversee and regularly update the training programs. These committees ensured that the learning materials remained relevant and aligned with the latest industry standards.
   - **Ethics roundtables**: Weekly roundtable discussions were introduced, where team members could share insights, discuss recent developments in AI ethics, and explore the ethical dimensions of their ongoing projects.

Step 2 – building ethical AI frameworks

Creating and implementing ethical AI frameworks involves developing structured policies and practices that guide ethical AI development and deployment. These frameworks should ensure that ethical considerations are embedded at every stage of the AI lifecycle.

Here are the implementation steps:

1. **Drafting policies**:

    - **Ethical guidelines**: We collaborated with APEX to develop comprehensive ethical guidelines tailored to their needs. These guidelines included standards for data usage, transparency, and accountability, ensuring that AI systems were designed and implemented ethically.
    - **Policy documentation**: These guidelines were thoroughly documented and accessible to all employees. They were also regularly updated to reflect evolving ethical standards and regulatory changes.

2. **Creating cross-functional teams**:

    - **Diverse teams**: We established cross-functional teams that included AI developers, legal experts, ethicists, data scientists, and customer representatives. This diversity ensured a broad perspective on ethical issues and promoted holistic decision-making.
    - **Regular meetings**: These teams were scheduled to discuss ongoing projects, review ethical concerns, and make collaborative decisions. Open communication and diverse viewpoints were encouraged to ensure comprehensive ethical oversight.

3. **Integrating ethical checks**:

    - **Ethical checkpoints**: Ethical checkpoints were embedded into the AI development process. At each key stage—data collection, model training, validation, and deployment—these checkpoints ensured that ethical standards were assessed and documented.
    - **Review boards**: Ethical review boards were established to audit AI systems periodically. These boards evaluated the systems against the established ethical guidelines and recommended necessary adjustments.

Step 3 – governance of AI solutions and capabilities

Effective governance structures and policies are essential for ethically managing AI systems. These structures provide ongoing oversight, ensure accountability, and maintain compliance with ethical standards and regulatory requirements.

The implementation steps are as follows:

1. **Establish governance committees**:

    - **AI ethics committee**: An AI ethics committee consisting of senior leaders, AI experts, and legal advisors. This committee oversaw all AI-related activities within APEX and made critical decisions regarding ethical concerns.

- **Roles and responsibilities**: Clear roles and responsibilities were defined for each committee member. This ensured accountability for monitoring and addressing ethical concerns, with the committee having the authority to make impactful decisions.

2. **Define governance policies**:

    - **Governance framework**: We helped APEX develop a comprehensive governance framework that outlined policies for data usage, transparency, accountability, and compliance. This framework was aligned with industry best practices and regulatory requirements.

    - **Documentation and communication**: These policies were documented and communicated across the organization. All team members were made aware of their responsibilities under the governance framework.

3. **Continuous monitoring and auditing**:

    - **Monitoring systems**: Advanced monitoring systems were implemented to oversee AI systems' compliance with ethical standards continuously. These systems included automated tools to detect bias and irregularity, providing real-time alerts for potential issues.

    - **Regular audits**: Regular audits of AI systems were conducted to ensure ongoing compliance with ethical guidelines and regulatory requirements. These audits assessed the systems against the governance framework, identified areas for improvement, and recommended necessary adjustments.

Results achieved

The steps discussed produced the following results:

- **Improved fairness and efficiency**: The predictive maintenance tool's recalibration reduced downtime by 20% and improved operational efficiency. This was achieved by ensuring the tool provided balanced attention to all equipment, addressing the initial bias.

- **Enhanced transparency and trust**: Implementing transparency protocols made APEX's AI decision-making processes transparent and understandable. This built trust among employees and stakeholders, fostering a more collaborative work environment and facilitating smoother AI adoption.

- **Strengthened data privacy and security**: Robust data governance policies were established, ensuring customer and operational data were used responsibly and securely. This addressed privacy concerns and enhanced customer trust and satisfaction, improving customer relationships.

- **Regulatory compliance**: The governance framework helped APEX stay ahead of regulatory changes, ensuring compliance across different jurisdictions. This proactive approach mitigated the risk of legal issues and financial penalties, providing a stable foundation for future growth.

During one of our workshops, a senior engineer shared a story about a malfunctioning predictive maintenance tool that failed to flag a critical issue, resulting in costly downtime. This incident caused significant frustration among the team. However, after integrating ethical checkpoints and recalibrating the tool, the same engineer reported a marked improvement in the system's performance. The tool now flagged potential issues accurately, preventing significant breakdowns. This turnaround saved costs and boosted team morale and trust in AI systems.

One of the most inspiring moments in a company-wide meeting came when the CEO of APEX highlighted the importance of ethical AI in shaping the company's future. She emphasized that while technology is a powerful tool, the ethical application of this technology will define their legacy. This message resonated deeply with employees, motivating them to embrace the new ethical frameworks and governance structures with purpose and responsibility.

Reflection and practical next steps

Before we conclude this chapter, it's important to take a moment to reflect on the key insights we've explored. Consider how these concepts resonate with your experiences developing or implementing AI systems. Have you encountered ethical challenges similar to those we discussed, such as bias in predictive models or lack of transparency in decision-making processes? How might the frameworks and governance structures we've examined reshape your approach to AI?

Think about a recent AI project you've been involved with. How might it have unfolded differently if you had applied the ethical considerations and governance practices we've discussed? Perhaps you would have caught potential bias earlier in the development process, or maybe you would have fostered greater trust among stakeholders through increased transparency. Imagine the positive impact these changes could have had on the project's outcomes and reception.

Now, let's challenge ourselves to assess our current situations critically:

- How well does your organization currently address AI ethics and governance? Are there gaps that need filling?
- What potential risks or ethical dilemmas might lurk in your AI systems that you haven't considered?
- How prepared is your team to handle emerging ethical challenges in AI?
- How could implementing more robust AI governance improve your organization's reputation and trustworthiness?
- How might a more ethical approach to AI development open up new opportunities or markets for your business?

These questions aren't meant to discourage but rather to inspire action and critical thinking. Every step towards more ethical AI is progress, no matter how small. The goal is to start a journey of continuous improvement and ethical consideration in your AI practices.

Consider these practical next steps to begin implementing what you've learned:

1. **Start a conversation**: Organize a meeting with your team to discuss AI ethics. Share the insights from this chapter and encourage open dialogue about potential ethical concerns in your current projects. This can be an informal lunch discussion or a more structured workshop. The key is to get people thinking and talking about these important issues.

2. **Conduct an ethics audit**: Review one of your existing AI systems through an ethical lens. Look for potential biases, transparency issues, or privacy concerns. This exercise can be eye-opening and provide immediate areas for improvement. Don't be discouraged if you find issues – identifying them is the first step towards addressing them.

3. **Draft initial guidelines**: Begin crafting ethical guidelines for AI development in your organization. They don't need to be perfect—the act of creating them will spark valuable discussions and set a foundation for future refinement. Consider involving team members from various departments to ensure diverse perspectives are included.

4. **Form a cross-functional ethics committee**: Identify colleagues from different departments who can bring diverse perspectives to AI ethics discussions. This could be the start of your AI governance structure. Include technical staff and people from legal, HR, marketing, and other relevant departments. Their varied viewpoints will be crucial in addressing the multifaceted challenges of AI ethics.

5. **Educate and train**: Plan a series of workshops or lunch-and-learn sessions to build AI ethics awareness across your organization. Ethical AI is everyone's responsibility, not just the tech teams'. Consider bringing in external experts or using online resources to supplement your team's knowledge.

6. **Integrate ethics into your development process**: Look for ways to incorporate ethical considerations at every stage of your AI development life cycle. This could involve adding ethical checkpoints to your project management process or including ethics-related questions in your code review practices.

7. **Engage with the wider community**: Look for opportunities to participate in industry discussions, conferences, or online forums about AI ethics. Sharing your experiences and learning from others can be invaluable in this rapidly evolving field.

8. **Create accountability measures**: Develop metrics and reporting structures to track your progress in implementing ethical AI practices. This could involve regular ethics audits, stakeholder feedback surveys, or other relevant measures.

Remember, implementing robust AI governance and ethics isn't an overnight process. It's a journey of continuous learning and improvement. You may face challenges along the way, such as resistance to change or difficulty quantifying the benefits of ethical practices. However, the long-term rewards—in terms of risk mitigation, stakeholder trust, and potential competitive advantage—make it a worthwhile endeavor.

As you embark on this journey, you'll likely find that ethical considerations mitigate risks and lead to more innovative, trustworthy, and successful AI solutions. By proactively addressing ethical concerns, you're future-proofing your AI initiatives and positioning your organization as a responsible leader in the field.

Moreover, embracing ethical AI practices can open up new opportunities. Customers and partners increasingly value companies that commit to responsible technology use. By prioritizing AI ethics, you could differentiate your organization in the market and attract talent and business opportunities.

So, what will your first step be? Perhaps it's as simple as scheduling that team meeting to discuss AI ethics. Or maybe you're ready to conduct an ethics audit of your current AI systems. Whatever it is, commit to taking action within the next week. Start small if needed, but start somewhere.

Summary

In this chapter, we navigated the complex landscape of AI governance and ethics, equipping you with the knowledge and tools to develop AI systems responsibly. We explored the importance of understanding AI ethics, building robust ethical frameworks, and implementing effective governance structures. Remember, ethical AI isn't just about compliance—it's about creating systems that benefit society while mitigating potential harms.

As you move forward, consider how you can apply these principles in your work. Whether fine-tuning a machine learning model or designing an AI-powered application, keep ethics at the forefront of your decision-making. By doing so, you're building better AI and shaping a more responsible and trustworthy technological future.

Our next chapter will delve into security in AI systems. Ethical considerations are crucial in AI development, but ensuring these systems' security is equally important. We'll explore how to protect AI from vulnerabilities and malicious attacks, further strengthening the foundation of responsible AI that we built in this chapter.

Questions

1. What are the four core principles of AI ethics mentioned in the chapter?
2. How can bias in AI systems perpetuate societal inequality? Provide an example.
3. What is the term "black box" to AI systems, and why is it problematic?
4. Describe two steps an organization can take to integrate ethical checks into their AI development process.
5. Why is having cross-functional teams involved in AI ethics discussions important?
6. What role does an AI ethics committee play in an organization's governance structure?
7. How can continuous monitoring and regular audits contribute to maintaining ethical AI systems?

8. In the APEX Manufacturing and Distribution case study, what was one of the key challenges they faced with their AI systems, and how did they address it?
9. Why is transparency important in AI decision-making processes, and how can it be improved?
10. How might implementing strong AI governance practices benefit an organization beyond ethical considerations?

References

1. everydayteching.io. *Ethical Implications of Automations.* https://everydayteching.io/ethical-implications-of-automations/
2. ginimachine.com. *Ethical AI in Finance: Striking a Harmony between Progress and Responsibility.* https://ginimachine.com/blog/ai-ethics-in-finance-balancing-innovation-with-responsibility/
3. walkersands.com. *Q&A with Rana el Kaliouby, CEO and Co-Founder of Affectiva, Author of Girl Decoded.* https://www.walkersands.com/about/blog/qa-rana-affectiva-girl-decoded/
4. mmcalumni.ca. *Common Problems of Artificial Intelligence in PDF Format.* https://mmcalumni.ca/blog/the-key-challenges-and-concerns-in-the-application-of-artificial-intelligence-insights-from-research-and-publications-in-pdf-format
5. technuovo.com. *NIST Compliance Across Industries Explained.* https://technuovo.com/nist-compliance-across-industries-explained/
6. technograte.com. *Chat GPT/ OpenAI based futuristic mobile operating system: Is it possible?* https://www.technograte.com/chat-gpt-openai-based-mobile/
7. skill-mine.com. *Digital Transformation in the Age of AI and Machine Learning.* https://skill-mine.com/digital-transformation-in-the-age-of-ai-and-machine-learning/

13
Security in AI Systems

AI security is about protecting AI systems from learning, doing and revealing the wrong thing. It is a set of practices to protect AI systems and lifecycles from digital attacks, theft and damage.

– General Paul Nakasone

Imagine this: you're at a bustling international airport, eagerly anticipating your flight. Suddenly, an urgent announcement crackles through the speakers, declaring that all flights are grounded due to a security breach in the AI system managing air traffic control. This isn't a scene from a science fiction thriller; it's a potential reality we will face if we neglect the security of AI systems.

The rapid expansion of the AI industry has led to its integration into critical sectors such as healthcare, financial services, and autonomous transportation. However, this swift growth also reveals a troubling truth – AI systems have become prime targets for sophisticated cyberattacks, and the consequences of such breaches can be devastating. The stakes are exceptionally high, from hacked autonomous vehicles causing fatal accidents to compromised medical devices leading to dangerous misdiagnoses.

Consider the 2019 incident where adversarial attacks were used to deceive an AI-powered medical imaging system, resulting in erroneous patient diagnoses. Or the case of an autonomous vehicle tricked into veering off course by a simple sticker placed on a road sign. These incidents underscore a critical truth: the security of AI systems transcends traditional IT concerns—it is a matter of public safety, operational continuity, and maintaining trust.

The unique vulnerabilities of AI systems demand our urgent attention. Unlike traditional software, AI models can be susceptible to adversarial attacks, data poisoning, and model inversion. Adversarial attacks involve manipulating input data to produce incorrect predictions. For example, researchers demonstrated this by subtly altering a stop sign's image in a nearly invisible way to the human eye, causing a state-of-the-art image recognition system to misclassify it as a yield sign. Imagine the potential consequences if such an attack were deployed against an autonomous vehicle navigating busy streets.

Data poisoning attacks involve injecting malicious data during training, causing AI models to learn incorrect behaviors or biases. This could lead to an AI diagnostic tool misinterpreting medical images in a healthcare setting, resulting in incorrect treatments. Model inversion attacks, meanwhile, seek to extract sensitive information from trained AI models, posing significant privacy risks by potentially revealing details about individuals whose data was used to train the models.

However, these challenges, while significant, are manageable. By understanding the specific vulnerabilities of AI systems and implementing robust security measures, we can protect these technologies from malicious actors. This chapter will explore the intricate landscape of AI security, examining the threats and providing practical, actionable solutions to safeguard your AI applications.

We will delve into real-world examples and cutting-edge research, offering strategies to fortify the security of your AI systems. Whether you are an AI developer, a business leader, or a security professional, the insights and guidance presented here will equip you with the knowledge and tools needed to defend against emerging threats.

As we navigate this complex topic, we blend rigorous analysis with engaging storytelling, making the discussion informative and accessible. In the realm of AI, security is not just a technical requirement—it is a fundamental pillar that underpins the integrity and trustworthiness of the entire ecosystem.

In this chapter, we will explore three crucial aspects of AI security:

- Securing AI models and data
- AI in cybersecurity
- Addressing AI vulnerabilities

By the end of this chapter, you will be able to implement comprehensive security measures for AI systems, including protecting sensitive data and models, leveraging AI for enhanced cybersecurity, and identifying and mitigating AI-specific vulnerabilities. You'll have the knowledge and tools to develop a robust AI security framework, ensuring your AI applications' integrity, confidentiality, and resilience in the face of evolving cyber threats.

The problem – pain points and challenges

As businesses increasingly integrate AI systems into their operations, they encounter numerous unique and formidable security challenges. Understanding these challenges is crucial to developing effective countermeasures. Let's delve deeper into AI security's key pain points and vulnerabilities.

Data breaches and privacy concerns

One of the most significant challenges in AI security is protecting sensitive data. AI systems often rely on vast amounts of data, including personal, financial, and healthcare information, to function effectively. This makes them prime targets for cybercriminals seeking to exploit data for monetary gain or other malicious purposes [1].

Consider the high-profile data breach at a leading healthcare organization where hackers infiltrated the AI system used for patient diagnostics. The breach exposed sensitive patient records, leading to identity theft and significant financial losses for the affected individuals. Moreover, the incident severely damaged the organization's reputation, causing a loss of trust among patients and stakeholders. According to a report by IBM Security, the healthcare sector's average cost of a data breach was $7.13 million in 2020, underscoring the financial and reputational risks associated with such incidents.

Model vulnerabilities and adversarial attacks

AI models, while powerful, are not infallible. They can be manipulated through adversarial attacks, where attackers introduce subtle changes to the input data that cause the AI system to make incorrect predictions or classifications. These vulnerabilities pose a substantial risk, particularly in critical applications such as autonomous vehicles and financial systems.

Researchers have demonstrated that placing small stickers on road signs can trick an autonomous vehicle's AI system into misinterpreting the signs, potentially leading to dangerous driving decisions. This example underscores the critical need for robust defenses against adversarial attacks to ensure the safety and reliability of AI systems. Even slight alterations can cause AI systems to fail, highlighting the inherent fragility of these models.

Data poisoning and integrity

Data poisoning attacks occur when attackers inject malicious data into the training dataset, causing the AI model to learn incorrect or harmful behaviors. This attack can be particularly insidious, as it compromises the model's integrity from the ground up, making it difficult to detect and rectify.

A significant financial institution experienced a data poisoning attack. The attackers introduced fraudulent transaction data into the AI system used for fraud detection. As a result, the model began to flag legitimate transactions as fraudulent while allowing actual fraudulent activities to go undetected. This resulted in financial losses and eroded customer trust in the institution's ability to protect assets. The institution had to comprehensively overhaul its data security measures, costing millions of dollars and significant time.

Model inversion and privacy risks

Model inversion attacks aim to extract sensitive information from an AI model by analyzing its outputs. This can lead to significant privacy risks, as attackers can reconstruct personal data to train the model [2].

For instance, in a study involving a facial recognition system, researchers demonstrated that they could infer details about the individuals in the training dataset by querying the model. This type of vulnerability highlights the need for rigorous privacy-preserving techniques to protect sensitive information in AI systems. The study by Fredrikson et al. (2015) showed how attackers could reconstruct faces from model outputs, emphasizing the privacy implications of AI systems.

Lack of explainability and transparency

Many AI models, especially those utilizing deep learning, operate as opaque systems, offering limited visibility into how they arrive at their decisions. This lack of transparency can hinder the detection and mitigation of security threats, as it is challenging to understand how and why an AI system arrived at a particular decision [3].

An insurance company using AI for claims processing faced significant challenges when customers began questioning the fairness of the AI's decisions. The company could have explained the rationale behind denied claims with transparency that led to customer dissatisfaction and regulatory scrutiny. This example underscores the importance of developing explainable AI systems to enhance transparency and accountability. A survey by O'Reilly Media found that 60% of AI practitioners consider explainability a critical factor in AI adoption.

The rapid evolution of threats

The threat landscape for AI systems is continually evolving, with attackers constantly developing new techniques to exploit vulnerabilities. This rapid evolution makes it difficult for organizations to stay ahead of potential threats, requiring continuous vigilance and adaptation.

A technology firm experienced this firsthand when its AI-powered cybersecurity system was outpaced by sophisticated new malware variants that exploited previously unknown vulnerabilities. Despite the firm's proactive security measures, the rapid development of new threats highlighted the need for an adaptable and resilient security strategy. According to the 2020 Verizon Data Breach Investigations Report, nearly 30% of all breaches involved using new or unknown attack methods, stressing the importance of adaptive security measures.

Personal anecdotes

In my experience working with AI systems, I encountered a scenario where a data poisoning attack compromised an AI model designed for predictive maintenance in manufacturing. The attackers introduced faulty data that caused the model to predict maintenance needs inaccurately, leading to unexpected equipment failures and production downtime. This incident reinforced the importance of securing the entire data pipeline and continuously monitoring for anomalies.

In another instance, while collaborating with a financial services company, we faced challenges with model explainability. Clients were skeptical of the AI-driven investment recommendations because they couldn't understand the underlying rationale. To address this, we implemented explainability tools that provided clear insights into the model's decision-making process, ultimately enhancing client trust and satisfaction. This experience underscored the value of transparency in building confidence and trust in AI systems.

The solution and process – implementation

To address the multifaceted security challenges outlined in the previous section, we need a comprehensive approach that covers three key areas: securing AI models and data, leveraging AI in cybersecurity, and addressing AI vulnerabilities. Here, we present unique solutions and actionable steps to implement these strategies effectively.

Securing AI models and data

Protecting AI models and data requires robust security measures to safeguard sensitive information and ensure the integrity of AI systems. This involves a combination of methodologies, tools, and frameworks to prevent unauthorized access, data breaches, and malicious attacks [4].

The implementation steps are as follows:

1. **Encryption techniques**:

   - **Data encryption**: Implement advanced encryption techniques to protect data at rest and in transit. Use robust encryption algorithms such as AES-256 to ensure that sensitive data remains secure even if intercepted.
   - **Model encryption**: Encrypt AI models to protect intellectual property and prevent tampering. This involves homomorphic encryption, which allows computation on encrypted data without decrypting it first.

2. **Access control mechanisms**:

   - **Role-based access control (RBAC)**: Implement RBAC to restrict access to AI models and data based on user roles. Ensure that only authorized personnel can access and modify critical AI systems.
   - **Multi-factor authentication (MFA)**: MFA adds an extra layer of security, ensuring that access to AI systems requires multiple forms of verification.

3. **Regular security audits**:

   - **Conduct security audits**: Perform regular security audits to identify vulnerabilities and ensure compliance with security policies [5]. Use tools such as Nessus or OpenVAS for comprehensive vulnerability scanning.
   - **Penetration testing**: Conduct penetration testing regularly to simulate attacks and identify potential weaknesses. Use frameworks such as OWASP ZAP to test the security of AI systems.

A healthcare provider implemented these measures to protect their AI diagnostic system. Encrypting patient data and using RBAC and MFA significantly reduced the risk of data breaches. Regular security audits and penetration testing helped them stay ahead of potential threats, ensuring the integrity and security of their AI systems [6].

AI in cybersecurity

AI can be a powerful ally in enhancing cybersecurity measures. By leveraging AI's capabilities in threat detection, incident response, and overall cybersecurity strategy, organizations can better protect themselves against evolving cyber threats.

Let's see the implementation steps:

1. **Selecting the right AI tools**:

    - **Threat detection tools**: Choose AI tools for threat detection, such as Darktrace or Cylance. These tools use machine learning algorithms to identify and respond to potential threats in real time.
    - **Incident response systems**: Implement AI-driven incident response systems such as IBM Resilient or Splunk Phantom to automate and streamline the response to security incidents.

2. **Training AI systems**:

    - **Data collection**: Gather a diverse and comprehensive dataset to train AI systems effectively. Ensure the data includes examples of both standard and malicious activities to improve threat detection accuracy.
    - **Continuous learning**: Implement continuous learning mechanisms to update AI systems with the latest threat intelligence. Use techniques such as reinforcement learning to enable AI systems to adapt to new threats.

3. **Monitoring and updating AI**:

    - **Continuous monitoring**: Set up constant monitoring systems to detect anomalies and suspicious activities. Use tools such as Splunk or Elastic Stack for real-time monitoring and analysis.
    - **Regular updates**: Regularly update AI systems with new threat signatures and patches to address emerging vulnerabilities. Implement an automated update process to ensure timely deployment of security patches.

A financial institution integrated AI into its cybersecurity measures by implementing Darktrace for threat detection and IBM Resilient for incident response. This integration allowed the institution to detect and respond to threats in real time, significantly reducing the impact of cyberattacks. Continuous monitoring and regular updates ensured their AI systems remained effective against new threats.

Addressing AI vulnerabilities

Identifying and mitigating vulnerabilities within AI systems is crucial to maintaining security. Regular vulnerability assessments and proactive mitigation strategies help ensure that AI systems remain resilient against attacks.

The implementation includes the following steps:

1. **Conducting vulnerability assessments**:

    - **Thorough assessments**: Conduct comprehensive vulnerability assessments using tools such as Nessus or OpenVAS. Focus on identifying weaknesses in data pipelines, model architectures, and deployment environments.
    - **Red team exercises**: Perform red team exercises to simulate real-world attacks and evaluate the resilience of AI systems [7]. Use insights from these exercises to improve security measures.

2. **Implementing patch management processes**:

    - **Patch management**: Establish a robust patch management process to ensure that all software components, including AI models and dependencies, are regularly updated. Use tools such as Microsoft SCCM or WSUS for automated patch management.
    - **Critical updates**: Prioritize the essential deployment of security updates to address high-risk vulnerabilities promptly.

3. **Establishing continuous monitoring systems**:

    - **Monitoring infrastructure**: Implement a comprehensive monitoring infrastructure to track the performance and security of AI systems. Use tools such as Prometheus or Grafana for real-time monitoring and alerting.
    - **Anomaly detection**: AI-driven anomaly detection systems are used to identify unusual activities that may indicate a security breach [8]. Implement solutions such as Splunk or Elastic Stack to detect and respond to anomalies quickly.

A technology firm conducted regular vulnerability assessments and red team exercises to identify weaknesses in its AI-powered cybersecurity system. By implementing a robust patch management process and continuous monitoring infrastructure, it was able to address vulnerabilities proactively and maintain the security of its AI systems.

To effectively secure your AI systems, consider the following key steps:

1. **Start with assessments**: Conduct thorough vulnerability assessments to identify the current state of your AI security.
2. **Implement robust security measures**: Use the actionable tips and tools to secure your AI models and data effectively.
3. **Leverage AI for cybersecurity**: Integrate AI into your cybersecurity strategy to enhance threat detection and incident response.
4. **Continuously monitor and update**: Establish continuous monitoring systems and ensure regular updates to maintain the security of your AI systems.

By following these steps, you can build a resilient AI security framework that protects your organization from the ever-evolving landscape of cyber threats. Let's move forward with a commitment to securing AI systems and safeguarding the future of technology.

Hypothetical case study – APEX Manufacturing and Distribution

To illustrate the successful application of our AI security framework, let's explore a hypothetical case study of APEX Manufacturing and Distribution, a leading global company in the manufacturing sector. This case study demonstrates how APEX navigated its initial challenges, implemented the recommended steps, and achieved significant results through robust AI security practices.

Client's initial situation

APEX Manufacturing and Distribution integrated AI systems into its operations, from predictive maintenance to supply chain optimization. However, they faced several critical security challenges:

- **Data vulnerability**: Sensitive manufacturing data, including proprietary designs and production schedules, was at risk of being exposed due to inadequate encryption and access controls
- **Adversarial attacks**: The AI models used for predictive maintenance were vulnerable to adversarial attacks, which could cause incorrect predictions and lead to unexpected equipment failures
- **Compliance issues**: APEX struggled with compliance requirements for data protection across multiple jurisdictions, putting them at risk of legal penalties and reputational damage

Steps taken

The following steps were implemented to tackle the security challenges observed.

Securing AI models and data

To enhance the security of their AI systems, APEX implemented the following key measures:

- **Implementing encryption techniques**:
  - **Data encryption**: APEX introduced advanced encryption techniques, such as AES-256, to protect data at rest and in transit [9]. This ensured that sensitive manufacturing data remained secure, even if intercepted.
  - **Model encryption**: They used homomorphic encryption to protect their AI models, allowing computations on encrypted data without decryption. This safeguarded the integrity and confidentiality of their AI algorithms.

- **Establishing access control mechanisms**:
  - **RBAC**: APEX implemented RBAC to restrict access to AI models and data based on user roles. This ensured that only authorized personnel could access critical systems.
  - **MFA**: To enhance their security measures, they implemented MFA, requiring users to complete multiple forms of verification to access AI systems [10].
- **Conducting regular security audits**:
  - **Security audits**: APEX performed comprehensive security audits using tools such as Nessus, identifying vulnerabilities and ensuring compliance with security policies
  - **Penetration testing**: Regular penetration testing with OWASP ZAP helped simulate attacks and identify potential weaknesses, allowing APEX to strengthen their security posture

Leveraging AI in cybersecurity

To leverage AI in strengthening their cybersecurity efforts, APEX implemented the following strategies:

- **Selecting the right AI tools**:
  - **Threat detection**: They implemented AI-driven threat detection tools such as Darktrace, which use machine learning algorithms to identify and respond to potential threats in real time
  - **Incident response**: AI-powered incident response systems such as IBM Resilient were deployed to automate and streamline responses to security incidents
- **Training AI systems**:
  - **Data collection**: They gathered diverse datasets, including examples of standard and malicious activities, to effectively train the AI systems
  - **Continuous learning**: Continuous learning mechanisms were implemented to keep AI systems updated with the latest threat intelligence, enabling them to adapt to new threats
- **Continuous monitoring and updating**:
  - **Monitoring systems**: They set up continuous monitoring systems that use tools such as Splunk to detect anomalies and suspicious activities in real time
  - **Regular updates**: Regular updates and automated patch management ensured that AI systems remained protected against emerging vulnerabilities

Addressing AI vulnerabilities

To proactively identify vulnerabilities and maintain robust security, APEX implemented the following measures:

- **Conducting vulnerability assessments**:

  - **Thorough assessments**: They used Nessus to conduct comprehensive vulnerability assessments, focusing on data pipelines, model architectures, and deployment environments
  - **Red team exercises**: Red team exercises were performed to simulate real-world attacks, providing valuable insights for improving security measures

- **Implementing patch management processes**:

  - **Patch management**: A robust patch management process was established, using tools such as Microsoft SCCM to ensure all software components, including AI models, were regularly updated
  - **Critical updates**: APEX prioritized deploying essential security updates to address high-risk vulnerabilities promptly

- **Establishing continuous monitoring systems**:

  - **Monitoring infrastructure**: A comprehensive monitoring infrastructure using Prometheus was implemented to track the performance and security of AI systems
  - **Anomaly detection**: AI-driven anomaly detection systems such as Elastic Stack were used to identify unusual activities that might indicate a security breach

Results achieved

As a result of their comprehensive security initiatives, APEX achieved the following significant benefits:

- **Enhanced data security**: APEX significantly reduced the risk of data breaches by implementing advanced encryption and access control mechanisms. Their sensitive manufacturing data and AI models were now securely protected, ensuring the integrity and confidentiality of critical information.
- **Improved threat detection and response**: Leveraging AI for threat detection and incident response enabled APEX to identify and respond to potential threats in real time. This proactive approach minimized the impact of cyberattacks, ensuring continuous and secure operations.
- **Increased compliance and trust**: Comprehensive security measures and regular audits ensured that APEX met compliance requirements across multiple jurisdictions. This mitigated legal risks and enhanced client, partner, and stakeholder trust.

- **Robust AI system security**: Conducting regular vulnerability assessments, implementing patch management processes, and establishing continuous monitoring systems fortified the security of APEX's AI systems. This proactive approach helped identify and mitigate vulnerabilities before they could be exploited.

Anecdote

During a penetration test, an adversarial attack on APEX's predictive maintenance AI system was simulated. Initially, the model was easily tricked into making incorrect maintenance predictions, leading to potential equipment failures. After implementing robust encryption and continuous monitoring, the test was rerun. This time, the AI system accurately detected the adversarial inputs and flagged them for review, preventing disruptions. This success story boosted the confidence of APEX's engineering team in the security of their AI systems.

One of the most inspiring moments came during a company-wide meeting, during which APEX's CEO highlighted the importance of AI security in their innovation strategy. They emphasized that while AI drives its competitive edge, ensuring its security underpins its commitment to operational excellence and client trust. This message resonated deeply with employees, motivating them to embrace the new security frameworks and practices with purpose and responsibility.

Reflection and practical next steps

Before we conclude this chapter, take a moment to reflect on the insights we've explored. The landscape of AI is rapidly evolving, bringing unprecedented opportunities and challenges. The security concerns we've discussed aren't just theoretical—they're real-world issues that organizations and individuals grapple with daily. Think about your own experiences with AI systems, whether you're developing them, implementing them in your business, or simply interacting with them as a user. How do the concepts we've covered resonate with your context?

Consider the AI systems you work with or encounter regularly. How might they be vulnerable to the threats we've discussed? Imagine a scenario where one of these systems is compromised. What would the immediate impact be? How would it affect your work, organization, or daily life? Now, envision a future where robust security measures are seamlessly integrated into these systems. Picture the peace of mind that comes with knowing your AI applications are resilient against attacks, that your data is protected, and that you can trust the outputs of your models.

This vision isn't just a comforting thought—it's an achievable reality. But it requires action, commitment, and a willingness to adapt. Think about your current approach to AI security. Are you proactive or reactive? Do you view security as an essential component of AI development and deployment, or is it an afterthought? Reflecting on these questions can help you identify areas where you can make meaningful improvements.

As you ponder these ideas, challenge yourself to think critically about your current practices. Are there gaps in your security measures that you've been aware of but haven't addressed? What small steps could you take today to start closing those gaps? Enhancing AI security doesn't always require a complete overhaul of your systems. Often, it's about making incremental improvements and fostering a culture of security awareness.

Consider the people around you—your team members, colleagues, or fellow students. How can you share these insights with them? Could you initiate discussions about AI security in your workplace or academic environment? Consider making these concepts accessible and relevant to others, even if they're not directly involved in AI development.

As you progress, remember that improving AI security is an ongoing journey. The threat landscape is constantly evolving, and so must our security approaches. Stay curious and keep learning. Engage with the broader AI community, participate in discussions, and stay informed about emerging threats and best practices. Your active involvement enhances your knowledge and contributes to the field's collective wisdom.

Think about the long-term impact of your actions. Every step you take to enhance AI security, no matter how small, contributes to a more secure and trustworthy AI ecosystem. You're not just protecting your systems or organization—you're playing a part in shaping the future of AI. Your efforts today could influence how AI is developed, deployed, and regulated in the future.

As you reflect on these ideas, consider setting some personal goals related to AI security. What do you want to learn more about? What changes do you want to implement in your work or studies? How can you contribute to raising awareness about AI security in your professional or personal circles? Setting clear, achievable goals can help turn your reflections into concrete actions.

Remember, the journey to robust AI security is a collective effort. While individual actions are important, real progress comes when we work together, share knowledge, and support each other in implementing best practices. As you take your next steps, think about how you can collaborate with others to create a more secure AI future.

The field of AI is full of exciting possibilities, and by prioritizing security, we ensure that we can harness its full potential responsibly and safely. Your commitment to AI security, no matter how big or small, is a crucial part of this endeavor. So, as you close this chapter, ask yourself: What will your contribution to the future of secure AI be? The possibilities are limitless, and your journey starts now.

Summary

In this chapter, we navigated the complex landscape of AI security, exploring the unique challenges and innovative solutions for protecting AI systems. You gained insights into securing AI models and data and understanding how encryption, access controls, and regular audits form the backbone of a robust security framework. We also explored how AI can be leveraged in cybersecurity, turning a potential vulnerability into a powerful defense mechanism. You learned the importance of addressing AI-specific vulnerabilities, from adversarial attacks to data poisoning, and how continuous monitoring and adaptive strategies are crucial in this ever-evolving field.

Remember, AI security isn't just about implementing technical solutions—it's about fostering a culture of vigilance and continuous improvement. Consider how these concepts apply to your work or projects as you reflect on this chapter. Whether you're developing AI systems, implementing them in your organization, or simply interacting with AI daily, the principles we discussed have far-reaching implications. Think about how you can start incorporating these security measures, even in small ways, to enhance the trustworthiness and resilience of the AI systems you encounter.

As we wrap up this exploration of AI security, take a moment to consider the broader implications. How might improved AI security change how we develop and deploy AI systems? What role can you play in advocating for more robust security measures in your professional or academic environment? These are the kinds of questions that will shape the future of AI, and your insights and actions matter.

The next chapter will explore AI ethics, focusing on how AI reshapes privacy. As AI's need for data grows, balancing this with individual privacy rights is critical. We'll examine solutions such as data minimization, privacy-preserving AI models, and how security and privacy intersect in ethical AI development.

Questions

1. What are the three key challenges in AI security discussed in the chapter?
2. How can encryption techniques protect AI models and data?
3. What role does AI play in enhancing cybersecurity measures?
4. Explain the concept of adversarial attacks in the context of AI security.
5. Why is the explainability of AI models necessary for security?
6. What is data poisoning, and how does it affect AI systems?
7. Describe two methods for implementing access control in AI systems.
8. How can continuous monitoring help in addressing AI vulnerabilities?
9. What are the potential consequences of a security breach in an AI system used for critical applications?
10. How does the rapid evolution of AI threats impact the approach to AI security?

References

1. havocshield.com. *Threat Actors View SMBs as Easy Targets – Learn How to Protect Your Company.* https://blog.havocshield.com/en-us/cyber-attackers-think-small-businesses-make-easy-targets-heres-how-to-prove-them-wrong
2. hrss.cpa. *Cyber Defense Adversarial AI for Government Security.* https://hrss.cpa/adversarial-ai-cyber-defense-government-security-digital/

3. simpleshow.com. *Navigating AI risks: Balancing innovation and responsibility.* `https://simpleshow.com/blog/navigating-ai-risks-balancing-innovation-responsibility/`

4. usediminish.com. *SaaS Maturity: Navigating Growth.* `https://www.usediminish.com/blog/saas-maturity-navigating-growth`

5. howcomtech.com. *Ensuring Data Security In The Cloud: Strategies For Protection And Preservation.* `https://www.howcomtech.com/ensuring-data-security-in-the-cloud-strategies-for-protection-and-preservation/`

6. ciocoverage.com. *Foresite Cybersecurity – SaaS Cybersecurity & Risk Management.* `https://www.ciocoverage.com/foresite-cybersecurity-saas-cybersecurity-risk-management/`

7. allsimcode.com. *Data Security and Confidentiality: Ensuring Robust Protection in Idea Management Software Platforms.* `https://allsimcode.com/data-security-and-confidentiality-ensuring-robust-protection-in-idea-management-software-platforms/`

8. eyer.ai. *Adopting AI for Anomaly Detection: A Primer.* `https://eyer.ai/blog/adopting-ai-for-anomaly-detection-a-primer/`

9. cameronmcguffie.com. *Cyber Security Best Practices: Securing Sensitive Data in a Digital World.* `https://cameronmcguffie.com/cyber-security/cyber-security-best-practices-securing-sensitive-data-in-a-digital-world/`

10. netrio.com. *What Should I Be Doing as an SMB to Protect My Organization from Cybersecurity Threats?.* `https://www.netrio.com/how-to-protect-my-smb-from-cybersecurity-threats/`

14

Privacy in the Age of AI

> *I think trust comes from transparency and control. You want to see the datasets that these models have been trained on. You want to see how this model has been built, what kind of biases it includes. That's how you can trust the system. It's really hard to trust something that you don't understand.*
>
> *– Clem Delangue*

Imagine being woken up each morning by your smart home assistant, who knows your morning routine to the smallest detail. It has already adjusted the thermostat to your preferred temperature, brewed your coffee how you like it, and queued up your favorite playlist to start your day on the right note. As you head out, it reminds you to take an umbrella because it has checked the weather and knows rain is on the horizon. An intricate data collection, processing, and analysis network powers this seamless convenience. But where does all this personal data go? Who has access to it, and how is it being used?

Welcome to the age of AI, where the unprecedented capabilities of intelligent systems bring equally unprecedented challenges to our privacy. Consider this staggering statistic: in 2020 alone, nearly 3 billion personal records were exposed due to data breaches. That's almost 40% of the global population potentially having their private information compromised. As AI systems evolve and integrate into every facet of our lives, the importance of maintaining robust privacy measures cannot be overstated.

Take a moment to think about the last time you used a navigation app. It tracked your location, knew your destination, and remembered your preferred routes. This data is essential for providing real-time traffic updates and efficient navigation, but it also constructs a comprehensive map of your daily habits and movements. Imagine this information falling into the wrong hands or being used for purposes you never agreed to. The implications are both far-reaching and deeply concerning.

Protecting privacy in the AI age is formidable but not impossible. By understanding the complexities of data privacy and implementing robust privacy measures, we can safeguard our personal information and maintain trust in these transformative technologies. This chapter delves into the multifaceted world of AI and privacy, exploring the risks and offering practical solutions to protect your data.

Our journey will blend in-depth research with compelling narratives to make the topic engaging and accessible. We will use relatable stories and a touch of humor to ensure that the discussion remains grounded in real-world implications while being intellectually stimulating. In the age of AI, protecting your privacy is not just a personal responsibility—it is a fundamental aspect of living in a digitally connected world.

In this chapter, we will explore the following key topics:

- Understanding AI and data privacy
- Implementing privacy-preserving AI
- Regulations and best practices

By the end of this chapter, you will be able to comprehend the fundamental principles of AI and data privacy, apply privacy-preserving techniques in AI systems, and navigate the complex landscape of data protection regulations. You'll also have gained practical insights into implementing best practices for safeguarding personal information in AI-driven environments, enabling you to develop and manage AI systems that respect user privacy and comply with legal requirements.

The problem – pain points and challenges

As businesses increasingly integrate AI systems into their operations, they face significant challenges related to data privacy. These challenges are complex and multifaceted, encompassing technical, ethical, legal, and operational aspects. Understanding these pain points is crucial for developing effective privacy strategies. Let's delve deeper into businesses' specific problems and challenges regarding AI and data privacy.

Data collection and consent

One of the most fundamental challenges in AI and data privacy is collecting personal data and obtaining informed consent from users. AI systems often require vast amounts of data to function effectively, leading businesses to collect extensive user information. However, ensuring that users fully understand what data is being collected, how it will be used, and how to obtain their explicit consent can be daunting.

Consider the controversy surrounding Facebook and Cambridge Analytica. In 2018, it was revealed that Cambridge Analytica had harvested data from millions of Facebook users without explicit consent and used it for political advertising [1]. This scandal highlighted the difficulties in ensuring transparent data collection practices and securing informed consent, leading to significant legal and reputational repercussions for Facebook.

To obtain meaningful consent, businesses must provide clear and accessible information about their data practices. This involves creating user-friendly privacy policies and consent forms that explain, in plain language, what data will be collected, how it will be used, who it will be shared with, and how long it will be retained. However, many users may still find these documents complex or may not take the time to read them thoroughly, leading to questions about the validity of the consent obtained.

Data security and breaches

Data security is critical, as AI systems often process sensitive personal information. Protecting this data from breaches and unauthorized access is paramount. Data breaches can lead to the exposure of personal information, causing financial and reputational damage to businesses and eroding user trust.

In 2017, Equifax, a leading credit reporting agency, suffered a data breach that compromised the personal information of 147 million individuals, including Social Security numbers, birth dates, and addresses [2]. The breach resulted in substantial financial losses and damaged Equifax's reputation. It underscored the importance of robust data security measures, especially when handling sensitive information.

To protect against data breaches, businesses must implement comprehensive security protocols, including encryption, firewalls, intrusion detection systems, and regular security audits. However, the rapidly evolving nature of cyber threats means that these measures must be continuously updated and enhanced. Human factors such as employee negligence or insider threats can also compromise data security, necessitating ongoing training and awareness programs.

Compliance with regulations

Navigating the complex landscape of data privacy regulations is another significant challenge. Regulations such as the **General Data Protection Regulation (GDPR)** in Europe and the **California Consumer Privacy Act (CCPA)** in the United States impose stringent requirements on how businesses collect, store, and process personal data [3]. Ensuring compliance with these regulations can be resource-intensive and complex.

A global e-commerce company had to overhaul its data-handling processes to comply with GDPR. This involved revising data collection methods, updating privacy policies, and implementing new data protection measures. Despite the considerable investment of time and resources, non-compliance could result in hefty fines and legal consequences, emphasizing the importance of regulatory adherence.

Compliance with data privacy regulations involves a thorough understanding of the legal requirements and a commitment to implementing the necessary changes. This can include appointing a **data protection officer (DPO)**, conducting **data protection impact assessments (DPIAs)**, and establishing mechanisms for data subject rights such as access, rectification, and erasure. Moreover, businesses must stay abreast of evolving regulations and be prepared to adapt their practices accordingly.

Data minimization and retention

AI systems thrive on large datasets, but collecting and storing more data than necessary can pose privacy risks. Data minimization involves limiting data collection to what is strictly required, and establishing clear data retention policies is essential. However, balancing the need for data with privacy considerations can be challenging.

A health tech start-up collecting patient data to train its AI diagnostic tool faced the challenge of data minimization. To comply with privacy regulations, the company had to carefully assess what data was essential and establish protocols for securely deleting data once it was no longer needed. This balance ensured that the AI system remained effective while protecting patient privacy.

Implementing data minimization requires businesses to critically evaluate their data needs and limit collection to the minimum data necessary. This involves restricting data collection at the outset and periodically reviewing and purging unnecessary data. Effective data retention policies must specify clear timelines for data deletion and include procedures for securely disposing of data to prevent unauthorized access.

Anonymization and de-identification

Anonymizing or de-identifying personal data is a common strategy to protect privacy while still leveraging data for AI. However, achieving adequate anonymization can be difficult, and there is always a risk of re-identification, where anonymized data is matched with other datasets to reveal personal information.

A transportation company used anonymized location data to improve route planning and reduce congestion. However, researchers demonstrated that by combining this data with publicly available information, they could re-identify individuals' travel patterns. This highlighted the limitations of anonymization and the need for robust de-identification techniques.

Effective anonymization involves removing or obfuscating identifiers in the data, but even then, additional steps are often needed to prevent re-identification. Techniques such as differential privacy can add noise to the data, making it harder to re-identify individuals while allowing for helpful analysis. However, businesses must balance the trade-off between data utility and privacy protection, ensuring that anonymization methods are rigorously tested and continuously improved.

Ethical use of AI and data

Beyond legal compliance, businesses must also consider the ethical implications of their AI and data practices. This includes ensuring AI systems do not reinforce biases or discriminate against certain groups. Ethical considerations are crucial for maintaining public trust and fostering a positive corporate image.

A hiring platform using AI for candidate screening faced backlash when it was discovered that the AI system disproportionately favored male candidates over female candidates. This bias arose from the historical data used to train the AI. Addressing this ethical challenge required revising the training data and algorithms to ensure fair and unbiased hiring practices.

Ethical AI practices involve regular audits of AI systems to detect and mitigate biases, transparency in AI decision-making processes, and the involvement of diverse teams in developing and overseeing AI technologies. Businesses should adopt frameworks such as the AI Ethics Guidelines developed by the European Commission, which provide principles and practical steps for responsible AI development. Engaging with stakeholders, including affected communities, can also help ensure that AI systems align with societal values and expectations.

The solution and process – implementation

To effectively address the complex challenges of AI and data privacy, businesses must adopt a comprehensive approach that covers understanding AI and data privacy principles, implementing privacy-preserving AI techniques, and adhering to relevant regulations and best practices. Here, we present unique solutions and a step-by-step guide to implementing these solutions in a detailed manner.

Understanding AI and data privacy

Understanding the principles of AI and data privacy is crucial for developing ethical AI systems. Data privacy is a legal requirement and a critical factor in maintaining user trust and ensuring compliance with regulations. It involves safeguarding personal data against unauthorized access and misuse while balancing the need for data to drive AI innovations.

Implementing AI and data privacy works as follows:

- **Educate your team and stakeholders**:

    - **Training sessions**: Organize comprehensive training sessions on AI and data privacy principles. Ensure that all employees, from developers to executives, understand the importance of data privacy and their roles in protecting it. Use real-world examples and case studies to illustrate the impact of data privacy breaches.

    - **Workshops and seminars**: Conduct workshops and seminars with privacy experts to discuss the latest trends, challenges, and solutions in data privacy. Encourage interactive discussions and Q&A sessions to deepen understanding. Workshops can be structured around encryption, consent management, and data minimization.

    - **Regular updates**: Provide regular updates on changes in privacy regulations and emerging best practices. Use newsletters, internal bulletins, and intranet portals to keep everyone informed. Create a dedicated section on your company's intranet for resources on data privacy.

    Consider a scenario where a marketing team plans to use AI to personalize customer interactions. Attending a data privacy training session teaches them the importance of obtaining explicit consent before collecting and using customer data. This knowledge helps them design more privacy-conscious marketing strategies, enhancing customer trust and regulation compliance.

- **Develop privacy policies and procedures**:

  - **Privacy policies**: Draft clear and concise privacy policies that outline your organization's data collection, usage, and protection practices. Make these policies easily accessible to all employees and customers.

  - **Procedures and protocols**: Establish detailed procedures and protocols for data handling. This includes guidelines for data collection, storage, processing, and deletion. Ensure that these procedures are aligned with legal requirements and industry best practices.

- **Promote a culture of privacy awareness**:

  - **Privacy champions**: Appoint privacy champions within each department to promote privacy awareness and ensure compliance with privacy policies. These champions can serve as points of contact for privacy-related questions and concerns.

  - **Awareness campaigns**: Run ongoing awareness campaigns to promote data privacy. Use posters, emails, and internal communications to reinforce the importance of data privacy.

Implementing privacy-preserving AI

Implementing privacy-preserving AI involves using methodologies, tools, and frameworks that protect user data while enabling AI functionality. Techniques such as differential privacy, federated learning, and encryption are essential for safeguarding personal information in AI systems.

Here is how privacy-preserving AI can be implemented:

- **Select appropriate privacy-preserving techniques**:

  - **Differential privacy**: Use differential privacy to add noise to data, ensuring that individual data points cannot be identified while allowing for meaningful analysis. This technique helps balance data utility with privacy protection. Implement differential privacy in your data-processing workflows using tools such as Google's TensorFlow Privacy.

  - **Federated learning**: Implement federated learning, which allows AI models to be trained across multiple decentralized devices using local data. This approach keeps data on local devices, reducing the risk of data breaches. Use frameworks such as PySyft to facilitate federated learning.

  - **Encryption**: Apply robust encryption methods to protect data in transit and at rest. Use advanced encryption algorithms such as AES-256 to ensure data security. Implement end-to-end encryption for communications and data transfers.

- **Set up privacy-preserving protocols**:

  - **Privacy by design**: Integrate privacy considerations into the AI development life cycle. Ensure that privacy is a core component of system architecture and design. Conduct **privacy impact assessments** (**PIAs**) at the beginning of each project to identify and mitigate privacy risks.

  - **Privacy audits**: Conduct regular privacy audits to identify and address potential vulnerabilities in AI systems. Use automated tools and manual reviews to ensure comprehensive assessments. Engage third-party auditors for unbiased evaluations.

- **Practical tips and tools**:

  - **Tool selection**: Choose tools and frameworks that support privacy-preserving AI, such as TensorFlow Privacy or PySyft. These tools provide built-in functionalities for implementing privacy techniques.

  - **Implementation guides**: Follow detailed implementation guides provided by privacy-preserving toolkits. These guides offer step-by-step instructions on integrating privacy techniques into AI models. Utilize online resources, tutorials, and community support to aid implementation.

Regulations and best practices

Adhering to regulations and best practices relevant to AI and data privacy ensures compliance and builds user trust. Regulations such as GDPR and CCPA provide a framework for protecting personal data, while best practices offer guidelines for ethical data handling.

The implementation of this is as follows:

- **Set up compliance frameworks**:

  - **Regulatory compliance**: Establish a compliance framework that aligns with relevant data privacy regulations. Appoint a DPO to oversee compliance efforts and act as a point of contact for regulatory authorities.

  - **DPIAs**: Conduct DPIAs to evaluate the impact of data-processing activities on privacy [4]. Use these assessments to identify risks and implement mitigation strategies. Document all DPIAs and keep records for regulatory audits.

- **Monitor regulatory updates**:

  - **Stay informed**: Monitor updates to data privacy regulations regularly and adjust policies accordingly. Subscribe to newsletters, join industry forums, and participate in regulatory briefings to stay current. Use regulatory tracking software to automate monitoring.

  - **Compliance audits**: Perform regular compliance audits to ensure ongoing adherence to regulations. Use both internal and external auditors to obtain comprehensive evaluations. Conduct gap analyses to identify areas needing improvement.

- **Continuously improve privacy measures**:
  - **Feedback loops**: Establish feedback loops to gather insights from stakeholders about the effectiveness of privacy measures. Use this feedback to make continuous improvements. Conduct surveys and focus groups to gather input from employees and customers.
  - **Best practice adoption**: Adopt industry best practices for data privacy, such as the NIST Privacy Framework. Incorporate these practices into your organization's privacy policies and procedures. Regularly review and update best practices to align with evolving standards.

Let's go through the detailed steps for staying compliant:

1. **Initial assessment**: Conduct a thorough initial assessment of your current data privacy practices to identify gaps and areas for improvement.
2. **Policy development**: Develop and document comprehensive data privacy policies that align with regulatory requirements and best practices.
3. **Training and awareness**: Conduct continuous training and awareness programs to ensure employees fully understand their responsibilities in safeguarding data privacy.
4. **Audit and monitor**: Regularly audit data privacy practices and monitor for compliance. Automated tools streamline the audit process and ensure continuous compliance.
5. **Review and adapt**: Review and adapt privacy policies and practices to address new challenges and regulatory changes. Engage with industry experts and stakeholders to stay informed about emerging trends and best practices.

Hypothetical case study – APEX Manufacturing and Distribution

To illustrate the successful application of our frameworks and solutions for AI and data privacy, let's delve into a hypothetical case study of APEX Manufacturing and Distribution. This case study demonstrates how APEX navigated its initial challenges, implemented the recommended steps, and achieved significant results through robust data privacy practices.

Client's initial situation

APEX Manufacturing and Distribution, a global leader in industrial machinery, integrated AI systems into various aspects of its operations, from predictive maintenance to supply chain optimization. However, they faced several critical data privacy challenges:

- **Data collection and consent**: APEX collected extensive data from customers and suppliers to optimize their operations. However, they needed help obtaining explicit consent and providing clear information on how the data would be used.

- **Data security and breaches**: The company experienced minor data breaches, raising concerns about the security of its AI systems and the sensitive data it processes.
- **Regulatory compliance**: Navigating the complex landscape of global data privacy regulations, such as GDPR and CCPA, was resource-intensive and challenging for APEX.
- **Ethical use of AI and data**: APEX was increasingly concerned that its AI systems did not reinforce biases or discriminate against certain groups.

Steps taken

Let's look at the various steps implemented to overcome the observed challenges.

Understanding AI and data privacy

Here is how APEX implemented a robust data privacy strategy across the organization:

- **Educating the team and stakeholders**:
  - **Training sessions**: APEX organized comprehensive training sessions on AI and data privacy principles for all employees, from executives to data scientists. These sessions covered the importance of data privacy, the impact of breaches, and each employee's role in protecting data. For example, one session included a detailed walk-through of high-profile data breaches and their consequences, reinforcing the importance of vigilant data-handling practices.
  - **Workshops and seminars**: Privacy experts conducted workshops and seminars to discuss the latest trends, challenges, and solutions in data privacy. Interactive discussions and Q&A sessions helped deepen understanding. A notable symposium featured a panel of industry leaders discussing emerging privacy-preserving technologies and their applications in various sectors.
  - **Regular updates**: APEX provided regular updates on changes in privacy regulations and emerging best practices through newsletters and internal bulletins. A dedicated section on APEX's intranet was created for resources on data privacy. This section included video tutorials, policy documents, and an FAQ page to address common concerns.

- **Developing privacy policies and procedures**:
  - **Privacy policies**: Clear and concise privacy policies were drafted, outlining APEX's data collection, usage, and protection practices. These policies were made easily accessible to all employees and customers. The policies included specific guidelines on data anonymization, encryption standards, and user consent protocols.
  - **Procedures and protocols**: Detailed procedures for data handling were established, including guidelines for data collection, storage, processing, and deletion. These procedures aligned with legal requirements and industry best practices and were designed to be scalable, allowing for easy updates as regulations evolved.

- **Promoting a culture of privacy awareness**:

  - **Privacy champions**: Privacy champions were appointed within each department to promote privacy awareness and ensure compliance with privacy policies. These champions conducted monthly check-ins to address privacy-related issues and provide ongoing support.

  - **Awareness campaigns**: Ongoing awareness campaigns were run to keep data privacy in mind, using posters, emails, and internal communications to reinforce the importance of data privacy. An engaging campaign theme, "Protecting Privacy Together," highlighted the collective responsibility of all employees in safeguarding data.

Implementing privacy-preserving AI

Here is how APEX selected and implemented safeguards across their operations:

1. **Selecting appropriate privacy-preserving techniques**:

   - **Differential privacy**: Differential privacy techniques were implemented to add noise to data, ensuring individual data points could not be identified while allowing meaningful analysis. This technique was integrated into APEX's data-processing workflows, particularly in customer analytics and predictive maintenance applications.

   - **Federated learning**: Federated learning was employed to train AI models across multiple decentralized devices using local data, reducing the risk of data breaches. This approach was particularly beneficial for APEX's global operations, as it minimized data transfers between regions.

   - **Encryption**: Strong encryption methods, using advanced encryption algorithms such as AES-256, were applied to protect data both in transit and at rest. End-to-end encryption was implemented for all communications and data transfers within APEX's network.

2. **Setting up privacy-preserving protocols**:

   - **Privacy by design**: Privacy considerations were integrated into the AI development life cycle. PIAs were conducted at the beginning of each project to identify and mitigate privacy risks. Each AI project included a dedicated privacy review phase, ensuring privacy concerns were addressed before deployment.

   - **Privacy audits**: Regular privacy audits were conducted to identify and address potential vulnerabilities in AI systems, using automated tools and manual reviews for comprehensive assessments [5]. These audits included testing for compliance with internal policies and external regulations.

3. **Practical tips and tools**:

    - **Tool selection**: Tools and frameworks that support privacy-preserving AI, such as TensorFlow Privacy and PySyft, were chosen for implementation. These tools provided built-in functionalities for implementing privacy techniques and were integrated into APEX's AI infrastructure.
    - **Implementation guides**: Detailed implementation guides from privacy-preserving toolkits were followed, offering step-by-step instructions on integrating privacy techniques into AI models. Additionally, internal documentation was created to ensure consistency across different teams and projects.

Regulations and best practices

Here is how APEX ensured they remained proactive and aligned with industry standards:

- **Set up compliance frameworks**:

    - **Regulatory compliance**: A compliance framework aligned with relevant data privacy regulations was established. A DPO was appointed to oversee compliance efforts and act as a point of contact for regulatory authorities. The DPO's responsibilities included conducting regular training sessions and staying updated on regulatory changes.
    - **DPIAs**: DPIAs were conducted to evaluate the impact of data-processing activities on privacy, identify risks, and implement mitigation strategies. DPIAs became a mandatory step in APEX's project management workflow, ensuring that privacy risks were evaluated early and often.

- **Monitored regulatory updates**:

    - **Stay informed**: Regular updates to data privacy regulations were monitored, and policies were adjusted accordingly. Regulatory tracking software was used to automate monitoring. The software provided alerts on upcoming regulatory changes, ensuring that APEX remained proactive in its compliance efforts.
    - **Compliance audits**: Regular compliance audits were performed to ensure adherence to ongoing regulations. These audits used internal and external auditors for comprehensive evaluations, thorough documentation reviews, and interviews with key personnel.

- **Continuously improved privacy measures**:

    - **Feedback loops**: Feedback loops were established to gather insights from stakeholders about the effectiveness of privacy measures, using this feedback for continuous improvements. Regular surveys and feedback sessions with employees and customers provided valuable insights into the practical application of privacy policies.
    - **Best practice adoption**: Industry best practices for data privacy, such as the NIST Privacy Framework, were adopted and incorporated into APEX's privacy policies and procedures. Periodic reviews of best practices ensured that APEX remained aligned with industry standards.

Results achieved

Implementation of these steps produced the following results:

- **Enhanced data collection and consent**: APEX educated its team and stakeholders on data privacy principles and developed clear and user-friendly consent forms. This ensured that customers and suppliers were fully informed about data collection practices and provided explicit consent, enhancing transparency and trust. APEX also implemented an easy-to-navigate online portal where customers could manage their data preferences and consent settings.

- **Strengthened data security**: Implementing robust encryption methods and regular privacy audits significantly improved the security of APEX's AI systems. The risk of data breaches was reduced considerably, safeguarding sensitive information and bolstering user confidence. APEX also introduced advanced threat detection systems that monitored network activity for signs of unauthorized access.

- **Improved regulatory compliance**: The comprehensive compliance framework ensured that APEX stayed ahead of regulatory requirements. Regular DPIAs and compliance audits helped identify and mitigate risks, avoiding significant fines and legal consequences. Compliance reports were generated quarterly, providing detailed insights into the company's adherence to data privacy regulations.

- **Ethical AI practices**: By integrating privacy-preserving techniques such as differential privacy and federated learning, APEX maintained high data privacy standards without compromising its AI systems' functionality. This ethical approach fostered a positive corporate image and public trust. APEX also developed an ethics committee to review AI projects, ensuring they met ethical standards before deployment.

During a privacy training session, a member of the APEX marketing team shared a story about a previous campaign that had faced backlash due to privacy concerns. The team had collected customer data without explicit consent, leading to negative publicity and customer distrust. The training session highlighted the importance of transparency and consent, inspiring the team to adopt more ethical data practices. This change improved their campaigns and strengthened their relationship with customers.

One of the most inspiring moments came during a company-wide meeting, during which APEX's CEO emphasized the importance of data privacy in their innovation strategy. They highlighted that while AI drives their competitive edge, ensuring data privacy underpins their commitment to ethical practices and customer trust. This message resonated deeply with employees, motivating them to embrace the new privacy frameworks and practices with purpose and responsibility.

Detailed implementation and continued success

After implementing the new privacy measures, APEX took several additional steps to ensure ongoing success and improvement:

- **Continuous education and training**:

    - **Refresher courses**: Regular refresher courses on data privacy were organized to keep employees updated on the latest best practices and regulatory changes. These sessions reinforced the importance of data privacy and provided practical examples of handling data ethically.

    - **Onboarding programs**: New hires received comprehensive training on data privacy as part of their onboarding process. This ensured that all employees understood the company's commitment to data privacy from day one, regardless of their role or department.

- **Advanced privacy technologies**:

    - **Privacy-enhancing technologies (PETs)**: APEX invested in advanced PETs to further protect customer data. This included adopting homomorphic encryption, which allows data to be processed without decrypting, ensuring that sensitive information remains secure even during computation.

    - **AI-driven privacy monitoring**: AI-driven tools were implemented to continuously monitor data flows and detect any anomalies that might indicate a potential data breach or misuse. These tools provided real-time alerts and automated responses to mitigate risks quickly.

- **Enhanced customer communication**:

    - **Transparent communication**: APEX made a concerted effort to communicate its data privacy practices transparently to customers. Detailed privacy notices were provided at every touchpoint, explaining how data was collected, used, and protected.

    - **Customer feedback channels**: Dedicated channels for customer feedback on privacy issues were established. This allowed customers to voice their concerns and suggestions, which APEX used to refine their privacy practices further.

- **Regular privacy assessments and audits**:

    - **Third-party audits**: Independent third-party audits were conducted annually to assess APEX's compliance with data privacy regulations and best practices. These audits provided an unbiased evaluation of the company's privacy measures and identified areas for improvement.

    - **Internal privacy reviews**: The privacy team conducted quarterly internal reviews to ensure all departments adhered to established privacy policies and procedures. These reviews included spot checks and random audits to maintain high data protection standards.

- **Ethical AI development**:
  - **Bias detection and mitigation**: APEX developed and implemented tools to detect and mitigate biases in its AI models. It also regularly audited AI algorithms to ensure fairness and prevent discrimination.
  - **Ethics committees**: Ethics committees were formed to review AI projects and ensure they aligned with the company's ethical guidelines. These committees included representatives from diverse backgrounds to provide various perspectives.

Long-term impact

The comprehensive approach to data privacy had a lasting positive impact on APEX Manufacturing and Distribution:

- **Increased customer trust and loyalty**: Customers appreciated the transparent communication and robust privacy measures, leading to increased trust and loyalty. APEX saw a significant improvement in customer satisfaction scores and reduced churn rates.
- **Competitive advantage**: APEX gained a competitive advantage in the market by prioritizing data privacy. Their commitment to ethical data practices attracted new customers and business partners, enhancing their reputation as a trustworthy and forward-thinking company.
- **Regulatory compliance and risk mitigation**: The thorough compliance framework ensured that APEX remained ahead of regulatory requirements, avoiding fines and legal challenges. This proactive approach to compliance also minimized the risk of data breaches and associated financial losses.
- **Innovation with integrity**: APEX's ethical AI practices enabled them to innovate with integrity. They developed cutting-edge AI solutions that respected privacy and fairness, contributing to their long-term success and sustainability.
- **Organizational culture of privacy**: The emphasis on data privacy fostered a culture of privacy awareness throughout the organization. Employees at all levels understood the importance of protecting personal information and proactively identified and mitigated privacy risks.

The APEX Manufacturing and Distribution case underscores the transformative impact of implementing robust data privacy measures. By addressing data collection and consent issues, enhancing data security, ensuring regulatory compliance, and adopting ethical AI practices, APEX safeguarded its operations, built trust, and maintained a positive reputation.

Reflection and practical next steps

Before we conclude this chapter, take a moment to reflect on the core insights we've explored. Consider how the principles of privacy-preserving AI and ethical data handling resonate with your own experiences.

Have you encountered situations where better privacy practices could have made a difference? Think about the potential impact of implementing these strategies in your work or personal projects. How might adopting a "privacy by design" approach change how you develop or interact with AI systems?

Now, let's challenge ourselves to critically assess our current practices. Are your data collection methods truly transparent and consent-driven? How robust are your data security measures in the face of evolving threats? Consider the ethical implications of your AI systems—are they free from biases and respectful of individual privacy? These questions aren't meant to overwhelm but to inspire action and improvement.

Identify one or two concrete steps to enhance privacy in your AI practices. Perhaps it's conducting a thorough DPIA on your next project or implementing differential privacy techniques in your data analysis. Maybe it's as simple as revisiting your privacy policies to ensure they're clear and accessible. Remember, progress doesn't have to be monumental to be meaningful. Even small changes, such as introducing regular privacy training for your team, can have a significant impact over time.

As you embark on this journey, remember the example of APEX Manufacturing and Distribution. Their commitment to privacy enhanced their security, built trust, and fostered innovation. You, too, can turn privacy challenges into opportunities for growth and excellence. Whether you're a developer, manager, or enthusiast, you have the power to champion ethical AI practices and set new standards in your field.

So, what will your first step be? Will you start by educating your team on privacy principles or exploring PETs? Whatever you choose, approach it with curiosity and determination. The path to privacy-conscious AI may seem complex, but each step you take brings you closer to a future where innovation and privacy go hand in hand. Remember, in the rapidly evolving world of AI, staying informed and adaptable is key. Embrace this opportunity to lead by example and make a positive impact in the realm of AI and data privacy.

Summary

In this chapter, we journeyed through the complex landscape of privacy in the age of AI. You gained insights into challenges in data collection, security, and ethical AI use and learned practical strategies to address these issues. From implementing privacy-preserving techniques such as differential privacy and federated learning to navigating regulatory compliance, you're now equipped with the knowledge to approach AI development with a privacy-first mindset. Protecting privacy isn't just about following rules—it is also about building trust and fostering innovation responsibly.

As we close this chapter, consider how you can apply these principles in your work. Whether you're fine-tuning data collection practices or rethinking AI model design, every step toward better privacy practices counts. In the next chapter, we'll build on this foundation as we dive into compliance, exploring how to navigate the regulatory landscape while keeping your AI innovations on track. Get ready to transform legal requirements into opportunities for excellence in AI development.

Questions

1. What is differential privacy, and how does it contribute to privacy-preserving AI?
2. Name two key challenges businesses face when implementing AI systems concerning data privacy.
3. How does federated learning help protect user privacy in AI systems?
4. What is a **data protection impact assessment** (**DPIA**) and when should it be conducted?
5. Explain the concept of "privacy by design" and its importance in AI development.
6. What role does encryption play in safeguarding data privacy in AI systems?
7. How can organizations foster a culture of privacy awareness among their employees?
8. What was one significant result of implementing robust data privacy measures in the APEX Manufacturing and Distribution case study?
9. Why is it important to regularly update and review privacy policies and practices in AI development?
10. How can ethical AI practices contribute to a company's competitive advantage?

References

1. pogowasright.org. *Judge Warns Facebook in Approving Record $5B Fine for Alleged Privacy Violations.* https://www.pogowasright.org/judge-warns-facebook-in-approving-record-5b-fine-for-alleged-privacy-violations.
2. thepuregoldcompany.co.uk. *Protecting yourself from a digital Armageddon.* https://thepuregoldcompany.co.uk/protecting-yourself-from-a-digital-armageddon.
3. *Re-Thinking Data Strategy and Integration for Artificial Intelligence: Concepts, Opportunities, and Challenges.* Aldoseri, A. & Al-Khalifa, K. (2023). 12, s.l. : Applied Sciences, Vol. 13. 708.
4. legalfoxess.com. Data privacy and protection. https://www.legalfoxess.com/data-privacy-and-protection
5. cyberdefensemagazine.com. *Cybersecurity Implications of AI.* https://www.cyberdefensemagazine.com/cybersecurity-implications-of-ai/

15
AI Compliance

Digital workplace leaders will proactively implement AI-based technologies such as virtual assistants or other NLP-based conversational agents and robots to support and augment employees' tasks and productivity. However, the AI agents must be properly monitored to prevent digital harassment and frustrating user experiences.

– Helen Poitevin

Imagine you've just developed a revolutionary AI application that has the potential to transform your industry. It's intelligent, efficient, and exactly what your customers need. But as you prepare to launch, you're hit with a daunting realization: the labyrinth of compliance requirements. Did you know that failing to comply with AI regulations can result in fines of up to 4% of global annual turnover or €20 million, whichever is higher, under the GDPR [1]? That's a staggering figure that can hurt even the most successful enterprises.

Welcome to the world of AI compliance, where navigating the intricate web of regulations and standards is as crucial as the technology itself. The rise of AI has brought incredible advancements. Still, it has also ushered in a complex regulatory landscape to protect consumers, ensure ethical practices, and foster trust in AI technologies.

Consider this: In 2020, a global financial institution faced a hefty fine of $100 million for non-compliance with AI-related data privacy regulations. The incident impacted their economic standing and tarnished their reputation, causing a loss of customer trust and market share. This stark example underscores the significance of robust AI compliance practices.

And it's not just about avoiding fines. Compliance plays a crucial role in building trust with your customers and stakeholders. Imagine you're using an AI-powered app that handles sensitive personal data, and you learn that the company behind it has been flagged for non-compliance with privacy regulations. Would you still feel comfortable using that app? Probably not. Ensuring compliance signals to your users that you take their privacy and security seriously, fostering trust and loyalty.

Another key area is transparency and explainability. Users should be informed about how their data is used and be able to understand AI decision-making processes. Implementing mechanisms to provide clear explanations of AI decisions is crucial. For instance, an insurance company using AI to assess claims can give the customers understandable explanations of how the AI arrived at its conclusion, enhancing transparency and trust.

Fairness and bias mitigation are also essential components of AI compliance. Regulations increasingly emphasize the need to address bias and ensure fairness in AI systems. This involves conducting bias assessments, implementing mitigation strategies, using diverse datasets, and regularly reviewing AI models for potential biases. For example, a hiring platform can use diverse training data and conduct bias audits to ensure its AI-driven recruitment processes do not unfairly discriminate against certain groups.

In this chapter, we will cover the following key topics:

- Ensuring AI compliance with industry standards
- Navigating legal and regulatory requirements
- Building a culture of compliance and accountability

By the end of this chapter, you will be able to implement comprehensive AI compliance strategies within your organization. You'll know how to align your AI systems with industry standards, navigate the complex landscape of AI regulations, and foster a robust culture of compliance and accountability across your teams. These skills will enable you to mitigate risks, build trust with stakeholders, and position your organization at the forefront of responsible AI adoption.

The problem – pain points and challenges

Navigating the labyrinth of AI compliance presents many challenges for businesses, ranging from data privacy concerns to the ever-evolving regulatory landscape. Understanding these pain points is crucial for developing effective compliance strategies. Let's delve into the problems and challenges businesses encounter regarding AI compliance.

Complex and evolving regulations

One of the most significant challenges that businesses face is the complexity and rapid evolution of AI regulations. Regulations such as GDPR in Europe, CCPA in California, and the upcoming EU AI Act impose stringent data handling, transparency, and accountability requirements. Keeping up with these regulations and ensuring compliance can take time and effort.

Consider the case of a multinational tech company fined €50 million under GDPR for not adequately informing users about how their data was being used for personalized ads. Despite investing heavily in compliance, the company struggled to keep pace with the evolving regulatory landscape and ensure that all its practices were current.

The fast pace of regulatory changes means that businesses must continuously monitor and adapt to new requirements. This can be resource-intensive and requires a dedicated compliance team or officer who can stay abreast of regulatory updates and ensure that the organization's practices align with the latest standards. Moreover, regulatory compliance isn't just a legal obligation and a strategic advantage. Companies that demonstrate robust compliance can build stronger relationships with regulators and customers, enhancing their reputation and market position.

Data privacy and security

Data privacy and security are at the core of AI compliance challenges. AI systems often require large amounts of personal data to function effectively, but this data must be handled per strict privacy regulations. Ensuring that data is collected, stored, and processed securely is essential to avoid breaches and penalties.

In 2019, British Airways faced a £20 million fine for a data breach that compromised the personal data of over 400,000 customers [2]. The breach resulted from poor security practices, highlighting the critical need for robust data protection measures in AI systems.

Data breaches can result in financial penalties and damage an organization's reputation. To mitigate these risks, robust encryption methods, regular security audits, and data handling practices that comply with relevant regulations are essential. Additionally, businesses must adopt a proactive stance on data privacy, integrating security measures into AI systems' design and development stages. This approach, known as privacy by design, ensures that privacy considerations are baked into the core functionality of AI applications [3].

Transparency and explainability

Transparency and explainability are crucial for building user trust and complying with regulations. Many AI systems operate as "black boxes," making decisions that are not easily understandable to users. This lack of transparency can lead to compliance issues and erode user trust.

A major social media platform faced backlash when its AI algorithm for content recommendation was found to amplify misleading information. The company needed help explaining how the algorithm worked, which led to public distrust and regulatory scrutiny.

Ensuring transparency and explainability in AI systems involves developing mechanisms to explain AI decisions clearly. This can include using **explainable AI (XAI)** techniques and providing users with detailed information about their data use. Transparency not only aids compliance but also enhances user trust and satisfaction. Furthermore, regulators are increasingly focusing on the explainability of AI decisions to ensure that automated systems do not produce unfair or discriminatory outcomes.

Bias and fairness

Bias in AI systems is a significant challenge that can lead to unfair and discriminatory outcomes. Ensuring that AI systems are fair and do not perpetuate biases is critical for regulatory compliance and ethical AI practices.

A recruitment platform that used AI to screen job applicants faced criticism when it was revealed that the AI system disproportionately favored male candidates over female candidates. This bias stemmed from the historical data used to train the AI, highlighting the need for rigorous bias detection and mitigation strategies.

Addressing bias in AI systems requires ongoing efforts, including using diverse training data, conducting regular bias audits, and implementing mitigation strategies. Ensuring fairness in AI systems is a regulatory and moral obligation to prevent discrimination and promote equality. Businesses must continuously monitor and update their AI models to identify and correct biases that may arise over time.

Accountability and governance

Establishing clear accountability and governance frameworks for AI systems is essential for compliance. This involves defining roles and responsibilities, implementing continuous monitoring, and conducting regular audits to ensure adherence to regulations.

An international retailer implemented an AI-driven supply chain management system. However, without a clear governance framework, the system led to significant operational disruptions due to unmonitored biases and errors. This lack of accountability resulted in financial losses and regulatory scrutiny.

Accountability and governance frameworks help ensure that AI systems are developed and operated responsibly. This includes assigning responsibility for compliance, conducting regular audits, and continuously monitoring AI systems for adherence to ethical and regulatory standards. Effective governance promotes transparency, accountability, and trust. Establishing an AI ethics committee or board can also provide oversight and ensure that AI initiatives align with broader organizational values and ethical standards.

Integration with existing systems and processes

Integrating AI compliance measures with existing systems and processes can be challenging. Many organizations have legacy systems that may not be designed to handle the complexities of AI and its associated compliance requirements.

A financial institution attempted to integrate an AI-based fraud detection system with its IT infrastructure. The integration process revealed numerous incompatibilities and data handling issues, leading to delays and compliance concerns.

Successful integration requires thorough planning and coordination across different departments. Organizations must assess their existing infrastructure and identify potential gaps hindering compliance. Collaboration between IT, legal, and compliance teams is crucial to ensure that AI systems are seamlessly integrated and compliant with relevant regulations.

Resource constraints

Implementing and maintaining AI compliance measures can be resource-intensive. Many organizations, including **small and medium-sized enterprises** (**SMEs**), may need help allocating resources for comprehensive compliance efforts.

A start-up developing an AI-driven health monitoring app faced significant challenges in meeting compliance requirements due to limited resources. The need for dedicated compliance staff and budget constraints made it difficult to implement robust compliance measures.

Resource constraints can be mitigated by leveraging external expertise and technology solutions. Engaging with compliance consultants, utilizing compliance software, and participating in industry collaborations can help organizations manage compliance more effectively. Additionally, prioritizing compliance efforts based on risk assessments can ensure that resources are allocated to the most critical areas.

In my experience working with various organizations, I have seen firsthand the difficulties businesses face in navigating AI compliance. At one organization, we implemented an AI-driven customer service tool that required access to customer interaction data. Ensuring that this data was collected with explicit consent and securely stored was significant. We had to update our privacy policies, enhance our data security measures, and conduct regular audits to maintain compliance with data protection regulations.

Another anecdote involves a project where we developed a personalized marketing AI system. The system needed detailed customer profiles to deliver tailored recommendations. To address privacy concerns, we employed data anonymization techniques and provided customers with precise opt-in mechanisms, allowing them to control their data usage. This not only ensured compliance but also enhanced customer trust and engagement.

The solution and process – implementation

A comprehensive approach that encompasses adherence to industry standards, navigating legal and regulatory requirements, and fostering a culture of compliance and accountability is essential to address the complex challenges of AI compliance. Here, we present unique solutions and a step-by-step guide to implementing these solutions effectively.

Ensuring AI compliance with industry standards

Following industry standards is crucial for maintaining credibility, operational excellence, and stakeholder trust. Industry standards provide a framework for best practices, ensuring that AI systems are developed and operated responsibly and ethically.

Let's see the implementation steps:

1. **Conduct compliance audits**:
   - **Regular audits**: Conduct regular compliance audits to evaluate whether your AI systems meet industry standards. Use both internal and external auditors to provide a comprehensive evaluation. For example, a financial services company can schedule quarterly audits to ensure its AI systems adhere to financial industry standards.
   - **Audit checklist**: Develop a detailed audit checklist based on relevant industry standards. This checklist should cover data privacy, security protocols, transparency, bias detection, and ethical considerations.
   - **Compliance gaps**: During the audit, identify gaps and areas of non-compliance. Develop a remediation plan to address these issues promptly.

2. **Implement standardized protocols**:
   - **Standard operating procedures** (SOPs): Develop and implement SOPs that align with industry standards. Ensure that these procedures are documented and accessible to all team members. SOPs should include guidelines for data handling, model development, and monitoring processes.
   - **Compliance management tools**: Utilize compliance management tools that automate and streamline the process of adhering to industry standards. These tools can track compliance activities, manage documentation, and provide real-time insights into compliance status.
   - **Regular reviews**: Schedule regular reviews of SOPs to ensure they remain current and relevant as industry standards evolve.

3. **Utilize frameworks and best practices**:
   - **Adopt frameworks**: Adopt well-established frameworks such as the NIST AI Risk Management Framework or the ISO/IEC 27001 standard for information security management. These frameworks provide structured approaches to managing AI risks and ensuring compliance.
   - **Best practices**: Incorporate industry best practices into your compliance strategy. This includes regular training, continuous monitoring, and proactive risk management. For instance, implementing a change management process can help track and manage updates to AI systems while ensuring continued compliance.

Navigating legal and regulatory requirements

Navigating the complex legal and regulatory landscape surrounding AI involves understanding applicable laws, setting up compliance teams, and continuously monitoring regulatory changes. Practical strategies and frameworks can ensure compliance with relevant regulations and avoid legal repercussions.

Here are the implementation steps:

1. **Identify applicable regulations**:

   - **Regulatory mapping**: Conduct a comprehensive mapping of applicable regulations based on your industry and geographic location. Identify critical regulations such as GDPR, CCPA, HIPAA, and the upcoming EU AI Act. This process should involve legal experts and compliance officers to ensure accuracy.

   - **Regulatory database**: Maintain an up-to-date database of applicable regulations and compliance requirements. This database should be easily accessible to all relevant stakeholders. Include summaries and links to full texts of rules for quick reference.

2. **Set up compliance teams**:

   - **Dedicated compliance team**: Establish a dedicated compliance team that is responsible for monitoring regulatory changes, conducting audits, and ensuring adherence to legal requirements. This team should include legal experts, compliance officers, and data protection officers. Define clear roles and responsibilities for each team member.

   - **Training and resources**: Provide regular training and resources to the compliance team to inform them about the latest regulatory developments. Encourage continuous learning and professional development. Offer access to industry conferences, webinars, and workshops.

3. **Continuous monitoring and adaptation**:

   - **Regulatory monitoring tools**: Utilize regulatory monitoring tools to stay updated on changes in laws and regulations. These tools can provide real-time alerts and updates, ensuring that your compliance team is always informed. Tools such as Thomson Reuters Regulatory Intelligence or OneTrust can be valuable assets.

   - **Compliance audits**: Conduct regular audits to evaluate adherence to legal requirements. Use the findings from these audits to make necessary adjustments and improvements to your compliance strategy. Develop a cycle of pre-audit preparation, audit execution, and post-audit follow-up to ensure continuous compliance.

Building a culture of compliance and accountability

Fostering a culture of compliance and accountability within an organization is essential for long-term success. This involves instilling ethical behavior, transparency, and responsibility values across all teams and departments.

The implementation steps are as follows:

1. **Develop training programs**:

    - **Comprehensive training**: Develop and implement comprehensive training programs that educate employees about compliance requirements, ethical considerations, and best practices. Training should be mandatory for all employees and tailored to specific roles and responsibilities. Incorporate interactive elements such as quizzes, case studies, and role-playing scenarios.
    - **Interactive workshops**: Conduct interactive workshops and seminars to reinforce compliance training. Use real-world scenarios and case studies to illustrate the importance of compliance and ethical behavior. Encourage participation and discussion to deepen understanding and engagement.

2. **Establish clear communication channels**:

    - **Open communication**: Establish open communication channels that allow employees to report compliance concerns and seek guidance. Ensure that these channels are confidential and encourage a speak-up culture. Implement anonymous reporting mechanisms such as hotlines or secure online portals.
    - **Regular updates**: Provide regular updates on compliance activities, regulatory changes, and best practices. Use newsletters, intranet portals, and team meetings to disseminate information. Highlight success stories and recognize employees who demonstrate exemplary compliance behavior.

3. **Set up accountability measures**:

    - **Clear roles and responsibilities**: Define clear roles and responsibilities for compliance activities. Assign accountability to specific individuals and teams and ensure that these responsibilities are documented and communicated. Develop role-specific compliance checklists and job aids.
    - **Performance metrics**: Establish performance metrics to evaluate compliance efforts. Use these metrics to track progress, identify areas for improvement, and recognize achievements. Metrics can include the number of compliance training sessions completed, audit findings, and incident reports.

Hypothetical case study – APEX Manufacturing and Distribution

To illustrate the successful application of our AI compliance framework, let's explore a hypothetical case study of APEX Manufacturing and Distribution. This case study demonstrates how APEX navigated its initial challenges, implemented our recommended steps, and achieved significant results in compliance with industry standards, legal and regulatory navigation, and building a culture of compliance.

Client's initial situation

APEX Manufacturing and Distribution, a global leader in industrial machinery, was experiencing rapid growth and integrated AI systems into various operations, from predictive maintenance to supply chain optimization. However, they faced several critical challenges:

- **Industry standards compliance**: APEX struggled to keep up with the evolving industry standards for AI, leading to inconsistencies in its compliance efforts across different regions and departments
- **Legal and regulatory navigation**: AI regulations' complex and ever-changing landscape posed significant challenges, especially with varying requirements across different jurisdictions
- **Culture of compliance**: Despite having basic compliance measures in place, APEX needed a cohesive culture of compliance and accountability across the organization

Steps taken

They executed the following steps to tackle the compliance-related challenges.

Ensuring AI compliance with industry standards

To ensure that APEX's AI systems adhere to the highest industry standards, we initiated key actions focused on the following:

1. **Conduct compliance audits**:

    - **Initial action**: We initiated a series of comprehensive compliance audits across APEX's AI systems to evaluate their adherence to industry standards. These audits were conducted by a combination of internal auditors and external consultants specializing in AI compliance.

    The implementation steps were as follows:

    - **Regular audits**: Quarterly audits were scheduled to ensure continuous monitoring and adherence to standards. Each audit cycle thoroughly reviewed data privacy practices, security protocols, and ethical considerations.
    - **Audit checklist**: We developed a detailed audit checklist based on industry standards such as the ISO/IEC 27001 for information security management and the NIST AI Risk Management Framework [4].
    - **Outcome**: The audits revealed several compliance gaps, particularly in data handling and security protocols. We identified these gaps early and implemented targeted remediation plans, ensuring that APEX's AI systems met the highest industry standards.

2. **Implement standardized protocols**:

    - **Initial action**: APEX had multiple teams working on AI projects, each with its own procedures. We standardized their protocols to streamline efforts and align them with industry best practices.

    The implementation steps were as follows:

    - **SOPs**: We developed and implemented SOPs tailored to APEX's specific needs while aligning with industry standards. These SOPs included guidelines for data handling, model development, and regular monitoring.

    - **Compliance management tools**: APEX adopted compliance management tools that automated and streamlined adherence to industry standards. These tools tracked compliance activities, managed documentation, and provided real-time insights.

    - **Outcome**: Implementing standardized protocols significantly improved consistency across APEX's AI projects. Compliance management tools provided clear visibility into compliance status, enabling proactive management of potential issues.

Navigating legal and regulatory requirements

To effectively navigate the complex regulatory landscape and ensure compliance, we focused on the following strategies:

1. **Identify applicable regulations**:

    - **Initial action**: To ensure accuracy, we comprehensively mapped applicable regulations based on APEX's industry and geographic locations, involving legal experts and compliance officers.

    The implementation steps included the following:

    - **Regulatory database**: We created a regulatory database that included summaries and full texts of relevant regulations such as GDPR, CCPA, HIPAA, and the upcoming EU AI Act. This database was accessible to all relevant stakeholders.

    - **Regulatory mapping**: Detailed mapping exercises were conducted to identify key regulations and compliance requirements, ensuring that APEX's practices were aligned with legal standards across different regions.

    - **Outcome**: The regulatory mapping exercise provided a clear understanding of the compliance landscape, enabling APEX to address regulatory requirements more effectively. The regulatory database became a vital resource for the compliance team, ensuring that they stayed informed about changes and updates.

2. **Set up compliance teams**:

    - **Initial action**: APEX had a basic compliance structure but needed a dedicated team focused on AI compliance. We established a dedicated compliance team that was responsible for monitoring regulatory changes and ensuring adherence.

    The implementation steps were as follows:

    - **Dedicated compliance team**: A team comprising legal experts, compliance officers, and data protection officers was formed. Roles and responsibilities were clearly defined, with team members trained in the latest regulatory developments.
    - **Training and resources**: We provided regular training sessions and resources to keep the compliance team updated on regulatory changes. We also facilitated access to industry conferences, webinars, and workshops.
    - **Outcome**: Establishing a dedicated compliance team significantly improved APEX's ability to navigate the complex regulatory landscape. The team's proactive approach ensured continuous compliance and minimized legal risks.

3. **Continuous monitoring and adaptation**:

    - **Initial action**: To ensure ongoing compliance, we needed a robust system for monitoring regulatory changes and adapting practices accordingly.

    The implementation steps were as follows:

    - **Regulatory monitoring tools**: APEX adopted regulatory monitoring tools such as Thomson Reuters Regulatory Intelligence and OneTrust, which provided real-time alerts and updates on changes in laws and regulations.
    - **Compliance audits**: Regular compliance audits were conducted to evaluate adherence to legal requirements. The findings were used to adjust APEX's compliance strategy.
    - **Outcome**: Continuous monitoring and regular audits ensured that APEX remained compliant with evolving regulations. Advanced regulatory monitoring tools enabled the compliance team to stay ahead of changes and proactively address potential issues.

Building a culture of compliance and accountability

To foster a robust culture of compliance within APEX, we focused on the following:

1. **Develop training programs**:

    - **Initial action**: APEX had basic training programs but needed comprehensive training to instill a solid organizational compliance culture.

Here are the implementation steps we followed:

- **Comprehensive training**: We developed and implemented extensive training programs that educated employees about compliance requirements, ethical considerations, and best practices. These programs included interactive quizzes, case studies, and role-playing scenarios.
- **Interactive workshops**: Regular interactive workshops and seminars were conducted to reinforce compliance training. Real-world scenarios and case studies illustrated the importance of compliance and ethical behavior.

- **Outcome**: The training programs significantly enhanced employees' understanding of compliance requirements and ethical considerations. Interactive workshops increased engagement and retention, fostering a culture of compliance throughout the organization.

2. **Establish clear communication channels**:

- **Initial action**: APEX needed to improve its communication channels to encourage open reporting of compliance concerns and provide clear guidance.

These are the implementation steps we followed:

- **Open communication**: We established open communication channels, including anonymous reporting mechanisms such as hotlines and secure online portals. These channels encouraged employees to report compliance concerns and seek guidance without fear of retribution.
- **Regular updates**: Regular updates on compliance activities, regulatory changes, and best practices were provided through newsletters, intranet portals, and team meetings. Success stories and exemplary compliance behavior were highlighted.

- **Outcome**: Establishing clear communication channels fostered a speak-up culture and ensured that compliance concerns were addressed promptly. Regular updates kept employees informed and engaged, reinforcing the importance of compliance.

3. **Set up accountability measures**:

- **Initial action**: APEX needed clear accountability measures to ensure compliance activities were effectively managed and monitored.

The implementation steps were as follows:

- **Clear roles and responsibilities**: We defined clear roles and responsibilities for compliance activities, assigning accountability to specific individuals and teams. These responsibilities were documented and communicated across the organization.
- **Performance metrics**: Performance metrics were established to evaluate compliance efforts. These metrics included the number of compliance training sessions completed, audit findings, and incident reports. Progress was tracked, and achievements were recognized.

- **Outcome**: Establishing accountability measures ensured that compliance activities were managed effectively and transparently. Performance metrics provided clear insights into compliance progress, enabling continuous improvement and recognition of exemplary efforts.

Results achieved

Through the successful implementation of our AI compliance framework, APEX Manufacturing and Distribution achieved significant results:

- **Industry standards compliance**:
  - **Enhanced adherence**: Regular audits, standardized protocols, and compliance management tools ensured that APEX's AI systems consistently met industry standards
  - **Operational excellence**: Adherence to industry standards enhanced operational excellence, building trust with customers and regulatory bodies

- **Legal and regulatory navigation**:
  - **Proactive compliance**: The dedicated compliance team, regulatory monitoring tools, and regular audits enabled APEX to navigate the complex regulatory landscape proactively
  - **Minimized legal risks**: Continuous monitoring and adaptation minimized legal risks, ensuring ongoing compliance with evolving regulations

- **Culture of compliance and accountability**:
  - **Strong compliance culture**: Comprehensive training programs, clear communication channels, and accountability measures fostered a strong culture of compliance and accountability across the organization
  - **Increased engagement**: Employees were more engaged and motivated to uphold compliance standards, contributing to the organization's overall success

The APEX Manufacturing and Distribution case underscores the transformative impact of implementing robust AI compliance measures. By addressing compliance with industry standards, navigating legal and regulatory requirements, and building a culture of compliance and accountability, APEX safeguarded its operations, built trust, and maintained a positive reputation.

Reflection and practical next steps

Before we conclude this chapter, take a moment to reflect on the core insights we've explored. Consider how the challenges of navigating complex regulations, ensuring data privacy, and fostering transparency in AI systems resonate with your own experiences. Have you encountered similar hurdles in your work with AI or perhaps witnessed the impact of non-compliance in your industry? Reflect on how the strategies we've discussed – from implementing standardized protocols to building a culture of accountability – could transform your approach to AI compliance.

Now, let's challenge ourselves to assess our current practices critically. Are your AI systems truly aligned with the latest industry standards? How confident are you in your organization's ability to adapt to rapidly evolving AI regulations? Consider the benefits of enhancing your compliance strategies: improved stakeholder trust, reduced legal risks, and a competitive edge in AI. What areas of your AI operations could benefit most from a compliance overhaul?

To translate these reflections into action, identify one concrete step you can take this week to improve AI compliance in your organization. Perhaps it's scheduling a comprehensive audit of your AI systems or initiating discussions about establishing a dedicated compliance team. Remember, progress doesn't have to be monumental to be meaningful. Even small actions, such as updating your data handling procedures or organizing a workshop on AI ethics, can set the stage for significant improvements.

As you move forward, stay curious and proactive. The field of AI is constantly evolving, and so too must our approach to compliance. Challenge yourself to stay informed about emerging regulations and best practices. Engage with your peers, share experiences, and contribute to the ongoing dialogue about responsible AI development. By doing so, you're not just protecting your organization – you're helping to shape a future where AI technology is trusted, ethical, and genuinely beneficial to society.

Remember, the journey toward robust AI compliance is ongoing, but with each step, you're building a stronger foundation for innovation and success. What will your next move be in this exciting challenge?

Summary

In this chapter, we navigated the complex landscape of AI compliance together. We explored how to align your AI systems with industry standards, tackle the ever-evolving regulatory requirements, and foster a culture of compliance within your organization. Remember, compliance isn't just about avoiding fines – it is also about building trust, ensuring fairness, and positioning your AI initiatives for long-term success. By implementing the strategies we discussed, from conducting regular audits to establishing clear communication channels, you're not just ticking boxes but also setting the foundation for responsible and ethical AI development.

As we wrap up our exploration of AI compliance, take a moment to reflect on how these insights apply to your specific context. What steps can you take today to enhance your AI compliance efforts? In our next and final chapter, we'll combine all the threads we've explored throughout this journey, offering a holistic view of the AI landscape and describing the road ahead for Chief AI Officers.

Questions

1. What is the maximum potential fine for non-compliance with GDPR?
2. Name three key areas of AI compliance discussed in the chapter.
3. What is the purpose of conducting regular compliance audits?
4. How can organizations address the challenge of evolving AI regulations?
5. What role does transparency play in AI compliance?
6. Describe one strategy for building an organization's compliance culture.
7. What tool was implemented to help with regulatory monitoring in the APEX Manufacturing case study?
8. Why is it important to have clear communication channels for compliance concerns?
9. How can performance metrics contribute to AI compliance efforts?
10. What potential benefits can an organization gain from improving its AI compliance strategies?

References

1. defensorum.com. *HITRUST Incorporates GDPR into the CSF.* https://www.defensorum.com/hitrust-gdpr-csf/
2. gxait.com. *Protecting Your Systems and Data with Business IT Solutions.* https://gxait.com/blog/protecting-your-systems-and-data-with-business-it-solutions/
3. kulurgroup.com. *Navigating Global Data Privacy for Disruptive Growth and Marketing Strategies.* https://kulurgroup.com/blog/navigating-global-data-privacy-for-disruptive-growth-and-marketing-strategies/
4. susocial.com. *Comprehensive Measures For Enhancing IoT Security.* https://susocial.com/comprehensive-measures-for-enhancing-iot-security/

Part 4: Empowering AI Leadership with Practical Tools and Insights

This part serves as a comprehensive guide for Chief AI Officers and business leaders, synthesizing the book's core themes while providing essential resources to drive AI transformation. It offers a reflective conclusion on the transformative potential of AI, followed by an appendix designed to equip you with actionable tools and knowledge.

This part has the following chapters:

- *Chapter 16, Conclusion*
- *Chapter 17, Appendix*

16
Conclusion

Our intelligence is what makes us human, and AI is an extension of that quality. Artificial intelligence is extending what we can do with our abilities. In this way, it's letting us become more human.

– Yann LeCun

As we conclude *The Chief AI Officer's Handbook*, it's time to reflect on AI's transformative power and chart the road ahead for **Chief AI Officers** (**CAIOs**). AI is not just an advancing technology; it is already reshaping industries, redefining how organizations solve complex challenges, innovate, and grow. AI drives profound shifts across sectors, from automating processes and enhancing customer experiences to enabling data-driven decision-making.

CAIOs play a pivotal role in aligning AI's potential with strategic goals, fostering a culture of innovation and ensuring responsible use. Through visionary leadership and ethical stewardship, CAIOs can harness AI's full potential to create sustainable and meaningful change in the business landscape.

We will reflect on the handbook's key insights:

- **AI's transformative power**: AI reshapes business, driving automation, better customer experiences, and data-driven decisions
- **Core themes**: CAIOs must balance technical expertise with ethical responsibility, asking "Can we?" and "Should we?"
- **Business strategy impact**: AI is central to modern strategy, with CAIOs as strategists and change agents
- **The road ahead**: The future demands CAIOs be adaptable, ethical, and committed to responsible AI for lasting impact

Let's lead purposefully, using AI for sustainable growth and meaningful change.

The transformative power of AI

AI is not just a technological advancement but a transformative force reshaping industries, economies, and societies. It drives unprecedented innovation and efficiency in healthcare, finance, manufacturing, and retail. The ability to analyze vast amounts of data, uncover hidden patterns, and make intelligent decisions is revolutionizing how businesses operate.

Consider the story of APEX Manufacturing and Distribution. Initially grappling with compliance challenges, APEX's journey to implement a robust AI compliance framework ensured regulatory adherence, enhanced operational excellence, and built stakeholder trust. This transformation underscores AI's potential to solve problems and create opportunities for growth and innovation.

AI's transformative power is reshaping individual organizations and entire industries, revolutionizing how they operate, compete, and deliver value to customers. By integrating AI strategically, companies across sectors are discovering new ways to enhance efficiency, drive innovation, and adapt to rapidly changing market demands. Consider how AI is making a tangible impact across various industries:

- **Healthcare**: AI-driven diagnostic tools and predictive analytics enable earlier disease detection, optimize treatment plans, and support personalized medicine, significantly improving patient outcomes.

- **Finance**: Advanced AI algorithms detect fraud with high accuracy, enhance risk assessment, and inform strategic investment decisions, fostering a safer and more efficient financial ecosystem.

- **Retail**: AI enhances every aspect of the customer journey. Personalized recommendations drive sales, while intelligent supply chain management predicts demand, optimizes inventory, and reduces costs.

- **Manufacturing**: Predictive maintenance algorithms prevent equipment failures, improve productivity, and reduce downtime. Quality control powered by computer vision raises product standards and consistency.

- **Transportation and logistics**: AI optimizes routing, enhances fleet management, and supports autonomous vehicles, resulting in faster, more reliable, and cost-effective deliveries.

- **Agriculture**: AI-powered systems monitor crop health, manage resources efficiently, and increase yields, promoting sustainable farming practices that address food security challenges.

- **Energy**: AI supports smart grid management, predictive maintenance, and optimization of renewable resources, boosting both efficiency and sustainability.

- **Education**: Personalized learning platforms driven by AI adapt to individual student needs, enhancing engagement and retention.

These examples underscore AI's profound, versatile impact across industries, demonstrating the transformative potential of strategic AI integration for growth, efficiency, and customer satisfaction.

Key themes and insights

Throughout this book, several key themes have emerged, each illustrating the multifaceted impact of AI:

- **Innovation and growth:** AI catalyzes innovation, driving new product development and opening up untapped markets. Businesses that leverage AI can build and innovate faster, stay ahead of competitors, and deliver unique value propositions.
- **Operational efficiency:** AI optimizes operations by automating routine tasks, predicting maintenance needs, and enhancing decision-making processes. This leads to cost savings, improved productivity, and better resource management [1].
- **Customer experience**: AI transforms customer interactions by providing personalized experiences, predictive insights, and proactive support. This enhances customer satisfaction, loyalty, and retention.
- **Strategic decision-making**: AI provides actionable insights derived from data, enabling informed strategic decisions. Organizations can better understand market trends, customer preferences, and operational challenges, leading to more effective strategies.

The profound impact on business strategies

AI's integration into business strategies is transformative. Companies that adopt AI improve their operational efficiencies and redefine their strategic goals. AI-driven insights allow businesses to pivot quickly, respond to market changes, and anticipate customer needs. For instance, a company using AI to analyze market trends can identify emerging opportunities and adjust its strategy accordingly, gaining a first-mover advantage.

Improving customer experiences

AI enhances customer experiences by delivering personalized, timely, and relevant interactions. Chatbots powered by natural language processing provide instant support, addressing customer queries efficiently [2]. AI algorithms that analyze customer behavior can predict needs and preferences, offering personalized recommendations and proactive solutions. This level of personalization builds strong customer relationships and fosters brand loyalty.

Enhancing operational efficiency

AI-driven automation and predictive analytics optimize operations across various functions. AI can optimize routes and manage inventory levels in logistics, ensuring timely deliveries and reducing costs. AI can streamline production processes, reduce waste, and improve quality control in manufacturing. This improved efficiency translates into significant cost savings and improved overall performance.

A clear vision of AI's potential

As we look ahead, AI's potential is boundless. It promises to continue transforming industries, creating new opportunities, and solving complex challenges. However, realizing this potential requires committing to ethical practices, continuous learning, and strategic innovation. CAIOs are at the forefront of this transformation, guiding their organizations through the AI revolution.

The road ahead for Chief AI Officers

As we look to the future, the CAIO's role will be pivotal in guiding organizations through the AI revolution. The road ahead is exciting and challenging, requiring CAIOs to be visionary leaders, ethical stewards, and strategic innovators.

Visionary leadership

CAIOs must be visionary leaders who foresee AI's transformative potential and align it with their organization's strategic goals. This involves staying abreast of AI advancements, understanding market trends, and anticipating future needs. Visionary leadership is about seeing the bigger picture and guiding the organization towards long-term success.

Here's some actionable advice:

- **Continuous learning**: Embrace ongoing education by staying up to date with AI research and advancements. Participate in AI conferences and webinars and engage with professional AI communities. Networking with industry experts can provide valuable insights and foster collaboration.
- **Strategic alignment**: Ensure AI initiatives align tightly with your organization's strategic goals. Each AI project should have a clear path to driving business value and enhancing competitive advantage. This includes regular assessments to verify that AI solutions remain relevant and continue to support the broader business mission.

Ethical stewardship

Ethical considerations are paramount in the age of AI. CAIOs must ensure that AI systems are developed and deployed ethically, protecting user privacy, preventing bias, and promoting transparency. Building ethical AI systems fosters trust with customers, employees, and regulators.

Here's some actionable advice:

- **Ethical frameworks**: Develop and implement comprehensive ethical frameworks and guidelines for AI projects. Integrate moral considerations, such as fairness, privacy, and inclusivity, at every stage of the AI life cycle to ensure that systems are designed with integrity from inception to deployment.

- **Transparency and accountability**: Encourage transparency by using explainable AI techniques that make the decision-making processes of AI systems understandable to stakeholders. Establish clear accountability measures, assigning responsibility for AI outcomes to uphold ethical standards and enhance trust within and outside the organization.

Strategic innovation

Innovation is at the heart of AI. CAIOs must drive strategic innovation by exploring new AI applications, experimenting with cutting-edge technologies, and fostering a culture of creativity and experimentation. Embracing innovation enables organizations to stay ahead of the curve and capitalize on new opportunities.

Here's some actionable advice:

- **Experimentation**: Promote a culture of experimentation by actively piloting new AI projects. Encourage teams to test and learn from both successes and setbacks, using these experiences to refine approaches and drive continuous improvement.

- **Innovation culture**: Cultivate a culture of innovation across the organization by encouraging collaboration, creativity, and open-mindedness [3]. Create opportunities for cross-functional teams to contribute to AI initiatives and reward creative problem-solving to sustain a dynamic, forward-thinking environment.

Summary

As we move forward into this AI-driven era, it's clear that the true power of AI lies not only in its capabilities but in how we choose to apply it. For CAIOs, this means continuously seeking ways to align AI solutions with organizational objectives and ethical standards, creating a balance between rapid innovation and responsible deployment. The role of a CAIO extends beyond technology to a broader vision of how AI can be leveraged to address pressing societal issues, improve lives, and contribute positively to our shared future.

The road ahead will not be without challenges. The dynamic nature of AI, coupled with its ethical and regulatory complexities, requires CAIOs to be adaptable, informed, and proactive. Building trust through transparency, upholding data privacy, and ensuring fairness in AI decisions will be essential components of this journey. By championing these values, CAIOs can guide their organizations toward industry leadership, public trust, and social responsibility.

CAIOs have the unique opportunity to shape the future of AI by making thoughtful, impactful decisions that balance innovation with integrity. In doing so, they will play a critical role in guiding their organizations—and the industry—toward a future where technology and humanity advance hand-in-hand, unlocking AI's transformative power for the benefit of all. The path is challenging but filled with possibility, and with the right vision, CAIOs can lead their organizations to unprecedented success and positive impact.

Thank you for joining me through *The Chief AI Officer's Handbook*. I hope you find the insights, strategies, and practical advice shared here valuable and inspiring as you navigate the exciting world of AI. The road ahead is full of possibilities, and I'm excited to see the incredible innovations and achievements in store for you and your organizations.

References

1. dnainspections.net. How Expert Consulting Elevates Projects. `https://dnainspections.net/how-expert-consulting-elevates-projects`

2. link-building-service.info. AI Revolution: Transforming and Enriching Everyday Life. `https://link-building-service.info/ai-revolution-transforming-and-enriching-everyday-life.html`

3. exitbuilt.com. Unlocking the Potential of Your Mid-Market Business: A Comprehensive Guide. `https://exitbuilt.com/unlocking-the-potential-of-your-mid-market-business-a-comprehensive-guide/`

17
Appendix

This appendix is designed to be a practical companion, offering essential tools and resources to support your journey in leading AI initiatives. Within, you'll find the following:

- **Glossary of AI terms**: Clear definitions of key concepts and terminology in AI
- **Recommended readings and resources**: A curated list of books, articles, and courses for expanding your AI knowledge
- **Templates and frameworks**: Ready-to-use tools for developing AI strategies, managing projects, and measuring impact effectively

These resources aim to equip you with the foundational knowledge and practical tools to drive meaningful and impactful AI transformation in your organization.

Glossary of AI terms

This glossary defines key terms and concepts in **artificial intelligence** (**AI**) relevant to **Chief AI Intelligence Officers** (**CAIOs**) and professionals involved in AI strategy and implementation. Use it as a reference to enhance your understanding of the AI landscape:

- **Artificial Intelligence (AI)**: The field focused on creating machines or systems that can perform tasks requiring human-like intelligence, such as understanding language, recognizing patterns, solving problems, and learning from experience.
- **Algorithm**: A specific set of step-by-step instructions a computer follows to solve a problem or accomplish a task, often used to process data or perform calculations.
- **Artificial General Intelligence (AGI)**: A theoretical form of AI where a machine can understand, learn, and apply knowledge across a wide range of tasks at a level comparable to a human being.
- **Artificial Neural Network (ANN)**: A computing model inspired by the human brain's neural networks, consisting of interconnected nodes (neurons) that work together to process information and recognize patterns within data.

- **Augmented Reality (AR)**: A technology that overlays digital information – such as images, sounds, or data – onto the real-world environment, enhancing one's perception of reality through computer-generated inputs.
- **Big data**: Extremely large and complex datasets that traditional data processing applications cannot handle efficiently, characterized by high volume, velocity, and variety of information.
- **Bias (algorithmic bias)**: A systematic error in an AI system that leads to unfair outcomes, often favoring one group over others due to prejudiced assumptions or flawed data.
- **Bot**: A software application that runs automated tasks over the internet, often performing repetitive actions much faster than a human could, such as crawling websites or simulating conversations.
- **Computer vision**: A branch of AI that enables computers to interpret and understand visual information from the world, such as images and videos, to make decisions or take actions.
- **Chatbot**: A computer program designed to simulate human conversation, allowing users to interact with technology using natural language through text or voice.
- **Cloud computing**: The delivery of computing services – such as servers, storage, databases, networking, and software – over the internet ("the cloud"), providing flexible resources and economies of scale.
- **Data mining**: The process of exploring and analyzing large datasets to discover meaningful patterns, correlations, and insights that can inform decision-making.
- **Deep learning**: A subset of machine learning that uses neural networks with many layers to model complex patterns in data, enabling tasks such as image and speech recognition.
- **Data science**: An interdisciplinary field combining statistics, computer science, and domain expertise to extract knowledge and insights from structured and unstructured data.
- **Expert system**: An AI program that emulates the decision-making ability of a human expert, using a knowledge base and inference rules to analyze information and solve specific problems.
- **Edge computing**: A computing paradigm that processes data near the source of generation (the "edge" of the network) to reduce latency and bandwidth use, improving response times.
- **Feature extraction**: The process of transforming raw data into measurable characteristics (features) that can be used for analysis while preserving essential information.
- **Federated learning**: A machine learning approach that trains algorithms across multiple decentralized devices holding local data samples without exchanging the data itself.
- **Generative Adversarial Network (GAN)**: A machine learning framework involving two neural networks – a generator and a discriminator – that compete against each other to produce increasingly realistic outputs.
- **Hyperparameter**: A configuration setting used to control the learning process of a machine learning model, set before training and not learned from the data.

- **Heuristic**: A problem-solving technique that employs a practical method or various shortcuts to produce solutions that may not be perfect but are sufficient for reaching an immediate goal.
- **Internet of Things (IoT)**: A network of interconnected physical devices embedded with sensors and software, enabling them to collect and exchange data over the internet.
- **Intelligent agent**: An autonomous entity that observes its environment, makes decisions, and takes actions to achieve specific goals, often using AI techniques.
- **Knowledge representation**: The area of AI focused on representing information about the world in a form that a computer system can use to solve complex tasks such as reasoning or understanding language.
- **K-means clustering**: A method in data analysis that partitions data into *k* distinct groups based on feature similarity, aiming to minimize the variance within each cluster.
- **Machine Learning (ML)**: A subset of AI where algorithms learn from data to improve their performance on a specific task over time, without being explicitly programmed for each outcome.
- **Logistic regression**: A statistical model for predicting a binary outcome's probability (such as yes/no) based on one or more predictor variables.
- **Model overfitting**: A modeling error in machine learning where a model learns the training data too well, capturing noise as if it were a true pattern, which harms its performance on new data.
- **Machine vision**: The technology and methods used to provide imaging-based automatic inspection and analysis, often used in industrial applications for quality control.
- **Natural Language Processing (NLP)**: A field of AI that focuses on enabling computers to understand, interpret, and generate human language in a valuable way.
- **Neural network**: A computational model composed of interconnected nodes (neurons) that process data by responding to inputs and transmitting information between layers, inspired by the human brain.
- **Optimization algorithm**: A method used to adjust the parameters of a machine learning model to minimize errors and improve performance during training.
- **Ontology**: In AI, a structured framework that represents knowledge as a set of concepts within a domain and the relationships between those concepts.
- **Predictive analytics**: Techniques that use historical data, statistical algorithms, and machine learning to predict future events or outcomes.
- **Python**: A high-level, versatile programming language known for its readability and extensive libraries, widely used in AI and machine learning applications.
- **Quantum computing**: A type of computing that leverages the principles of quantum mechanics to process information, potentially solving complex problems faster than classical computers.

- **Q-learning**: A reinforcement learning algorithm that seeks to learn the value of actions in particular states, aiming to find the optimal policy for decision-making.
- **Reinforcement Learning (RL)**: An area of machine learning where an agent learns to make decisions by performing actions and receiving feedback as rewards or penalties.
- **Robotics**: The field concerned with the design, construction, operation, and use of robots, often integrating computer systems for control and information processing.
- **Supervised learning**: A machine learning approach where models are trained on labeled data, learning to predict outcomes based on input-output pairs.
- **Swarm intelligence**: The collective behavior of decentralized, self-organized systems, often observed in nature, used in AI to solve optimization problems through the interaction of simple agents.
- **Semantic analysis**: The process of understanding and interpreting the meanings of words, phrases, and sentences in context, crucial for language comprehension.
- **TensorFlow**: An open source software library developed by Google for numerical computation and machine learning, particularly suited for building and training neural networks.
- **Transfer learning**: A machine learning technique where a model developed for one task is reused as the starting point for a model on a related task, reducing training time.
- **Unsupervised learning**: A type of machine learning that analyzes unlabeled data to discover hidden patterns or intrinsic structures without predefined categories or labels.
- **User interface (UI)**: The point of interaction between a user and a computer system, encompassing the visual elements and controls designed for effective and intuitive use.
- **Virtual reality (VR)**: A simulated experience created by computer technology that immerses the user in a virtual environment, often using special equipment such as headsets.
- **Voice recognition**: The capability of a machine or program to identify and process spoken language, allowing for voice commands and dictation.
- **Weak AI (narrow AI)**: AI systems designed to perform a specific task or a limited range of tasks, operating under predefined constraints without consciousness or self-awareness.
- **Word embedding**: A technique in natural language processing where words are represented as numerical vectors in a continuous vector space, capturing semantic relationships.
- **Explainable AI (XAI)**: AI systems that provide clear and understandable explanations of their decision-making processes to human users.
- **Yield optimization**: The use of AI and analytical methods to maximize outputs or efficiency in various industries, such as increasing crop production in agriculture.
- **Zero-shot learning**: A machine learning scenario where a model is expected to recognize and classify data from classes it hasn't seen during training, using knowledge from related information.

Glossary of AI terms 265

Here are a few additional terms:

- **Application Programming Interface (API)**: A collection of protocols and tools that allows different software applications to communicate with each other, enabling developers to build programs that can access features or data from other operating systems, applications, or services.
- **Backpropagation**: A learning algorithm used in neural networks where errors are propagated backward through the system to adjust the weights of connections, helping the model learn by minimizing the difference between predicted and actual outputs.
- **Cognitive computing**: Technology designed to replicate human thought processes in a computerized model, enabling systems to simulate reasoning, learning, and decision-making similar to the human mind.
- **Data lake**: A large storage repository that holds vast amounts of raw data in its original format, keeping it available for future processing and analysis as needed.
- **Ethical AI**: The practice of developing and implementing artificial intelligence systems in ways that prioritize fairness, accountability, transparency, and adherence to human values and ethical principles.
- **Hyperparameter tuning**: The process of optimizing the settings that control how a machine learning model learns, known as hyperparameters, to improve its performance on a given task.
- **Intelligent automation**: Combining artificial intelligence with automation technologies to perform tasks that previously required human intelligence, enhancing efficiency and decision-making processes.
- **K-Nearest Neighbors (KNN)**: A straightforward, supervised machine learning algorithm used for classification and regression, which predicts outcomes based on the closest data points in the feature space.
- **Latent Dirichlet Allocation (LDA)**: A statistical method that uncovers hidden thematic structures in large sets of data, such as grouping similar topics within a collection of documents by analyzing word patterns.
- **Monte Carlo simulation**: A computational technique that uses random sampling and statistical modeling to estimate mathematical functions and predict the behavior of complex systems under uncertainty.
- **Natural Language Generation (NLG)**: The use of artificial intelligence to automatically produce human-like written or spoken narratives from structured data.
- **Ontology engineering**: The field dedicated to designing and managing ontologies, which are formal representations of a set of concepts within a domain and the relationships between those concepts, to facilitate better data integration and understanding.
- **Predictive modeling**: Developing and testing mathematical models that use historical data to forecast future events or trends.

- **Quantum machine learning**: An emerging field that integrates quantum computing algorithms with machine learning techniques to potentially solve complex problems more efficiently than classical computers.
- **Recurrent Neural Network (RNN)**: A type of neural network where connections between nodes form directed cycles, allowing the network to maintain a memory of previous inputs and making it effective for sequential data processing.
- **Support Vector Machine (SVM)**: A supervised learning model that analyzes data for classification and regression tasks by finding the optimal boundary that separates different classes in the dataset.
- **Tokenization**: The process of breaking down text into smaller units called tokens – such as words, phrases, or symbols – for easier analysis in natural language processing tasks.
- **Underfitting**: A situation where a machine learning model is too simple to capture the underlying structure of the data, leading to poor performance on both training and new, unseen data.
- **Validation set**: A subset of data used during model training to evaluate and fine-tune the model's parameters, helping to prevent overfitting and improve its ability to generalize to new data.

Recommended readings and resources

This section provides a curated list of books, articles, courses, websites, and other resources to enhance your understanding of artificial intelligence and its strategic implementation. These materials are valuable for CAIOs and professionals involved in AI leadership roles.

Books

- *Artificial Intelligence: A Modern Approach* by Stuart Russell and Peter Norvig: A comprehensive textbook covering the theory and practice of AI, suitable for both beginners and experienced practitioners.
- *Prediction Machines: The Simple Economics of Artificial Intelligence* by Ajay Agrawal, Joshua Gans, and Avi Goldfarb: Explores the economic implications of AI and how it affects business decisions and strategy.
- *Human + Machine: Reimagining Work in the Age of AI* by Paul R. Daugherty and H. James Wilson: Discusses how AI technologies are transforming business processes and the future of work.
- *Applied Artificial Intelligence: A Handbook for Business Leaders* by Mariya Yao, Adelyn Zhou, and Marlene Jia: Provides practical guidance on implementing AI solutions in business settings.
- *The Master Algorithm* by Pedro Domingos: An accessible introduction to machine learning and its impact on various industries.
- *AI Superpowers: China, Silicon Valley, and the New World Order* by Kai-Fu Lee: Analyzes the competitive landscape of AI development between China and the United States.

Academic papers and articles

- *Building the AI-Powered Organization* by Tim Fountaine, Brian McCarthy, and Tamim Saleh (Harvard Business Review): Discusses strategies for integrating AI into organizational structures effectively.

- *The Future of Employment: How susceptible are jobs to computerisation?* by Carl Benedikt Frey and Michael A. Osborne: Investigates the potential impact of AI on the labor market and job automation.

- *Artificial Intelligence and Life in 2030* (One Hundred Year Study on Artificial Intelligence): Examines the potential societal impacts of AI over the next decade.

Online courses and tutorials

- *Machine Learning* by Andrew Ng (Coursera): A foundational course covering key concepts in machine learning, including supervised and unsupervised learning.

- *Deep Learning Specialization* by Andrew Ng (Coursera): An in-depth series on deep learning techniques and applications, including neural networks and sequence models.

- *AI for Everyone* by Andrew Ng (Coursera): Designed for non-technical professionals to understand AI technologies and their business implications.

- *Introduction to Artificial Intelligence (AI)* by IBM (edX): Provides an overview of AI concepts, including machine learning and neural networks.

- *Elements of AI* (University of Helsinki): A free online course aimed at demystifying AI for the general public and professionals.

Websites and blogs

- *OpenAI Blog*: Features research updates, insights, and discussions on AI advancements.

- *MIT Technology Review – AI Section*: Covers the latest news and analysis on AI technologies and their societal impact.

- *AI Trends*: Provides industry news, case studies, and insights into AI applications across various sectors.

- *Towards Data Science*: A platform for sharing ideas and learning about data science, machine learning, and AI.

- *KDnuggets*: Offers tutorials, opinions, and resources in AI, data science, and machine learning.

Professional organizations and communities

- **Association for the Advancement of Artificial Intelligence (AAAI)**: A scientific society dedicated to advancing the understanding of AI.
- **IEEE Computational Intelligence Society**: Focuses on the theory, design, application, and development of biologically and linguistically motivated computational paradigms.
- **Artificial Intelligence Group on LinkedIn**: An online community for professionals to discuss AI trends, challenges, and networking opportunities.
- **International Joint Conferences on Artificial Intelligence (IJCAI)**: Promotes global AI research and collaboration through conferences and publications.

Conferences and events

- **NeurIPS (Neural Information Processing Systems)**: A premier conference on machine learning and computational neuroscience.
- **International Conference on Machine Learning (ICML)**: Focuses on all aspects of machine learning, from theoretical advances to practical applications.
- **AI Summit Series**: A global series of events bringing together AI innovators and practitioners across industries.
- **AAAI Conference on Artificial Intelligence**: Showcases the latest research and developments in AI from academia and industry.

Podcasts and videos

- **The AI Podcast** by NVIDIA: Features interviews with AI researchers and practitioners discussing the latest trends and breakthroughs.
- **Artificial Intelligence** playlist by TED Talks: A collection of talks exploring various facets of AI, ethics, and its impact on society.
- **Lex Fridman podcast**: In-depth conversations about AI, technology, and society with leading experts in the field.

Government and regulatory resources

- **Ethics Guidelines for Trustworthy AI** by the European Commission: Outlines key requirements for developing ethical and trustworthy AI systems.
- **AI Ethics and Governance Toolkit** by the Singapore Government: Provides practical guidance for organizations to deploy AI responsibly and ethically.

- **The National Artificial Intelligence Research and Development Strategic Plan** by the U.S. National Science and Technology Council: A framework guiding AI research and development investments in the United States.

Research institutions

- **Stanford Artificial Intelligence Laboratory (SAIL)**: Conducts research in a broad range of AI areas, including robotics and machine learning.
- **MIT Computer Science and Artificial Intelligence Laboratory (CSAIL)**: Focuses on AI, robotics, and computational theory, pushing the boundaries of what's possible.
- **Carnegie Mellon University School of Computer Science**: Known for pioneering research in AI, machine learning, and human-computer interaction.

Tools and platforms

- **TensorFlow**: An open source machine learning framework developed by Google, widely used for building AI applications.
- **PyTorch**: An open source machine learning library for Python, developed by Facebook's AI Research lab, known for its flexibility and ease of use.
- **Google Cloud AI Platform**: Provides tools and services for building, deploying, and managing AI applications in the cloud.
- **Microsoft Azure AI**: Offers AI services, including machine learning, cognitive services, and bot services, to accelerate AI development.
- **Amazon Web Services (AWS) Machine Learning**: A suite of AI services and tools provided by AWS to build intelligent applications.

Additional resources

- **AI Now report**: Annual reports that examine the social implications of AI technologies and provide recommendations.
- **The State of AI report**: An annual report that analyzes the latest developments in AI research, talent, and industry.
- **OpenAI GPT Models**: Advanced language models that can be used for various natural language processing tasks.
- **Deep Learning** by Ian Goodfellow, Yoshua Bengio, and Aaron Courville: A definitive text on deep learning methods and applications.

Educational platforms

- **Udacity**: Offers nanodegree programs in AI and machine learning, including practical projects and mentorship.
- **DataCamp**: Provides interactive courses in data science and AI with hands-on coding exercises.
- **edX**: Hosts courses from leading institutions on AI, machine learning, and related fields.

Community forums

- **Stack Overflow**: An online community where developers and programmers come together to ask questions, share solutions, and discuss topics related to coding, software development, and artificial intelligence.
- **Reddit – machine learning community**: A forum for news, discussions, and questions about machine learning.
- **Kaggle**: A community of data scientists and machine learning practitioners, offering datasets and competitions.

Ethics and policy resources

- **Partnership on AI**: An organization that brings together diverse voices to address AI's opportunities and challenges.
- **AI Ethics Lab**: Provides resources and consulting on integrating ethics into AI development.
- **The IEEE Global Initiative on Ethics of Autonomous and Intelligent Systems**: Offers guidelines and standards for ethical AI practices.

Industry reports

- **McKinsey Global Institute – AI Reports**: Provides insights into AI's economic impact and its role in business transformation.
- **Gartner's Hype Cycle for Artificial Intelligence**: An annual report analyzing the maturity and adoption of AI technologies.
- **Accenture – AI Research**: Explores how AI can drive innovation and growth in various industries.

Key journals and publications

- **Journal of Artificial Intelligence Research (JAIR)**: Publishes state-of-the-art research articles in all areas of AI.
- **Machine Learning Journal**: Focuses on research developments in machine learning methodologies.

- **IEEE Transactions on Pattern Analysis and Machine Intelligence**: Covers the latest in computer vision and pattern recognition.

Templates and frameworks

In this section, we will present a collection of templates and frameworks designed to assist CAIOs in strategizing, implementing, and governing AI initiatives within their organizations. These tools offer structured approaches to AI project management, risk assessment, ethical considerations, and more. By incorporating established frameworks such as the NIST AI Risk Management Framework, organizations can ensure that their AI systems are effective, trustworthy, and aligned with organizational goals and societal values.

NIST AI Risk Management Framework (AI RMF)

The **National Institute of Standards and Technology (NIST)** developed the **AI Risk Management Framework (AI RMF)** to help organizations manage the risks associated with artificial intelligence systems. This comprehensive framework guides integrating risk management processes throughout the AI lifecycle, promoting developing and deploying trustworthy and responsible AI solutions.

Key components

The NIST AI RMF is organized around four core functions:

- **Map**: This function involves understanding the context, objectives, and environment in which the AI system operates. Organizations are encouraged to identify the purpose and scope of the AI system, recognize stakeholders, and consider potential impacts. This includes defining legal, ethical, and societal considerations that may affect the system's deployment.
- **Measure**: In this phase, organizations assess and analyze the AI system to identify and evaluate risks. This includes developing metrics for performance, fairness, and security, conducting thorough testing and validation, and monitoring for unintended outcomes or behaviors that could pose risks.
- **Manage**: This function focuses on prioritizing and responding to identified risks to minimize negative impacts. Organizations implement risk mitigation strategies, adjust the AI system based on feedback and findings, and document changes and updates to maintain transparency and accountability.
- **Govern**: The governance function involves establishing policies, procedures, and oversight mechanisms to support risk management. This includes defining roles and responsibilities, ensuring compliance with relevant regulations, and promoting a culture of risk awareness and ethical considerations throughout the organization.

Application

By following the NIST AI RMF, organizations can enhance trust in their AI systems, ensure regulatory compliance, reduce risks, and improve overall performance. Implementing the framework involves mapping out the AI system's objectives and context, measuring its performance and associated risks, managing those risks through proactive strategies, and establishing governance structures to oversee the entire process. This comprehensive approach helps organizations develop AI systems that are not only effective but also aligned with ethical standards and societal expectations.

AI strategy development template

Developing a robust AI strategy is essential for organizations leveraging artificial intelligence effectively. This template guides CAIOs in formulating an AI strategy that aligns with organizational objectives, drives business value, and fosters innovation.

Components

An effective AI strategy should encompass the following elements:

- **Executive summary**: Provide an overview of the AI strategy, highlighting its alignment with business goals and the anticipated benefits.
- **Vision and mission**: Articulate a clear vision for AI within the organization and the mission that will guide the approach to achieving this vision. This will set the strategic direction and establish a shared understanding among stakeholders.
- **Strategic objectives**: Define specific, measurable goals the AI initiatives aim to achieve. These objectives should be aligned with the broader organizational strategy and include **key performance indicators** (**KPIs**) for tracking progress.
- **Current state assessment**: Conduct a thorough analysis of the organization's **strengths**, **weaknesses**, **opportunities**, and **threats** (**SWOT**) related to AI capabilities. Evaluate existing technology infrastructure, data assets, talent, and processes to identify gaps and areas for improvement.
- **Opportunity identification**: Identify areas where AI can add significant value to the organization, such as enhancing customer experience, optimizing operations, reducing costs, or enabling new business models.
- **Strategic initiatives**: Outline key projects and programs to pursue, prioritizing them based on potential impact, feasibility, and alignment with strategic objectives.
- **Roadmap**: Develop a timeline that outlines the AI initiatives' milestones, deliverables, and dependencies. This roadmap should provide a clear path forward and facilitate coordination across different teams and departments.

- **Resource allocation**: Detail the budgeting and allocation of resources necessary for executing the AI strategy. This includes technology investments, staffing needs, training programs, and potential partnerships.
- **Risk management**: Identify potential risks associated with AI initiatives, such as technical challenges, ethical concerns, or market uncertainties. Develop mitigation strategies to address these risks proactively.
- **Governance and ethics**: Establish policies and frameworks for ethical AI use, data governance, and compliance with relevant regulations. Define roles and responsibilities to ensure accountability.
- **Performance metrics**: Specify the KPIs and metrics that will be used to measure the success of AI initiatives. Regular monitoring and reporting on these metrics will enable continuous improvement.

Implementation

To implement this AI strategy template effectively, CAIOs should begin by engaging with key organizational stakeholders to ensure alignment and buy-in. Communicating the AI vision and strategic objectives helps build a shared understanding and commitment. The strategy should be reviewed and adapted regularly to respond to changing business environments, technological advancements, and feedback from ongoing AI projects.

AI Project Management Framework

Effective management of AI projects requires a structured approach that guides the project from conception to deployment, ensuring it meets objectives and delivers tangible value. The AI Project Management Framework provides a roadmap for planning, executing, and overseeing AI initiatives within an organization.

Phases

The framework comprises several key phases:

1. **Initiation**: Define the project's scope, objectives, deliverables, and success criteria. This involves clarifying the project's aims and how it aligns with the organization's strategic goals. Assembling a skilled project team and assigning clear roles and responsibilities are critical.
2. **Planning**: Develop a comprehensive project plan that outlines tasks, timelines, resource requirements, and budget estimates. Conduct a risk assessment to identify potential obstacles, dependencies, and constraints. Establish communication plans and stakeholder engagement strategies.
3. **Execution**: Conduct the project plan by collecting and preparing data, developing AI models, and integrating necessary technologies. This phase involves iterative model training, testing, and validation to ensure the AI system meets performance and quality standards.

4. **Monitoring and Control**: Continuously track project progress against the plan using performance metrics and status reports. Implement quality assurance processes to maintain high standards and make adjustments as necessary to address issues or changes in scope.
5. **Closure**: Deploy the AI solution into operational environments and ensure it is fully integrated with existing systems. Conduct a post-implementation review to evaluate the project's outcomes against objectives, document lessons learned, and identify best practices for future projects.

Key considerations

Throughout the project lifecycle, effective communication with stakeholders is vital to manage expectations and foster collaboration. Adopting agile methodologies can provide flexibility and adaptability, allowing teams to promptly respond to changes and new insights. Additionally, incorporating change management practices prepares the organization for adopting the latest AI solutions, ensuring user acceptance and maximizing the benefits.

Ethical AI Implementation Framework

As AI systems become more integrated into organizational processes, ensuring their ethical development and deployment is paramount. The Ethical AI Implementation Framework provides guidelines for embedding ethical principles into AI initiatives, promoting responsible use, and fostering stakeholder trust.

Framework elements

The framework focuses on several key ethical principles:

- **Fairness**: AI systems should be designed to avoid biases and discrimination. This involves using diverse and representative datasets, regularly auditing models for potential biases, and implementing techniques to mitigate any identified unfairness.
- **Transparency**: Organizations should strive for transparency in how AI systems operate. Documenting data sources, model architectures, and decision-making processes allows for better understanding and accountability. Providing explanations for AI-driven decisions helps build trust with users and stakeholders.
- **Accountability**: Clear ownership and responsibility for AI systems and their outcomes should be established within the organization. This includes defining roles for oversight, establishing processes for reporting and addressing issues, and ensuring that there are mechanisms to hold individuals and teams accountable for ethical considerations.
- **Privacy**: Protecting personal and sensitive data is crucial. Organizations must comply with data protection regulations, such as GDPR or CCPA, and implement data anonymization and access controls to safeguard privacy.

- **Inclusivity**: AI systems should be accessible and considerate of diverse user groups. Engaging with stakeholders from different backgrounds, designing for accessibility, and being mindful of cultural sensitivities help ensure that AI solutions effectively serve a broad audience.
- **Safety and security**: It is essential to ensure that AI systems are robust against errors, failures, and malicious attacks. This includes thorough testing, implementing security measures, and planning for safe operation under various conditions.

Implementation guidelines

Organizations should provide ethics training to team members involved in AI projects to raise awareness and understanding of ethical considerations. Establishing an ethical review board or committee can provide oversight and guidance on ethical issues. Continuous monitoring and regular assessments of AI systems help ensure ongoing compliance with ethical standards and allow for timely adjustments as needed.

Data Governance Framework

Data is the lifeblood of AI systems, and effective data governance is foundational to successful AI initiatives. The Data Governance Framework provides a structured approach to managing data assets, ensuring data quality, integrity, and security throughout the AI lifecycle.

Key components

Effective data governance is crucial for AI success, ensuring data quality, security, and alignment with business goals. A strong Data Governance Framework offers a structured approach to managing data assets through key components such as strategy, architecture, quality management, and security. Key components include the following:

- **Data strategy**: Align data management practices with organizational objectives. This involves defining a clear vision for how data supports business goals, establishing data policies and standards, and prioritizing data initiatives appropriately.
- **Data architecture**: Design data models, storage solutions, and data flows supporting scalability, integration, and efficient processing. A well-defined data architecture facilitates seamless data movement and accessibility across the organization.
- **Data quality management**: The practice of using processes and tools to make sure that data is accurate, consistent, and dependable. This involves setting up rules to validate data, regularly cleaning and correcting datasets, and tracking metrics to monitor data quality, all aimed at maintaining high standards for the information used.
- **Metadata management**: Documenting data lineage, ownership, and attributes through metadata enhances data understanding and discoverability. Metadata management supports transparency and enables users to make informed decisions about data usage.

- **Data security and privacy**: Protect data assets by implementing security measures such as encryption, access controls, and intrusion detection systems. Regular audits and compliance checks help ensure adherence to data protection regulations.

- **Data lifecycle management**: Define processes for data creation, storage, usage, retention, and disposal. Effective lifecycle management ensures that data remains relevant and that outdated or unnecessary data is appropriately handled.

- **Roles and responsibilities**: Assign data stewardship roles and define accountability structures. Clear roles help ensure that data governance practices are consistently applied and that data assets are owned.

Implementation steps

Organizations should start by assessing their current data governance practices to identify strengths and areas for improvement. It is crucial to develop a comprehensive data governance policy that outlines standards, procedures, and guidelines. Implementing data governance tools and technologies can automate and enforce policies, improving efficiency and compliance. Engaging stakeholders from various departments fosters collaboration and ensures that data governance aligns with organizational needs.

AI Capability Maturity Model

The AI Capability Maturity Model helps organizations assess their maturity in AI adoption and provides a roadmap for progression. By evaluating current capabilities and identifying areas for improvement, organizations can systematically enhance their AI practices and achieve greater value from AI initiatives.

Maturity levels

The AI Capability Maturity Model defines five levels of AI adoption, guiding organizations from ad hoc efforts to optimized, strategic use:

- **Level 1: Ad hoc**: AI initiatives are sporadic, uncoordinated, and lack formal processes. Individual teams may drive isolated projects without overarching strategy or governance.

- **Level 2: Managed**: Basic project management practices exist, and AI projects have defined objectives. Some coordination exists, but processes are still largely informal.

- **Level 3: Defined**: AI processes and methodologies are standardized and documented across the organization. Best practices are shared, and there is a consistent approach to AI development and deployment.

- **Level 4: Quantitatively managed**: Metrics and data measure AI performance and inform decision-making. Processes are adjusted based on empirical evidence to optimize outcomes.

- **Level 5: Optimized**: There is a culture of continuous improvement, with AI innovations driving strategic advantages. The organization proactively seeks opportunities to leverage AI and stays at the forefront of technological advancements.

Assessment areas

Organizations should evaluate their maturity across several domains:

- **Strategy and leadership**: Alignment of AI initiatives with business strategy and support from leadership.
- **Culture and talent development**: Organizational culture supporting AI innovation and investment in AI skills development.
- **Technology and infrastructure**: Availability of appropriate technology platforms, tools, and infrastructure to support AI.
- **Process and methodology**: Existence of standardized processes, methodologies, and best practices for AI development.
- **Governance and compliance**: Effective governance structures, policies, and compliance mechanisms for AI initiatives.

Advancement strategies

To progress through the maturity levels, organizations can do the following:

- **Invest in training**: Develop AI competencies within the workforce through training programs and professional development.
- **Standardize processes**: Create and implement standardized methodologies and frameworks for AI projects to ensure consistency and quality.
- **Measure performance**: Use KPIs and metrics to monitor AI initiatives, enabling data-driven decision-making and continuous improvement.
- **Foster innovation**: Encourage experimentation, collaboration, and the exploration of new AI technologies and approaches.

AI Vendor Selection Framework

Selecting the right AI vendors is critical for the success of AI initiatives. The AI Vendor Selection Framework provides a structured approach to evaluating and choosing vendors that align with organizational needs, values, and strategic goals.

Evaluation criteria

Key criteria to consider when evaluating AI vendors include the following:

- **Technical capability**: Assess whether the vendor's solutions are compatible with existing systems, scalable to meet future needs, and capable of delivering the required technical performance.

- **Domain expertise**: Evaluate the vendor's experience and expertise in the relevant industry or application area. A proven track record of successful implementations can indicate reliability.
- **Support and services**: Consider the quality and availability of customer support, training resources, and professional services offered by the vendor.
- **Cost structure**: Examine the vendor's pricing models, including upfront costs, subscription fees, and total cost of ownership. Transparency and flexibility in pricing are important for budgeting and long-term planning.
- **Security and compliance**: Verify that the vendor adheres to industry standards for security and compliance and that their data handling practices align with your organization's policies.
- **Reputation and references**: Research client testimonials, case studies, and the vendor's market position. Speaking with existing clients can provide valuable insights into the vendor's reliability and performance.

Selection process

The vendor selection process typically involves the following steps:

1. **Define requirements**: Clearly outline your organization's needs, expectations, and evaluation criteria for the AI solution
2. **Shortlist vendors**: Create a shortlist of potential vendors based on initial research and the defined criteria
3. **Request proposals**: Solicit detailed proposals from the shortlisted vendors, requesting specific information about their solutions and capabilities
4. **Evaluate proposals**: Assess the proposals using a standardized scoring system to ensure objective vendor comparison
5. **Conduct demos**: Arrange demonstrations or proof-of-concept projects to see the vendor's solution and evaluate its usability and effectiveness
6. **Negotiate and finalize**: Discuss terms, conditions, and pricing with the preferred vendor(s) and reach an agreement that aligns with your organization's requirements

AI Ethics and Compliance Checklist

The AI Ethics and Compliance Checklist is a practical tool designed to ensure that AI projects adhere to ethical standards and legal requirements throughout their lifecycle. It helps organizations proactively address potential issues related to data privacy, fairness, accountability, and more.

Checklist items

Key areas covered in the checklist include the following:

- **Data privacy and security**: Confirm that data collection practices comply with relevant regulations and that data storage and transmission are secure. Evaluate whether appropriate consent has been obtained and whether data usage aligns with stated purposes.
- **Bias and fairness**: Evaluate datasets and models for potential biases. Implement strategies to detect, mitigate, and monitor biases to promote fairness in AI outcomes.
- **Transparency and explainability**: Ensure that AI systems explain their decisions and that documentation is available for auditing purposes. Transparent communication builds trust with users and stakeholders.
- **Accountability and governance**: Define clear roles and responsibilities for AI initiatives. Establish processes for reporting issues, addressing concerns, and ensuring oversight.
- **Legal compliance**: Verify that the AI system complies with all relevant laws and regulations, including data protection, intellectual property, and industry-specific requirements.
- **User consent and awareness**: Inform users about using AI systems and obtain consent where necessary. Clear communication about AI interactions enhances user trust and satisfaction.
- **Robustness and safety**: Assess the AI system's resilience to errors, adversarial attacks, and unexpected inputs. Implement safeguards and fail-safe mechanisms to maintain safety.
- **Environmental impact**: Consider AI systems' energy consumption and environmental footprint. Adopt sustainable practices where possible to reduce negative impacts.

Implementation guidelines

Organizations should conduct regular audits and assessments using the checklist to ensure ongoing compliance. Engaging stakeholders from diverse backgrounds can provide broader perspectives and help identify potential ethical issues. Keeping ethical guidelines updated with evolving standards and regulations ensures that the organization remains compliant and responsive to new challenges.

AI Skills and Competency Framework

The AI Skills and Competency Framework helps organizations identify the necessary skills and competencies for AI-related roles. It serves as a guide for recruiting, developing talent, and assessing performance, ensuring the organization has the expertise to successfully execute AI initiatives.

Competency areas

Key competency areas include the following:

- **Technical skills**: Proficiency in programming languages such as Python or R, experience with machine learning algorithms and frameworks, and knowledge of data processing and database systems are essential for technical AI roles.
- **Analytical skills**: It is crucial to interpret complex data, understand model outputs, and apply statistical analysis techniques. Strong problem-solving skills enable professionals to address challenges creatively.
- **Business acumen**: Understanding the organization's industry, market dynamics, and business processes helps align AI initiatives with strategic goals. Strategic thinking and the ability to identify opportunities for AI applications are valuable.
- **Ethics and compliance**: Knowledge of legal and regulatory requirements affecting AI and the ability to make decisions considering ethical implications and societal impacts is important for responsible AI development.
- **Communication and collaboration**: Effective communication skills enable professionals to explain technical concepts to non-technical stakeholders, and collaboration skills facilitate teamwork across multidisciplinary groups.
- **Project management**: Skills in planning, organizing, and executing projects help ensure that AI initiatives are completed on time, within budget, and meet quality standards.

Usage

Organizations can use the framework to develop detailed job descriptions and hiring criteria, ensuring candidates possess the required competencies. It can also inform the design of training and development programs to build internal capabilities. Regular performance evaluations against the competency framework help identify strengths and areas for growth among team members.

AI Investment Evaluation Template

Evaluating the financial viability of AI initiatives is essential for making informed decisions about resource allocation. The AI Investment Evaluation Template provides a structured approach to assessing the potential **return on investment (ROI)** and associated risks of AI projects.

Components

The template includes the following elements:

- **Project overview**: A concise description of the AI initiative, including its objectives, scope, and expected outcomes.

- **Financial analysis**:
  - Costs:
    - **Initial investment**: Estimate costs for technology acquisition, infrastructure setup, personnel hiring or training, and any external consulting.
    - **Operational costs**: Include ongoing expenses such as maintenance, software licensing, cloud services, and support.
  - Benefits:
    - **Revenue generation**: Project potential new income streams from the AI initiative, such as increased sales or market share.
    - **Cost savings**: Identify areas where the AI system can reduce expenses, improve efficiency, or optimize resource utilization.
- **ROI metrics**:
  - **Payback period**: Calculate the time required to recoup the initial investment through net cash inflows.
  - **Net Present Value (NPV)**: Determine the present value of future cash flows generated by the project, discounted back to today's dollars.
  - **Internal Rate of Return (IRR)**: Estimate the expected rate of growth the project is anticipated to generate.
- **Risk assessment**:
  - **Market risks**: Consider changes in market conditions, customer preferences, or competitive dynamics that could impact the project's success.
  - **Technical risks**: Assess the feasibility of the AI solution, potential integration challenges, and technology limitations.
  - **Regulatory risks**: Evaluate potential legal or compliance issues affecting project implementation.
- **Strategic alignment**: Analyze how the AI project supports the organization's strategic objectives, mission, and long-term goals.
- **Recommendation**: Based on the analysis, provide a recommendation to proceed with, revise, or decline the project. Include justifications and any conditions that should be met.

Implementation steps

To utilize the template effectively, organizations should do the following:

1. **Collect data**: Gather accurate and comprehensive financial and operational information relevant to the project
2. **Analyze scenarios**: Consider different scenarios (best-case, expected, and worst-case) to understand potential outcome variations
3. **Validate assumptions**: Engage with key stakeholders and subject matter experts to verify the assumptions used in the analysis
4. **Document findings**: Prepare a detailed report summarizing the evaluation, including data sources, methodologies, and key insights
5. **Review and approve**: Present the evaluation to decision-makers for review and approval, facilitating informed and transparent decision-making

Assessments

Chapter 1 – Why Every Company Needs a Chief AI Officer

1. The primary role of a CAIO is to align AI strategies with business goals, drive innovation, and ensure that AI initiatives deliver measurable value. It is essential because AI is transforming industries, and having focused leadership ensures these initiatives are both effective and sustainable.

2. A CAIO bridges the gap by translating complex technical concepts into actionable business strategies that resonate with executives, ensuring AI projects receive the necessary support and resources while maintaining a focus on business outcomes.

3. A CAIO drives innovation by fostering a culture of experimentation, staying updated on the latest AI advancements, and encouraging teams to explore new AI applications that can enhance efficiency and solve business challenges.

4. Aligning AI initiatives with business goals ensures that AI efforts drive meaningful results, such as improving customer experiences or operational efficiency. Without alignment, projects may become disjointed and fail to deliver expected value, wasting resources and potential.

5. A CAIO ensures compliance by staying informed about evolving regulations, setting up governance frameworks, and conducting audits to prevent ethical issues such as bias or privacy violations in AI systems.

6. A CAIO builds a data-driven culture by promoting data literacy across all levels of the organization, ensuring decisions are informed by data, and making AI-generated insights accessible. This culture is critical for leveraging AI effectively and staying competitive.

7. Challenges include resistance to change, integrating AI with existing systems, and managing ethical concerns. A CAIO overcomes these by fostering collaboration, communicating AI's benefits, and ensuring proper training and support for teams involved in AI projects.

8. Continuous improvement is crucial because AI technologies evolve rapidly. A CAIO fosters this by promoting a culture of learning, regularly reviewing AI strategies, and adapting to new developments and business needs to ensure AI initiatives remain relevant.

9. AI can enhance decision-making by providing predictive analytics, real-time data insights, and reducing uncertainty in business decisions. The CAIO ensures that AI tools are effectively integrated into decision-making processes and accessible to leadership.

10. A CAIO ensures cross-functional collaboration by establishing clear communication channels, fostering teamwork across departments, and ensuring that AI initiatives reflect the needs and goals of various functions within the organization.

Chapter 2 – Key Responsibilities of a Chief AI Officer

1. The three main topics covered in this chapter are the following:

    - **Challenges of AI integration**: Covered the complexities of implementing AI, including technological hurdles, ethical and regulatory concerns, and workforce resistance.
    - **Practical AI implementation**: Provided a structured, step-by-step guide for developing an AI vision, aligning initiatives with business goals, and addressing skill gaps.
    - **Case study application**: Demonstrated AI's impact through APEX Manufacturing's transformation, showcasing improvements in efficiency, customer satisfaction, and growth

2. Three key responsibilities of a CAIO include the following:

    - Developing a clear AI vision and strategy
    - Navigating technological complexity
    - Addressing ethical and regulatory challenges

3. Developing a clear AI vision is important because it aligns AI initiatives with overall business goals, provides direction for AI projects, and helps prioritize resources and efforts.

4. Ethical considerations a CAIO should address include the following:

    - Ensuring AI systems are fair and unbiased
    - Maintaining transparency in AI decision-making processes
    - Protecting data privacy and security
    - Ensuring compliance with relevant regulations (for example, GDPR)

5. A CAIO can foster a culture of AI adoption in the following ways:

    - Implementing comprehensive training programs
    - Communicating the benefits of AI clearly across the organization
    - Highlighting success stories and early wins
    - Addressing employee concerns and misconceptions about AI

6. In the APEX case study, the first AI solution implemented was a predictive maintenance system. It reduced equipment downtime by 40%, leading to significant cost savings.

7. Two challenges a CAIO might face when navigating AI complexity are as follows:

    - Keeping up with rapid technological advancements
    - Integrating AI solutions with existing systems and processes

8. A CAIO contributes to aligning AI initiatives with business goals in the following ways:
    - Collaborating with executive leadership to understand business priorities
    - Developing AI strategies that directly support these priorities
    - Establishing measurable outcomes for AI projects that tie to business objectives
9. One strategy to address the skill gap could be to implement a comprehensive AI training program for existing employees, combined with strategic hiring of AI specialists to build internal capabilities.
10. The various steps for a CAIO to ensure ethical compliance in AI implementations are as follows:
    - Develop and enforce clear ethical guidelines for AI development and use
    - Establish an AI ethics committee or task force
    - Implement regular audits of AI systems for bias and fairness
    - Ensure transparency in AI decision-making processes
    - Engage with diverse stakeholders to understand and address ethical concerns

Chapter 3 – Crafting a Winning AI Strategy

1. The primary goal is to align AI initiatives with business objectives, ensuring AI investments drive measurable business value, enhance operational efficiency, and create a competitive advantage.
2. The chapter suggests developing a clear AI vision that aligns with the organization's overall goals, involving executive leadership in setting strategic AI objectives and creating a detailed implementation roadmap.
3. KPIs play a crucial role in measuring the success of AI initiatives. They provide specific, measurable targets that help organizations track progress and demonstrate the value of their AI investments.
4. Many organizations struggle because some AI benefits (such as improved decision-making) are intangible, and quantifying long-term impacts is difficult. The chapter emphasizes the importance of developing a robust framework for measuring tangible and intangible benefits.
5. A phased approach allows for manageable implementation, quick wins, and iterative improvements. It helps manage risks, demonstrate value, and maintain stakeholder engagement throughout the AI implementation process.
6. Organizations can address the AI talent gap by developing strategic plans to attract top talent, implementing comprehensive training programs to upskill existing employees, and creating retention strategies to motivate AI professionals.

7. Poor data quality can severely undermine AI efforts, leading to inaccurate insights, suboptimal decision-making, and failed AI initiatives. The chapter stresses the importance of proper data governance and quality management.

8. One significant result was a 35% reduction in production bottlenecks, which led to more consistent production schedules and enhanced operational efficiency.

9. The chapter recommends conducting a gap analysis to identify areas where current processes need adaptation, implementing a comprehensive change management strategy, and using iterative development cycles to integrate AI into business processes gradually.

10. The first step would be to engage with executive leadership to develop a clear AI vision that aligns with the organization's overall business objectives. This ensures that AI initiatives are strategically aligned from the outset.

Chapter 4 – Building High-Performing AI Teams

1. Curiosity, creativity, and imagination are the three key characteristics to look for when identifying the right talent for your AI team.

2. Providing team members with a sense of impact and control is crucial because it fosters a sense of purpose, engagement, and fulfillment, which drives motivation and excellence in their work.

3. You can leverage multiple recruitment channels to attract top AI talent, such as job boards, social media, university partnerships, AI conferences, and proactive talent sourcing on platforms such as LinkedIn, GitHub, and Kaggle.

4. Creating cross-functional AI teams brings together diverse skill sets and expertise, enabling comprehensive problem-solving, fostering innovation, and ensuring AI initiatives align with business goals.

5. Implementing agile methodologies such as Scrum or Kanban helps manage AI projects by allowing for iterative development, continuous feedback, quick adjustments to changing requirements, and ensuring projects remain aligned with business objectives.

6. To encourage experimentation and foster a culture of innovation within your AI team, you can create a safe environment for taking calculated risks, provide continuous learning opportunities, implement a mentorship program, and celebrate successes while learning from failures.

7. A gap analysis before integrating AI initiatives with existing business processes is important because it helps identify areas where AI can add the most value and determines the necessary changes for effective integration.

8. You can measure the success of your AI projects by defining clear, SMART KPIs that align with business goals, conducting regular performance reviews, communicating results to stakeholders, and continuously iterating based on feedback and insights. Measuring success is crucial for demonstrating value, securing ongoing investment, and driving continuous improvement.

9. In the hypothetical case study of APEX Manufacturing, some key results achieved by implementing the AI team-building strategies included enhanced production efficiency, improved product quality, reduced operational costs, increased revenue, and a fostered culture of innovation.

10. To apply the insights from this chapter to your context, start by critically assessing your current situation, identifying areas for improvement in your AI team-building practices, and then implementing the strategies discussed, such as revamping your recruitment process, restructuring your team for better collaboration, fostering a culture of innovation, integrating AI with business processes, and measuring success. Take concrete, achievable steps to transform your AI team and gradually drive meaningful progress.

Chapter 5 – Data – the Lifeblood of AI

1. Data is crucial for AI implementation as it forms the foundation for all AI capabilities. Without reliable, high-quality data, even the most advanced AI algorithms cannot deliver accurate insights or predictions.

2. Three common challenges are as follows:

    - Data collection from diverse sources and legacy systems
    - Ensuring data quality and consistency
    - Breaking down data silos across different departments

3. Data standardization ensures that data from various sources is converted into a common format. This allows for easier integration, analysis, and use in AI models, particularly when dealing with data from different systems or machines.

4. IoT sensors enable real-time data collection from equipment, providing continuous operational insights such as vibration levels and temperature. This data is essential for applications such as predictive maintenance.

5. Data enrichment involves integrating additional external sources to provide a broader context. For example, enriching internal production data with market trends, supplier performance metrics, and weather data can help in more accurate forecasting and better operational insights.

6. A data governance framework establishes clear ownership, access rights, and usage guidelines for data. It ensures that data is used ethically and legally, and helps maintain data quality and integrity over time.

7. Scalable storage solutions, such as cloud-based data lakes, are crucial for managing big data as they can handle the volume, velocity, and variety of data generated in modern manufacturing environments. They allow for storage of both structured and unstructured data and can grow with the organization's needs.

8. Continuous monitoring and retraining of AI models is important because it ensures the models remain accurate and relevant as new data becomes available, and as conditions in the operating environment change.

9. Organizations can foster a data-driven culture in the following ways:

    - Investing in training to improve data literacy across the organization
    - Encouraging cross-departmental collaboration on data projects
    - Demonstrating the value of data-driven decisions through pilot projects

10. Initial steps to start a data management journey for AI implementation include the following:

    - Conducting a comprehensive data audit
    - Starting small with IoT implementation on critical equipment
    - Implementing data cleaning protocols
    - Exploring cloud-based storage solutions
    - Developing a data governance framework

Chapter 6 – AI Project Management

1. Artifacts should be substantial (>15 lines), likely to be modified or reused, self-contained, and intended for use outside the conversation. They shouldn't be used for simple, informational, or short content.

2. This chapter recommends regular skill assessments, dynamic resource allocation based on project needs, and forming cross-functional teams to combine diverse skill sets.

3. Data augmentation is suggested to fill gaps and enhance datasets, potentially using external sources to gain additional insights not captured in internal data.

4. Sprint planning involves breaking the project into manageable sprints (typically 2 to 4 weeks long), each focused on delivering a specific component of the project.

5. This chapter recommends deploying the AI system in a controlled environment, starting with a limited scope (for example, a single product line), and closely monitoring its performance before full-scale rollout.

6. It suggests forming cross-functional teams that combine technical experts (such as data scientists and engineers) with domain experts to enhance collaboration and problem-solving.

7. This chapter emphasizes continuously monitoring the AI system's performance, making regular updates, and retraining to ensure the system remains effective as new data becomes available.

8. It recommends conducting thorough pre-project assessments of technological compatibility, adopting standardized data formats, and implementing incremental integration strategies.

9. Feasibility assessment is crucial for evaluating the project's technical and economic viability, including assessing data availability, technical requirements, and potential ROI.

10. This chapter suggests developing a comprehensive change management plan, involving employees early in the project, providing clear communication, and offering training programs to help employees adapt to new AI systems.

Chapter 7 – Understanding Deterministic, Probabilistic, and Generative AI

1. The three main types of AI that were discussed in this chapter were deterministic AI, probabilistic AI, and generative AI.

2. Deterministic AI makes decisions based on fixed rules and produces consistent outputs for given inputs, while probabilistic AI makes decisions based on statistical models and can handle uncertainty and variability.

3. Deterministic AI is most effectively applied in scenarios requiring high precision and consistency, such as manufacturing quality control, financial compliance checks, and automated inventory management systems.

4. A key challenge in implementing probabilistic AI is ensuring data quality. This can be addressed by investing in data cleaning, consistency checks, and establishing robust data governance processes.

5. Generative AI can contribute to creative processes and innovation by rapidly generating new ideas or designs, assisting in customization, providing inspiration to creative teams, and helping us to explore a wider range of possibilities in shorter timeframes.

6. Data quality is particularly important for probabilistic and generative AI models because these models learn patterns and make predictions based on the data they're trained on. Poor quality data can lead to inaccurate predictions or biased outputs.

7. The following two practical next steps were suggested:

    - Conduct an AI readiness assessment to evaluate current processes, data infrastructure, and team capabilities

    - Start a pilot project by choosing a small-scale problem to tackle with AI

Chapter 8 – AI Agents and Agentic Systems

1. The four key characteristics of AI agents are as follows:

    - Autonomy

    - Reactivity

    - Proactivity

    - Social ability

2. Reactive agents operate based on predefined rules and respond to environmental changes without internal state representation. They are suitable for straightforward tasks. Deliberative agents maintain an internal model of their environment and use it to plan their actions, making them capable of more complex decision-making processes.

3. AI agents enhance efficiency in the following ways:

    - Automating routine tasks
    - Processing vast amounts of data quickly
    - Making real-time decisions
    - Optimizing resource allocation
    - Predicting and preventing issues before they occur

4. ML plays a crucial role in developing AI agents by enabling them to learn from data, improve their performance over time, and adapt to new situations. Techniques such as reinforcement learning allow agents to optimize their behavior through trial and error.

5. Three potential applications of AI agents include the following:

    - Supply chain optimization and inventory management
    - Predictive maintenance in manufacturing
    - Customer service chatbots and virtual assistants

6. The main challenges in implementing AI agents and agentic systems include the following:

    - Complexity of integration with existing systems
    - Ensuring data privacy and security
    - Addressing ethical considerations and potential biases
    - Overcoming resistance to change from employees
    - High initial costs and uncertainty about ROI
    - Lack of expertise in AI technologies

7. In the APEX case study, AI agents were implemented in the following areas:

    - Supply chain optimization
    - Predictive maintenance
    - Enhanced customer service

8. Businesses can address employee resistance by doing the following:

    - Providing clear communication about the role of AI
    - Offering training and support for transitioning to new ways of working
    - Emphasizing how AI will augment human capabilities rather than replace jobs
    - Involving employees in the AI integration process

9. Data quality is crucial for AI agents for the following reasons:

    - High-quality data ensures accurate decision-making
    - It helps prevent biases in AI systems
    - Good data is essential for effective ML and model training
    - It enables AI agents to adapt to changing conditions and improve over time

10. Ethical considerations for AI agentic systems include the following:

    - Ensuring fairness and avoiding discrimination in decision-making
    - Protecting data privacy and security
    - Maintaining transparency in AI decision processes
    - Addressing potential job displacement concerns
    - Ensuring AI agents align with human values and societal norms

Chapter 9 – Designing AI Systems

1. The chapter compares designing AI systems to planning a road trip across a new continent.
2. The three main challenges discussed are data quality and bias, complexity and integration, and ethical and legal concerns. (Other valid answers include scalability and maintenance, human-AI collaboration, and security risks.)
3. APEX's primary goal was to optimize its supply chain using AI to reduce costs and improve efficiency.
4. Defining clear objectives is crucial as it provides a roadmap for the entire project, ensuring all stakeholders understand the goals and expected outcomes.
5. The chapter suggests implementing fairness checks to detect and mitigate biases, ensuring the AI system provides equal benefits across all operations segments.
6. Human-centered AI design involves engaging diverse teams in the design process, conducting impact assessments, and establishing clear guidelines for ethical AI use. It focuses on creating systems that augment human capabilities and foster trust.

7. Two significant areas of improvement were a reduction in inventory holding costs (surpassing their initial goal) and a decrease in delays due to accurate prediction of potential supply chain disruptions.

Chapter 10 – Training AI Models

1. The chapter compares data selection for AI model training to selecting ingredients for a gourmet meal.
2. Feature engineering enhances model performance by selecting relevant variables, creating new features, and transforming existing ones to make them more beneficial for learning.
3. The training process is iterative because it involves starting with an initial model, evaluating its performance, making adjustments, and repeating the cycle until desired results are achieved.
4. Accuracy, precision, recall, and F1 score are mentioned as evaluation metrics.
5. In medical diagnosis, a false negative (missing a disease) is often more critical than a false positive, making recall (sensitivity) a crucial metric.
6. Continuous learning and improvement in AI models are compared to tending a garden, which requires constant nurturing to keep the models flourishing.
7. The AI model discovered that umbrella sales spike during rainy days and on days with high pollen counts.
8. Training AI models requires technical expertise to handle the complexities of algorithms and data and creativity to engineer features, interpret results, and solve unexpected problems.
9. Poor data quality, such as a dataset including only young, healthy individuals, could lead to inaccurate predictions for older or chronically ill patients.
10. The chapter suggested developing a structured plan for regularly updating and retraining models, setting up automated data pipelines, scheduling periodic model reviews, and establishing a feedback loop with end users.

Chapter 11 – Deploying AI Solutions

1. One main challenge in scaling an AI prototype to production is handling increased data volume and variability in real-world conditions, which can impact model performance.
2. Two key components of a CI/CD pipeline for AI projects are automated testing (including model validation) and artifact management (storing and versioning trained models).
3. Ongoing monitoring is crucial because it helps detect issues such as model drift, ensures continued performance, and allows for timely AI system updates and maintenance.
4. APEX Manufacturing faced inefficient inventory management, leading to frequent stockouts and overstock situations, which caused production delays and increased costs.

5. APEX used a phased deployment strategy, starting with a small subset of products before a full-scale launch. This allowed them to monitor performance and make necessary adjustments.

6. Version control can be implemented using Git for code versioning and specialized tools such as DVC for managing datasets and model files.

7. Two potential consequences of not properly maintaining an AI system after deployment are degradation in model performance over time (model drift) and the system becoming misaligned with changing business needs or data patterns.

Chapter 12 – AI Governance and Ethics

1. The four core principles of AI ethics mentioned are fairness, accountability, transparency, and privacy.

2. AI systems trained on historical data can reflect and amplify existing bias. For example, an AI hiring tool might favor male candidates if trained on historical hiring data where men were predominantly hired.

3. "Black box" refers to AI systems that make decisions without providing clear, understandable explanations. This lack of transparency makes it difficult to identify and rectify potential biases or errors in decision-making.

4. Two steps to integrate ethical checks are as follows:

    I. Establish ethical checkpoints at key stages of the AI development life cycle (data collection, model training, validation, and deployment)

    II. Set up ethical review boards to periodically audit AI systems against established ethical guidelines

5. Cross-functional teams bring diverse perspectives to AI ethics discussions, ensuring a more comprehensive consideration of potential ethical issues across the organization's various aspects and stakeholders.

6. An AI ethics committee oversees all AI-related activities within the organization, makes critical decisions regarding ethical concerns, and ensures accountability in monitoring and addressing these concerns.

7. Continuous monitoring helps detect bias and irregularity in real time, while regular audits ensure ongoing compliance with ethical guidelines and regulatory requirements, allowing for timely adjustments and improvements.

8. One key challenge was bias in their predictive maintenance tool. They addressed this by recalibrating the tool to provide balanced attention to all equipment, which reduced downtime by 20% and improved operational efficiency.

9. Transparency is important because it builds trust among stakeholders and allows for better understanding and scrutiny of AI decisions. It can be improved by implementing protocols that make AI decision-making processes more explainable and understandable.

10. Strong AI governance can improve an organization's reputation, enhance customer trust, mitigate legal and financial risks, foster innovation, attract talent, and potentially open up new market opportunities by positioning the organization as a responsible leader in AI development.

Chapter 13 – Security in AI Systems

1. The three key challenges in AI security discussed are data breaches and privacy concerns, model vulnerabilities and adversarial attacks, and data poisoning and integrity issues.

2. There are encryption techniques that can be applied, for example, using advanced algorithms such as AES-256 to protect data at rest and in transit and homomorphic encryption to allow computations on encrypted data without decryption.

3. AI can enhance cybersecurity by improving threat detection, automating incident response, and adapting to new threats through continuous learning.

4. Adversarial attacks involve manipulating input data to cause AI systems to make incorrect predictions or classifications, potentially leading to dangerous outcomes in critical applications.

5. Explainability in AI models is important for security because it allows for a better understanding of how decisions are made, facilitating the detection and mitigation of potential security threats.

6. Data poisoning is an attack in which malicious data is injected into the training dataset, causing the AI model to learn incorrect or harmful behaviors and compromising its integrity.

7. Two methods for implementing access control in AI systems are RBAC, which restricts access based on user roles, and MFA, which requires multiple forms of verification for access.

8. Continuous monitoring helps address AI vulnerabilities by enabling real-time detection of anomalies and suspicious activities, allowing for quick response to potential security breaches.

9. Potential consequences of a security breach in critical AI applications could include financial losses, compromised safety (for example, in autonomous vehicles or medical diagnosis systems), damage to reputation, and erosion of trust in AI technologies.

10. The rapid evolution of AI threats requires organizations to maintain continuous vigilance, regularly update security measures, and adopt adaptive strategies to stay ahead of potential attackers.

Chapter 14 – Privacy in the Age of AI

1. Differential privacy is a technique that adds controlled noise to data, ensuring individual data points cannot be identified while still allowing for meaningful analysis. It contributes to privacy-preserving AI by protecting individual privacy while maintaining data utility.

2. Two key challenges are obtaining informed consent for data collection and use and ensuring compliance with complex data privacy regulations such as GDPR and CCPA.
3. Federated learning allows AI models to be trained across multiple decentralized devices using local data, keeping sensitive information on individual devices and reducing the risk of data breaches.
4. A DPIA is an assessment to evaluate the impact of data-processing activities on privacy. It should be conducted at the beginning of new AI projects or when significant changes are made to existing data-processing activities.
5. "Privacy by design" involves integrating privacy considerations into the AI development life cycle rather than as an afterthought. This is important because it ensures privacy is a core component of system architecture and design, leading to more robust privacy protection.
6. Encryption protects data in transit and at rest, thus making it unreadable to unauthorized parties. In AI systems, it helps safeguard sensitive information during data collection, storage, and processing.
7. Organizations can foster a culture of privacy awareness through regular training sessions, appointing privacy champions in each department, running awareness campaigns, and integrating privacy considerations into daily operations.
8. One significant result was increased customer trust and loyalty, improved customer satisfaction scores, and reduced churn rates.
9. Regular updates and reviews are important because privacy regulations and best practices evolve rapidly. Staying current ensures continued compliance and effectiveness of privacy measures in the face of new challenges and technologies.
10. Ethical AI practices can contribute to a competitive advantage by building customer trust, attracting privacy-conscious clients, reducing the risk of regulatory fines and reputational damage, and fostering innovation that respects user privacy.

Chapter 15 – AI Compliance

1. The maximum potential fine is up to 4% of global annual turnover or €20 million, whichever is higher.
2. The key three areas of AI compliance are data privacy and security, transparency and explainability, and fairness and bias mitigation.
3. Regular compliance audits help evaluate adherence to industry standards, identify gaps, and ensure continuous monitoring of AI systems.
4. Organizations can address evolving regulations by setting up dedicated compliance teams, using regulatory monitoring tools, and conducting regular audits.
5. Transparency in AI systems helps build user trust, comply with regulations, and explain AI decision-making processes clearly.

6. One strategy is developing comprehensive training programs that educate employees about compliance requirements, ethical considerations, and best practices.
7. APEX Manufacturing implemented regulatory monitoring tools such as Thomson Reuters Regulatory Intelligence and OneTrust.
8. Clear communication channels encourage employees to report compliance concerns without fear of retribution and ensure prompt addressing of issues.
9. Performance metrics help track progress, identify areas for improvement, and recognize achievements in compliance efforts.
10. Benefits include improved stakeholder trust, reduced legal risks, enhanced operational excellence, and a competitive edge in AI.

Index

A

agentic systems 123
AI agents 122
   challenges 126-130
   core capabilities 122
   deliberative agents 123
   evolution 123
   hybrid agents 123
   integration with IoT 124
   key characteristics 122
   potential applications 124
   reactive agents 123
   real-world applications 124-126
   role, of machine learning 124
AI agents, solution and implementation
   architecture, selecting 131
   continuous improvement 133
   decision-making algorithms, implementing 132
   deployment 132
   monitoring 132
   objectives and goals, defining 130
   perception and action mechanisms, developing 131
   testing methods 132
   tips and best practices 133
   validation 132
AI and data privacy
   challenges 222-225
   works, implementing 225, 226
AI Capability Maturity Model 276
   advancement strategies 277
   assessment areas 277
   levels 276
AI compliance
   challenges 238-241
   culture of compliance and accountability, building 243, 244
   ensuring, with industry standards 241, 242
   implementation 241
   legal and regulatory requirements 242, 243
AI-driven insights
   big data, best practices 76
   big data, harnessing 76
   data collection and management 72
   data collection, best practices 73
   data collection, challenges addressing 72
   data integrity, best practices 75
   data integrity, maintaining 75
   data management, best practices 73, 74
   data quality, best practices 74, 75
   data quality, ensuring 74

Index

AI ethics 196, 200
   implementing 196-200
AI Ethics and Compliance Checklist 278
   checklist items 279
   implementation guidelines 279
AI governance
   solutions and capabilities 199
AI governance solutions and capabilities 198, 201
   AI ethics 200
   ethical AI frameworks, building 200
   implementing 201, 202
AI initiatives, with business goals
   aligning 11
   alignment culture, building 13
   clear objectives and metrics, defining 12
   continuous evaluation and adjustment 12
   cross-functional collaboration and alignment 12
   data and insights, using 13
   leadership role 13
   strategic impact 13
   strategic vision and AI integration 11
AI Investment Evaluation Template 280
   elements 280, 281
   implementation steps 282
AI leadership strategy 8
   AI decision-making process 10
   AI implementation challenges 9
   business AI integration 8
   business future 11
   continuous improvement and adaptability 9, 10
   cross-functional collaboration 9
   technical aspects 10
AI learning curve 107
AI model training 158
   challenges 160
   continuous learning and improvement 159
   data selection, significance 158
   feature engineering 158
   model evaluation 159
   solution and process 163
   training process 159
   unexpected insights 159
AI model training challenges
   AI solutions, scaling 163
   computational resources 161
   continuous learning and maintenance 162
   data quality and availability 160
   ethical and legal considerations 162
   feature engineering complexity 160
   integration, with business processes 162
   interpretability and trust 161
   model selection and tuning 160, 161
   user adoption and feedback 163
AI model training, solution and process
   algorithms, selecting 163-165
   bias and fairness, handling in AI 167, 168
   model training and optimization 165-167
AI Project Management Framework 273
   considerations 274
   phases 273
AI projects management
   agile methodologies, applying 93, 94
   APEX Manufacturing and Distribution 97-100
   challenges 88-91
   challenges, identifying and mitigating checklist 96
   challenges, overcoming 94, 95
   solution and implementation 91-96
AI Risk Management Framework (AI RMF) 271
AI security 207
   insights 217, 218
   models and data, security 211

Index 299

pain points and challenges 208
solution and process 211
AI Skills and Competency Framework 279
competency areas 280
usage 280
AI solutions deployment
implementation process 178-182
pain points and challenges 176-178
AI strategy approach 23
AI culture adoption 25
AI vision and strategy, developing 23
ethical and regulatory challenges 24
resource allocation and skill development 25
robust infrastructure and processes, defining 26
technological complexity, navigating 24
AI strategy development template 272
components 272, 273
implementation 273
AI system
best practices 203-205
AI systems, problem 143, 194
accountability 194
bias 194
complexity and integration 143
compliance standards 195
data privacy and security 195
data quality and bias 143
ethical and legal concerns 144
ethical decision-making 195
high stakes 145
human-AI collaboration 144
market trends, predicting 144
personal anecdotes 196
regulatory compliance 195
scalability and maintenance 144
security risks 144
transparency 194

AI systems, solution 145
algorithms and tools, selecting 146
best practices 148
clear objectives, defining 145
ethical considerations 147
human-centered AI design 148, 149
integration and deployment 147
model developing 146
model training 146
monitoring and maintenance 148
quality data, preparing 146
AI technologies
deterministic AI 108
generative AI 111
implementing 108
probabilistic AI 109
AI terms
glossary 261-266
AI type
integrating, into business processes 107
AI Vendor Selection Framework 277
evaluation criteria 277, 278
selection process 278
AI vulnerabilities
addressing 212, 213
Amazon Web Services (AWS) 165
APEX Manufacturing and Distribution 41, 77, 112, 149, 199
AI governance solutions and capabilities 201
AI solutions, implementing 149
AI talent, sustaining 43
big data and advanced analytics, leveraging 80
case study 182-188
challenges 149
clear AI vision and strategy, developing 41
client's initial situation 199
data collection and management 78, 79

data quality and integrity, ensuring 79, 80
detailed roadmap, creating 42
deterministic AI for inventory management, implementing 114
deterministic AI for predictive maintenance, implementing 115
deterministic AI for quality control, implementing 113
generative AI for design innovation, implementing 115, 116
hypothetical case study 97
implementing 200
improvements 27
initial situation 41, 97
KPIs, identifying 42
memorable insights 81
motivational insights 99, 100
operational efficiency 26
operations, identifying 113
operations, transforming 26
relatable anecdotes 99, 100
results 30, 152, 202, 203
results achieved 81, 99
results, archiving 44
ROI, measuring 43
seamless integration, ensuring 43
step-by-step implementation 97-99
transformative results 116, 117

APEX Manufacturing and Distribution, AI solutions
algorithms and tools, selecting 150
clear objectives, defining 149
ethical considerations 151
integration and deployment 151
model training and development 150, 151
monitoring and maintenance 152
quality data, preparing 150

APEX Manufacturing and Distribution case study 169
AI, leveraging in cybersecurity 215
AI vulnerabilities, addressing 216
algorithms, selecting 170
challenges, tackling 214, 215
client's initial solution 214
continuous monitoring and maintenance 171
data preprocessing and feature engineering 170
initial situation 169
legal and regulatory requirements navigating 246, 247
model evaluation and deployment 171
problem and data collection 169
result benefits 216, 217
results 172

APEX Manufacturing and Distribution, case study 228, 244
AI and data privacy 229, 230
AI compliance, ensuring with industry standards 245, 246
client's initial situation 228, 229, 245
continued success 233, 234
culture of compliance and accountability, building 247-249
culture of results 249
detailed implementation 233, 234
long-term impact 234
privacy-preserving AI, implementing 230, 231
regulations and best practices 231
results 232

APEX Manufacturing and Distribution, improvements
clear AI vision, developing 27, 28
detailed roadmap, creating 28
phases, implementing 28

Index   301

APEX Manufacturing and Distribution, phases
integration and training 29
predictive maintenance systems, deploying 28
real-time monitoring 29

APEX, manufacturing and distribution with AI 58
AI initiatives, integrating with business processes 59, 60
AI team, structuring for success 59
culture of innovation and collaboration, fostering 59
results 60, 61
success and iterate, measuring 60
top AI talent, recruiting 58, 59

Application Programming Interface (API) 265

artificial intelligence (AI) 3, 67, 103, 261
in cybersecurity 212
key themes 257
recommended readings and resources 266-271
transformative power 256

Autoencoders (AEs) 150

automated machine learning (AutoML) 77, 161

AutoRegressive Integrated Moving Average (ARIMA) 150, 170

B

big data
leveraging 71

business strategies, AI impact on 257
clear vision 258
customer experiences, improving 257
operational efficiency, enhancing 257

C

California Consumer Privacy Act (CCPA) 162, 223

challenges, AI and data privacy 222
anonymization 224
breaches 223
data collection 222
data consent 222
data minimization 223
data retention 224
data security 223
de-identification 224
ethical considerations 224, 225
regulations, compliance 223

challenges, AI compliance 238
accountability and governance 240
bias and fairness 240
complex, and evolving regulations 238
data privacy, and security 239
integration, with existing systems and processes 240
resource constraints 241
transparency and explainability 239

challenges, for assembling AI teams
AI initiatives, integrating with existing business processes 52
culture of innovation, fostering 51
significance 53
structuring 51
success, measuring 52
talent scarcity 50

Chief AI Officer (CAIO), problem and challenges 20
AI technologies 20
ethical and regulatory considerations 21
technological advancements 21

Index

Chief AI Officer (CAIO) strategy 4
   advantage 6
   AI ecosystem, navigating 7
   AI efforts 5
   AI era 8
   business goals 4
   compliance and ethical AI 5
   data and AI landscape 6
   data-driven culture, building 6, 7
   innovation 4
   role 7
Chief AI Officers (CAIOs) 3, 19, 255, 261
   ethical stewardship 258
   strategic innovation 259
   visionary leadership 258
CI/CD, for AI
   managing 177
continuous integration and continuous deployment (CI/CD) pipeline 151
convolutional neural networks (CNNs) 164
cost-benefit analysis (CBA) 39
customer relationship management (CRM) 163

D

data analytics, for AI
   leveraging 76, 77
   leveraging, best practices 77
data collection 69
data collection and management 72
   best practices 73
   methodologies and tools 72
Data Governance Framework 275
   components 275, 276
   implementation steps 276

data in AI implementation, data-related challenges
   big data, leveraging 71
   data collection 69
   data integrity, maintaining 70, 71
   data management 69
   data quality, ensuring 70
data integrity
   maintaining 70-75
data management 69, 73
   best practices 74
data protection impact assessments (DPIAs) 223
data protection officer (DPO) 223
data quality
   ensuring 70, 74
   ensuring, best practices 74, 75
Data Version Control (DVC) 179
deep learning (DL) 163
deep neural networks (DNNs) 161
deep Q-networks (DQNs) 164
deliberative agents 123
Density-Based Spatial Clustering of Applications with Noise (DBSCAN) 164
deterministic AI 104, 108
   actionable tips 109
   challenges 107
   implementation 108
   key insights 108
   overview 105
   uses 108

E

ethical AI frameworks
   building 197, 200
   implementing 201

ethical AI Implementation Framework 274
  elements 274, 275
  implementation guidelines 275
exceptional AI teams, building
  control 54
  creativity 53
  curiosity 53
  imagination 54
  impact 54
explainable AI (XAI) techniques 239, 264

G

Gaussian mixture models (GMMs) 164
General Data Protection Regulation (GDPR) 22, 162, 195, 223
  AI culture adoption 22
  AI vision, need for 23
  resource allocation and skill gaps 22
generative adversarial networks (GANs) 104, 262
generative AI (GenAI) 37, 104, 111
  actionable tips 112
  implementation 111, 112
  key insights 111
  overview 106
  uses 111
gradient-boosting machines (GBMs) 161

H

high-performing AI team, step-by-step implementation
  AI initiatives, integrating with business processes 56, 57
  AI team, structuring for success 55, 56
  culture of innovation and collaboration, fostering 56

  tips, for measuring success and iterating 57
  top AI talent, recruiting 55
hybrid agents 123
hypothetical case study, APEX Manufacturing and Distribution 134
  initial situation 134
  results 135, 136
  steps 134, 135

I

identify bias
  algorithmic bias 168
  data bias 168
  label bias 168
industrial internet of things (IIoT) 69
Internet of Things (IoT) 7, 124, 263

K

key performance indicators (KPIs) 35, 272
K-Nearest Neighbors (KNN) 265

L

Latent Dirichlet Allocation (LDA) 265
Least Absolute Shrinkage or Selection Operator (LASSO) 164
Long Short-Term Memory (LSTM) 150, 170

M

machine learning (ML) 6, 37, 123, 263
machine learning (ML) algorithms 150
  inventory optimization 150
  supply chain prediction 150
Machine Learning Operations (MLOps) 162

Index

Mean Absolute Error (MAE) 171
multi-factor authentication (MFA) 211

N

National Institute of Standards and Technology (NIST) 271
Natural Language Generation (NLG) 265
natural language processing (NLP) 135, 166, 263
neural networks (NNs) 146
NIST AI Risk Management Framework (AI RMF) 271
   application 272
   components 271

O

overall equipment effectiveness (OEE) 68

P

pain points and challenges, AI security
   data breaches and privacy concerns 208
   data poisoning and integrity 209
   lack of explainability and transparency 210
   model inversion and privacy risks 209
   model vulnerabilities and adversarial attacks 209
   personal anecdotes 210
   rapid evolution of threats 210
privacy-enhancing technologies (PETs) 233
privacy impact assessments (PIAs) 227
privacy-preserving AI
   implementing 226, 227
   regulations and best practices 227, 228

probabilistic AI 104, 109
   actionable tips 110
   implementation 110
   key insights 109
   overview 105
   uses 110
proof-of-concept (PoC) 150

R

reactive agents 123
real-world applications, of AI agents 124
   algorithmic trading 125
   chatbots and virtual assistants 126
   customer service 126
   diagnostic assistance 125
   finance 125
   fraud detection 125
   healthcare 124
   inventory management 125
   logistics and supply chain management 125
   patient monitoring and care 125
   route optimization 126
   sentiment analysis 126
receiver operating characteristic (ROC) 167
recurrent neural networks (RNNs) 164, 266
reinforcement learning (RL) 150, 164, 264
return on investment (ROI) 5, 35, 280
role-based access control (RBAC) 73, 211

S

Security and Privacy in Emerging Technologies (SPET) 209
Shapley Additive exPlanations (SHAP) 161

small and medium-sized enterprises (SMEs) 69, 241
specific, measurable, achievable, relevant, and time-bound (SMART) 12, 39, 57, 92
standard operating procedures (SOPs) 242
stochastic gradient descent (SGD) 167
strengths, weaknesses, opportunities, and threats (SWOT) 272
support vector machines (SVMs) 146, 164

T

tool recommendation 146
transformative power, of AI 256

V

variational autoencoders (VAEs) 104

W

winning AI strategy
AI talent, sustaining 40
AI vision and strategy, developing 38
detailed roadmap, creating 38
hypothetical case study 41
KPIs, identifying 39
pain points and challenges 36
ROI, measuring 39
seamless integration, ensuring 40
solutions, to pain points and challenges 38
winning AI strategy, pain points and challenges
data quality and governance 37
integration, with existing processes 37
lack of clear KPIs 36
misaligned objectives 36
ROI, measuring 37
significance 37, 38
talent gap 37

<packt>

packtpub.com

Subscribe to our online digital library for full access to over 7,000 books and videos, as well as industry leading tools to help you plan your personal development and advance your career. For more information, please visit our website.

Why subscribe?

- Spend less time learning and more time coding with practical eBooks and Videos from over 4,000 industry professionals
- Improve your learning with Skill Plans built especially for you
- Get a free eBook or video every month
- Fully searchable for easy access to vital information
- Copy and paste, print, and bookmark content

Did you know that Packt offers eBook versions of every book published, with PDF and ePub files available? You can upgrade to the eBook version at packtpub.com and as a print book customer, you are entitled to a discount on the eBook copy. Get in touch with us at customercare@packtpub.com for more details.

At www.packtpub.com, you can also read a collection of free technical articles, sign up for a range of free newsletters, and receive exclusive discounts and offers on Packt books and eBooks.

Other Books You May Enjoy

If you enjoyed this book, you may be interested in these other books by Packt:

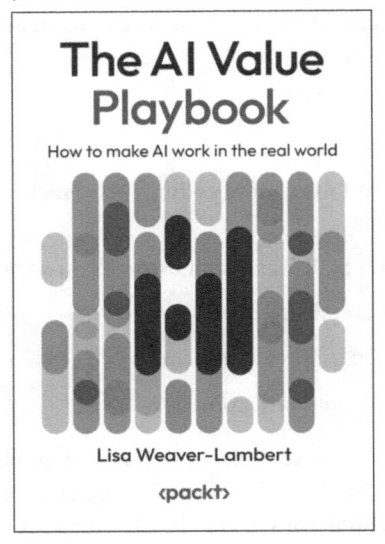

The AI Value Playbook

Lisa Weaver-Lambert

ISBN: 978-1-83546-175-4

- Fundamentals of AI concepts and the tech stack
- How AI works with real-world practical applications
- How to integrate into your company's overall strategy
- How to incorporate generative AI in your processes
- How to drive value with sector-wide examples
- How to organize an AI-driven operating model
- How to use AI for competitive advantage
- The dos and don'ts of AI application

LLM Engineer's Handbook

Paul Iusztin, Maxime Labonne

ISBN: 978-1-83620-006-2

- Implement robust data pipelines and manage LLM training cycles
- Create your own LLM and refine it with the help of hands-on examples
- Get started with LLMOps by diving into core MLOps principles such as orchestrators and prompt monitoring
- Perform supervised fine-tuning and LLM evaluation
- Deploy end-to-end LLM solutions using AWS and other tools
- Design scalable and modular LLM systems
- Learn about RAG applications by building a feature and inference pipeline

Packt is searching for authors like you

If you're interested in becoming an author for Packt, please visit `authors.packtpub.com` and apply today. We have worked with thousands of developers and tech professionals, just like you, to help them share their insight with the global tech community. You can make a general application, apply for a specific hot topic that we are recruiting an author for, or submit your own idea.

Share Your Thoughts

Now you've finished *The Chief AI Officer's Handbook*, we'd love to hear your thoughts! Scan the QR code below to go straight to the Amazon review page for this book and share your feedback or leave a review on the site that you purchased it from.

`https://packt.link/r/1-836-20085-4`

Your review is important to us and the tech community and will help us make sure we're delivering excellent quality content.

Download a free PDF copy of this book

Thanks for purchasing this book!

Do you like to read on the go but are unable to carry your print books everywhere?

Is your eBook purchase not compatible with the device of your choice?

Don't worry, now with every Packt book you get a DRM-free PDF version of that book at no cost.

Read anywhere, any place, on any device. Search, copy, and paste code from your favorite technical books directly into your application.

The perks don't stop there, you can get exclusive access to discounts, newsletters, and great free content in your inbox daily

Follow these simple steps to get the benefits:

1. Scan the QR code or visit the link below

   https://packt.link/free-ebook/9781836200857

2. Submit your proof of purchase
3. That's it! We'll send your free PDF and other benefits to your email directly

Made in United States
Cleveland, OH
29 May 2025